Sony CLIÉ®
FOR
DUMMIES®

by Denny Atkin

WILEY

Wiley Publishing, Inc.

Sony CLIÉ® For Dummies®

Published by
Wiley Publishing, Inc.
111 River Street
Hoboken, NJ 07030-5774

Copyright © 2004 by Wiley Publishing, Inc., Indianapolis, Indiana

Published by Wiley Publishing, Inc., Indianapolis, Indiana

Published simultaneously in Canada

For general information on our other products and services or to obtain technical support, please contact our Customer Care Department within the U.S. at 800-762-2974, outside the U.S. at 317-572-3993, or fax 317-572-4002.

Wiley also publishes its books in a variety of electronic formats. Some content that appears in print may not be available in electronic books.

Library of Congress Control Number: 2004102596

ISBN: 0-7645-7199-0

Manufactured in the United States of America

10 9 8 7 6 5 4 3 2 1

1O/RR/QW/QU/IN

WILEY

About the Author

Denny Atkin has been writing about technology since 1987, a primitive age where pioneer computer users toyed with Atari 800s and Commodore Amigas and actually typed in programs printed in magazines instead of downloading them. His articles have appeared in a variety of magazines ranging from pioneering technology/science publications *Compute!* and *OMNI* to *Wired, Entertainment Weekly, Computer Gaming World, Computer Shopper,* and *Handheld Computing* magazine. He has written a number of books, such as the one you're holding, and has appeared on Tech TV and CNN.

He's been using handhelds since the days of the original Apple "I don't understand what you're trying to write" Newton. He practices what he preaches, typically traveling with a CLIÉ, a folding keyboard, and a Bluetooth cell phone instead of a bulky laptop.

Atkin lives with his wife and son in Vermont, where he's doing long-term tests of the CLIÉ's ability to operate during ridiculously lengthy periods of sub-zero temperatures.

Dedication

To my supportive, creative, and astonishing wife Dawn, who kept me sane and laughing and kept the world running while I wrote this book.

Author's Acknowledgments

This book owes its existence to the CLIÉ community, which has been amazingly helpful in its production. I'd like to offer my sincere thanks to these folks:

Tiffany Franklin for giving me the opportunity to do this book, and for her patience as Murphy decided to use my office to enforce his Law.

Paul Levesque for making sure this book was up to the high standards you expect from a *For Dummies* title. Virginia Sanders for doing a brilliant copy-editing job and actually increasing the number of puns in the book. Darren Gladstone for an excellent technical review.

Sony's Eric Geruldsen, who provided invaluable help and ensured that this book had the most up-to-date info on the latest CLIÉ models.

Christie Burgner, Lisa Burnett, Sebastian Dijmarescu, Jonathan Fernstad, Kathleen Gilpatrick, Andrew Golden, Alexis Hinds, Mitch Kneppers, Jonathan Korzen, Candice Kwok, David Levitt, Parker Minardo, Aaron Roth, Moto Watanabe, Mike Wong, and Ellen Yeomans for ensuring that I had access to the best CLIÉ software and hardware.

Props to the CLIÉSource gaming gang — sj22Gam3r (aka Mac Tyler), orol, rightfuture, Remier, and fssia — for making sure that I had all the most addictive handheld games covered.

And, of course, to Dr. Carol Shuman, Denny Atkin Sr., and Don Thorburn for introducing me to publishing and technology and for providing years of inspiration and encouragement.

Publisher's Acknowledgments

We're proud of this book; please send us your comments through our online registration form located at www.dummies.com/register/.

Some of the people who helped bring this book to market include the following:

Acquisitions, Editorial, and Media Development

Project Editor: Paul Levesque

Acquisitions Editor: Tiffany Franklin

Copy Editor: Virginia Sanders

Technical Editor: Darren Gladstone

Editorial Manager: Kevin Kirschner

Permissions Editor: Laura Moss

Media Development Manager: Laura VanWinkle

Media Development Supervisor: Richard Graves

Editorial Assistant: Amanda Foxworth

Cartoons: Rich Tennant (www.the5thwave.com)

Composition

Project Coordinator: Courtney MacIntyre

Layout and Graphics: Amanda Carter, Andrea Dahl, Lauren Goddard, Stephanie D. Jumper, Jacque Schneider

Proofreaders: Laura Albert, TECHBOOKS Production Services

Indexer: TECHBOOKS Production Services

Publishing and Editorial for Technology Dummies

Richard Swadley, Vice President and Executive Group Publisher

Andy Cummings, Vice President and Publisher

Mary C. Corder, Editorial Director

Publishing for Consumer Dummies

Diane Graves Steele, Vice President and Publisher

Joyce Pepple, Acquisitions Director

Composition Services

Gerry Fahey, Vice President of Production Services

Debbie Stailey, Director of Composition Services

Contents at a Glance

Table of Contents

Introduction

*I*f you bought a Sony CLIÉ expecting it to be nothing more than a personal
organizer, boy, are you in for a pleasant surprise. After all, the somewhat
oddball CLIÉ name stands for Communication, Link, Information, and
Entertainment. (Or is that Éntertainment?) That's promising a lot for a handheld computer, but Sony delivers.

Although this device is small enough to fit in your pocket, it's more than a
replacement for the dog-eared day planner. The CLIÉ is also a miniature game
arcade, a library, and an office computer. Some models even manage to
squeeze in a photo studio, a movie theater, a concert hall, and an Internet ter-
minal. Heck, the CLIÉ outpaces the expectations of science fiction authors
from not long ago.

The CLIÉ is a very useful tool, but it's also lots of fun. In this book, I point out
the dozens of amazing things that you can do with this electronic wonder.
The CLIÉ has come a long way since it first arrived on the scene way back in
2000, and the newest models are so versatile that I even discovered some
cool new applications for them during the writing of this book.

About This Book

Sony CLIÉ For Dummies is designed to be a comprehensive reference and
tutorial for discovering how to use your CLIÉ. It progresses from the very
basics to advanced topics, from setting up your CLIÉ and entering information by using the stylus and keyboard to using wireless technology and setting security features. Along the way, I also show you how to play games,
watch movies, and listen to your favorite tunes.

If you're new to the CLIÉ, you can start from the first chapter and work your
way through the book, cover to cover. If you've already mastered the basics,
feel free to skip around and read the chapters that cover topics that are new
or useful to you. Alternatively, you could use this book as a handy reference
for the next time that you try to do something with the CLIÉ and you're
stumped. Each chapter is designed to stand by itself, and if I do cover a
related topic somewhere else in the book, I make sure to point you there.

Sony CLIÉ For Dummies focuses on the newest CLIÉ models that are running Palm OS 5. It's the first book to cover the newest developments, such as built-in wireless and Sony's innovative CLIÉ Organizer software. Even if you have an older CLIÉ, you can find plenty of helpful information here. The bundled software and precise design of particular programs might vary somewhat from the newest CLIÉs, but most of what I cover here applies to Palm OS 4 CLIÉs as well.

Who Are You?

In writing this book, I made a few assumptions about you, which is always risky. (You might have heard the old adage about what happens when you assume.) Nevertheless, this book is for you if some of these are true:

- ✔ You have a Sony CLIÉ and you want to find out how to get the most from it.

- ✔ You don't have a Sony CLIÉ yet, and you're wondering just what one could do for you.

- ✔ You're looking for a book that doesn't assume (there's that word again) that you know all the jargon and tech terms used in the PDA industry. (PDA stands for Personal Digital Assistant, by the way.)

- ✔ You want a reference that shows you *how,* step by step, to do useful and cool things with the CLIÉ without bogging you down with unnecessary background or theory.

- ✔ You're tired of hauling your 10-pound laptop with you on trips, and you're wondering how to turn your CLIÉ into a miniature traveling office.

- ✔ You no longer want to be tied to your desktop system for the critical activities in your life, such as playing games, watching movies, and surfing the Internet.

- ✔ You want to know how to pronounce CLIÉ. (It's *KLEE-a̅*. Now aren't you glad you bought this book?)

- ✔ You're looking for the secret Deluxe Macaroni and Cheese tip hidden in one of this book's figures.

What's in This Book

CLIÉ For Dummies is organized in seven parts, and each part is further divided into chapters that are related to the part's theme. And of course, the handy section headers (like the one a few lines up from this sentence) quickly lead you to specific topics.

Part I: Getting to Know Your CLIÉ

Part I starts with the absolute basics, the stuff that too many manuals assume you somehow learned by osmosis the first time you picked up your CLIÉ. To get you jazzed up to find out more, I start with a brief overview of all the amazingly cool things that the CLIÉ can do for you. Next, you discover how to interact with your CLIÉ and why it doesn't automatically understand your handwriting. Part I wraps up with a look at how your CLIÉ and your desktop system work together and how you can install all sorts of slick add-on programs.

Part II: Getting Organized

Part II covers the applications that PDAs are best known for: the personal organizer programs. You find out how to enter and manage your Address Book, create appointments, wrangle your To Do list, and get rid of all the yellow sticky notes cluttering your desk. After that, you'll have all sorts of extra free time, right? Not after you see the fun that I have in store for you in Part III.

Part III: Multimedia and Entertainment

Part III is where things get fun and creative. I show you how to manage your photos on your CLIÉ — and how to shoot new ones with the built-in camera. The fun doesn't stop with stills, as you find out after you discover how to convert and watch movies on your CLIÉ. If your CLIÉ's equipped to play music, Part III is the place to go to find the full scoop on music players and how to transfer tunes to a Memory Stick. The real fun begins with a look at the best CLIÉ games, and I wrap up on a literary note with eBooks and audiobooks.

Part IV: An Office in Your Pocket

Part IV is where you discover how you can often leave the laptop at home but still have full access to your Word documents and Excel spreadsheets — and even plug in an adapter that lets you do PowerPoint presentations right from your CLIÉ. You work step by step through the office suite that was probably bundled with your CLIÉ, and I explore the best third-party office add-ons.

Part V: Reaching Outside the CLIÉ Box

Part V shows you how to enhance your CLIÉ and connect it to the outside world. You find out about the various types of Memory Sticks, why you want one, and how you can use one to manage your files. You see the various ways that you can connect to the Internet with a variety of wireless technologies and then take a look at how to take advantage of your CLIÉ's online software. After you expand your CLIÉ and teach it how to talk to the outside world, I show you what else you need to make it the only computing device that you need when you hit the road.

Part VI: Securing and Protecting Your CLIÉ

Part VI delves into how to protect your CLIÉ's data from prying eyes — and from dead batteries and system crashes. After spending a good portion of the book convincing you that you can pretty much organize your life, manage your business, and centralize your entertainment on your CLIÉ, I'd be doing you a disservice if I didn't show you how to protect this now-vital tool. You find out about file encryption, data backups, emergency power sources, and how to protect your CLIÉ from physical damage.

Part VII: The Part of Tens

Part VII focuses on some useful Top Ten lists. You find out about the very best add-on programs, the best Web sites, and the must-have hardware accessories. And you find solutions to ten of the most vexing problems a CLIÉ owner can encounter, and maybe an Easter egg or two to wrap things up.

Your CLIÉ may vary

With 33 CLIÉs released in less than four years, these little electronic marvels vary from model to model. Of those 33 CLIÉs, not a single one has *every* feature that I cover in this book. In several instances, I point out the models that boast more unique features, but if I did that every time, this book would be about 100 pages thicker and that much harder to find a spot for in the bathroom. For the most part, you can quickly find out whether a CLIÉ has a feature that's discussed here. The easiest way to tell is to look for the icon for the application you're reading about in the Program Launcher. If you don't see it listed, your CLIÉ didn't include that particular option.

Icons in This Book

This book rarely delves into the geeky, technical details, but when it does, this icon warns you. Read on if you want to get under the hood a little or just skip ahead if you aren't interested in the gory details.

Here's where you can find shortcuts, commands, and other tricks that can make you a CLIÉ power user in no time. Pay special attention to the paragraphs with this icon to get the most out of your CLIÉ.

This icon highlights an important point that you don't want to forget because it just might come up again. I'd never be so cruel as to spring a pop quiz on you, but paying attention to these details can definitely help you.

Danger, Will Robinson! Don't pass over these crucial points; they could save you from screaming, tears, hair-pulling, or lost data.

Where to Go from Here

If you have comments or questions on this book, or you want to suggest the next big *For Dummies* project, visit the publisher's Web site at www. dummies.com, send an e-mail to customer@wiley.com, or drop a note to Wiley Publishing, Inc., 10475 Crosspoint Boulevard, Indianapolis, IN 46256.

Now you can dive in! Give Chapter 1 a quick look to get at least an idea of where this book takes you, and then feel free to head straight to your chapter of choice.

Part I

Getting to Know Your CLIÉ

The 5th Wave
By Rich Tennant

"OK antidote, antidote, what would an antidote icon look like? You know, I still haven't got this Sony CLIÉ the way I want it."

In this part . . .

In this section, you find out what your CLIÉ is and isn't. It's a personal organizer. It's a game machine. It's an entertainment system. It's a productivity tool. However, it is neither a dessert topping nor a floor wax.

This first part also discusses how to communicate with your CLIÉ by using Graffiti 2, the keyboard, and all the buttons and dials festooning the device. You also discover how to connect and synchronize your CLIÉ's contents with your desktop system — because even computers need friends.

Chapter 1

It's CLIÉ but Not Cliché

• •

• •

In the broadest sense, a Sony CLIÉ is a Personal Digital Assistant (PDA). But categorizing the CLIÉ as just a PDA is like calling J.Lo just a singer. Sure, these little electronic wonders are useful for the stuff that people have been doing with PDAs since the early days: organizing schedules, tracking phone numbers, managing To Do lists, and introducing users to the entertaining game of Find the Misplaced Stylus. But Sony created the CLIÉ to do more than the typical PDA. The name is actually an acronym for Communication, Link, Information, Entertainment — and as Sony has added new models to the mix, the company has occasionally reworded the acronym to include the words *Lifestyle* and *Emotion*. Yes, this device is too versatile for its own acronym.

The emphasis on entertainment makes the CLIÉ different from the typical PDA. No other PDA comes so loaded to the gills with built-in features for viewing digital images, listening to music, playing games, and various other fun stuff. So unless your idea of fun is rescheduling conflicting meetings, the CLIÉ is a natural choice. Sure, you can watch videos or take pictures with a Palm or a Pocket PC, but doing so often involves gathering, installing, and configuring a ton of add-on programs and accessories. Thanks, but I'd rather spend the time actually having fun or even being — gasp — productive.

Today's CLIÉs wrap the functions of numerous devices into one pocket-sized unit. The CLIÉ can do many things that a desktop computer can do, such as surf the Web, play games, or edit word processing and spreadsheet files. Many models of these versatile handhelds can also take the place of MP3 music players, voice recorders, digital cameras, and camcorders. You can do dozens of things with the PDA the moment you take it out of the box (well, after you charge the battery), but that's just the beginning. With dozens of add-ons available and literally thousands of third-party programs only a download away, the CLIÉ can do things even its designers never dreamed of.

Most of this book focuses on what you can do with your CLIÉ the moment you take it out of the box — which is a *lot*. Besides, my choices were either focus on the built-in stuff or write *Sony CLIÉ For Dummies: The 10 Volume Set,* which would have been much harder to cram into your briefcase.

What Your CLIÉ Can Do for You

Over the next few pages, I take a look at some of the more useful — or just plain cool — tasks and tricks that you can do with your CLIÉ. I cover each of these in more depth later in the book, so when you find something that intrigues you, feel free to skip ahead. But before you do, here are a few basics to keep in mind as you read this book:

- ✔ **Cost:** Not all CLIÉs are created equal; just look at the differences in the models pictured in Figure 1-1. Over the course of writing this book, 12 models were available, ranging in price from $149 to $799. High-end models have a wide variety of enhancements, such as built-in digital cameras or wireless features, that may not be available in midrange or entry-level CLIÉs.

- ✔ **Standard features:** Despite the differences in built-in features, all CLIÉ models offer a beefy set of standard capabilities: high-resolution color screens, enhanced contact-management software, a rich set of bundled applications, and the ability to run all Palm OS programs. So fear not — the majority of this book does apply no matter which model you own.

- ✔ **Enhanced features:** On the occasions when I do write about features that are unique to only a few CLIÉ models, I mention the model numbers in the discussion. However, given that Sony typically releases an average of one new CLIÉ model every *month,* not seeing your model mentioned doesn't mean that it lacks those features. When in doubt, be sure to check the specifications of your specific model to see if it has the feature in question.

- ✔ **Tweaks:** Sony often makes minor tweaks to the programs that come with every CLIÉ when it releases new models, so screen configurations or menu items may differ slightly on your CLIÉ from what you see here.

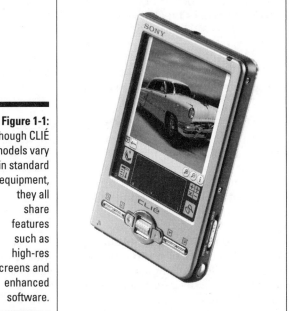

Figure 1-1:
Though CLIÉ
models vary
in standard
equipment,
they all
share
features
such as
high-res
screens and
enhanced
software.

When a CLIÉ is a Palm

All Sony CLIÉ models run the Palm Operating System, typically called Palm OS. Palm OS 5 is the latest version of the software originally designed for the very first mainstream PDA, the Palm Pilot. This is great news for CLIÉ owners because the Palm OS is the most popular operating system for handheld computers, and over 20,000 programs are available for it.

In general, you want to look for Palm OS programs rather than for CLIÉ software. Although many of the Palm OS programs have enhancements to take advantage of the CLIÉ's special features, they also work on other Palm OS PDAs, such as the Palm Zire and the Handspring Treo.

The CLIÉ doesn't run programs written for the Microsoft Pocket PC operating system. But that's no reason for concern. Pocket PCs have far fewer programs available than Palm OS devices. The CLIÉ gives you access to the widest selection of handheld software available. And just as important, the CLIÉ (like all Palm OS devices and Pocket PCs) can connect to desktop computers running Microsoft Windows and synchronize data such as appointments and address books.

Note that the CLIÉ does have one thing in common with the Pocket PC: Neither device comes equipped with support for connecting to a Macintosh. Third-party programs can make your CLIÉ and Mac get along swimmingly, however. I cover those in Chapter 3.

Now, don't get jealous because your CLIÉ PEG-ZXR8000 didn't include the holographic projector and tailfins found on the PEG-ZXR9000XT. Even a supposedly average CLIÉ still blows the socks off a more corporate PDA when it comes to fun per ounce.

Manage Your Personal Information

Although I brag about the CLIÉ's special abilities with the enthusiasm of a new parent pointing out how his baby isn't all scrunched like the others in the nursery, the device isn't all about the bells and whistles. At the core of Sony's little multimedia marvel is a top-notch personal information manager that can keep track of all your contacts, appointments, To Do items, and notes. (See Figure 1-2.) So add that paper day timer to the list of items that you can toss in the closet.

If you're already keeping all your contact and schedule information on your desktop system, fear not — you don't have to reenter your entire database with a stylus or tiny keyboard. A key feature of the CLIÉ (as with almost all PDAs) is the ability to share data with a desktop computer. In this case, the process is called HotSyncing.

Your CLIÉ and your desktop system always contain the same personal organizer data after a sync. So as long as you remember to HotSync regularly, you always have your latest appointment and contact information in your pocket. You can use the desktop system's keyboard to enter new information when you're at your desk — which beats a stylus or thumb keyboard any day. When you add a new contact on the road, HotSyncing copies that information to your desktop computer.

My favorite feature is the ability to HotSync with more than one computer. If you purchase an extra cradle, you can HotSync your CLIÉ at home and at work. Doing so ensures that you have identical personal organizer information at home, at work, and on the road. With up-to-date schedules and appointment alarms, you'll never have an excuse to miss an appointment again — which is usually a good thing. I give you the full scoop on HotSyncing in Chapter 3.

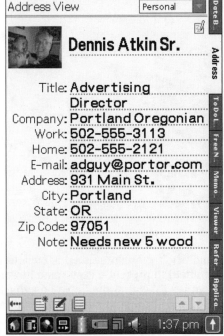

Figure 1-2:
The CLIÉ's
Address
Book lets
you add
a photo
of your
contact.

Show Off Your Pictures and Play Video

With its high-resolution screen, the CLIÉ is a natural for showing off pictures. Slideshows created using Sony's PhotoStand software are a heck of a lot more impressive than showing someone old-fashioned pictures stored in a yellowing plastic wallet holder.

And just try carrying a movie in your wallet! Your CLIÉ can play full-screen videos, as shown in Figure 1-3. Carry short videos of the kids along or entertain yourself on your next flight with episodes of *The Simpsons* taped with Sony's Memory Stick video recorder.

Plus, many CLIÉ models boast built-in cameras, so you can add to your photo album — or even shoot short videos — while you're on the road.

Figure 1-3:
Sure, you
can carry
pictures in
your wallet,
but the
CLIÉ lets
you carry
movies, too.

When you're talking to someone who's more interested in business than baby pictures, you can use your handheld to present a very small PowerPoint slideshow. Or, as you see in Chapter 13, with a simple add-on you can even connect your CLIÉ to a projector and show your PowerPoint slides (or vacation pictures) on the big screen.

Rock Out or Listen to a Good Book

Most CLIÉ models are equipped with a headphone jack and support for playing MP3 music. You can *rip* (digital music lingo for convert) songs from your CD collection into MP3 files or download them from the Internet. MP3 files take up much less space than the original songs on CDs, allowing you to fit about two hours of music on a typical 128MB Memory Stick. Figure 1-4 shows the Audio Player application built into many CLIÉs.

Of course, shrinking the files does reduce quality somewhat, but it's a small price to pay for portability — and only serious audiophiles are likely to notice the difference. The CLIÉ has built-in support for MP3 and ATRAC3 songs; the latter is a propriety Sony format that's better ignored. The only downside to the CLIÉ's music capabilities is that it doesn't support legally downloaded music from sites like the Apple iTunes store (www.apple.com/itunes)and Napster 2.0 (www.napster.com). Fear not, though — in Chapter 10, I show you how to get around this limitation and give you the full scoop on CLIÉ music support.

Audio Player MP3

| Continue | REP OFF | A→B |

TRACK
5

TIME
0:51

Old Joe's Place / The Folksmen

ALBUM
A Mighty Wind: The Album

MP3, 44.1 kHz, 192 kbps

AVLS | BASS 3

Vol

1:34 pm

Figure 1-4:
Don't buy an
iPod. Spend
the money
on a big
Memory
Stick and
use your
CLIÉ to play
your music.

Some CLIÉ models also support audiobooks from Audible (`audible.com`). You can choose from a huge selection of audiobook adaptations of best-sellers, as well as a wide variety of radio shows, all at a fraction of the price you'd pay for an audiobook on CD or cassette. Using a cassette or FM adapter with the CLIÉ's headphone jack, you can even listen to books while you drive.

Keep in Touch with Work and Friends

The first letter in CLIÉ stands for *Communication,* so it's no surprise that the device makes a great companion for people who want to stay in touch with friends or the office when they're on the go. You can read and respond to e-mail while sitting in a waiting room or check the local movie times while you're out eating dinner.

Best of all, you can do all this even if your CLIÉ doesn't have built-in wireless networking. Sony's CLIÉ Mail application lets you download your e-mail messages when you HotSync to your desktop system. On the next sync, you can upload any responses that you've written. And using applications like AvantGo and HandStory Suite, you can even download your favorite Web pages and read them offline with no live connection to the Internet.

Many CLIÉ models have built-in support for wireless Internet connections, or you can easily gain wireless access by adding a wireless card or by connecting the PDA to a cell phone. Wireless access means that you can check your e-mail, look something up on the Web, or see how your eBay auction is progressing — all using a pocket-sized device! And this stuff is about ten-times easier to do with a CLIÉ than with so-called smartphones. Figure 1-5 shows CLIÉ's wireless access at work.

Figure 1-5:
Web pages can feel a little cramped on a PDA, but "anywhere" access to the Web makes the slight compromise worthwhile.

Play Games, Read eBooks, and More!

This chapter just skims the surface of the thousands of uses people have put their CLIÉs to. Among other popular CLIÉ pastimes are

- ✔ **Gaming:** With its bright, high-resolution color screen, excellent audio support, and even an optional add-on game controller available for some models, the CLIÉ is an excellent time-killer. Games range from adaptations of classic arcade titles to detailed role-playing games to fast-paced, real-time strategy titles like Warfare Incorporated, as shown in Figure 1-6.

Figure 1-6:
Programs like Warfare Incorporated rival the quality of desktop games.

✔ **Reading eBooks:** The CLIÉ is a surprisingly good companion for book-worms. Thousands of titles (best-sellers, science fiction books, periodi-cals, and much more) are available in downloadable eBook format from sites like Palm Digital Media (www.palmdigitalmedia.com) and Fictionwise (www.fictionwise.com). And you can even download public-domain classics, such as works by Mark Twain and H.G. Wells, free of charge. The CLIÉ's crisp, backlit liquid crystal display (LCD) screen is as easy to read in a variety of conditions. Plus, because you always have the device with you, you can sneak in a few pages while waiting in a line or otherwise killing time.

✔ **Traveling:** With companion applications like Vindigo (you can find a demo version on your CLIÉ Installation CD), you can locate the best restaurants, night spots, bookstores, and other vital locations when traveling to major cities. And with the aid of a plug-in Global Positioning System (GPS) module, you'll never get lost again.

✔ **And much, much more:** Track your diet and exercise, keep your budget in check, control your home entertainment system, or even replace your bulky laptop computer.

As you're starting to see, the sky's the limit for CLIÉ users. So sit back, strap in, and get ready for takeoff!

Chapter 2

Communicating with Your CLIÉ

In This Chapter

▶ Pushing the right buttons
▶ Mastering the stylus
▶ Powering up
▶ Entering text with Graffiti 2, Decuma, and the keyboard

*W*orking with your CLIÉ is a lot like working with a desktop computer. Well, except for the lack of a keyboard. And a mouse. And disk drives. And a power plug. Well, okay, it's not *exactly* like working with a desktop computer. But any PC or Mac users will be instantly comfortable with the CLIÉ's icons, drop-down menus, on-screen buttons, and other interface components.

Although it runs the Palm OS, the interface on your CLIÉ might seem somewhat unfamiliar if you're upgrading from a Palm or Handspring device — or even an older CLIÉ. The standard Palm OS main screen of today — called the Program Launcher or just plain Launcher — differs little from the original Palm Pilots released in 1996. Sony, on the other hand, continually innovates and experiments with its interface design. Three variations on the Program Launcher are in use on the current models. Fear not, however — they all offer point-and-click simplicity. Most CLIÉ functions require just a couple taps of the stylus or a single press of a button.

In this chapter, I cover working with the CLIÉ from top to bottom: from switches and slots to writing with the stylus to keeping it in sync with your desktop computer.

Before you even turn on your trusty CLIÉ, though, I want you to familiarize yourself with the lay of the land. (Don't worry; you have me as your guide, your scout, your cicerone, your docent, your . . . you get the idea.)

Pushing the Right Buttons

Before you launch the stylus from its silo, go ahead and take a look at the CLIÉ's buttons, which give you one-touch access to your favorite applications.

The exact layout of these buttons differs among various CLIÉ models. No other Personal Digital Assistant (PDA) manufacturer comes close to the variety of device configurations that Sony offers. CLIÉs come in standard PDA forms: twist-and-flip models, mini-notebook styles, and with or without built-in mini-keyboards. They typically include the same basic buttons and switches but with minor variations in placement. The UX series mini-laptop-style models diverge more dramatically from the Palm standard, but these differences are mostly of concern to game players who might not find the right buttons available for zapping evil aliens. If variety is the spice of life, the Sony CLIÉ line is like a pile of electronic habeñero hot peppers.

The primary controls on all CLIÉ models are the *application hard buttons*. Despite the name, they're amazingly easy to use — *hard* refers to the fact that they're actual, physical buttons that you press with your fingers, rather than the buttons on the screen or in the silk-screened writing area that are designed to be activated with the stylus. The hard buttons give you one-touch access to the organizer application so that you can very quickly, say, look up an address. They even turn on the CLIÉ when you press them. Some CLIÉ models with folding screens actually feature two sets of application hard buttons, as shown in Figure 2-1.

If a hard button is set to launch an application that you don't use very often — say, Memo Pad — you can redefine it to launch your favorite program. Just launch the Prefs application (I'm getting ahead of myself here, but you can find out all about launching applications in the later section "Icon Do It!") and choose Buttons from the drop-down menu at the top-right corner of the screen. Now, tap the pop-up menu next to any of the button icons on the screen and select an application from the list that appears. Choose wisely, though, grasshopper. You don't want to set a button to launch your favorite game and then have your CLIÉ erupt with the Pac-Man theme during the middle of a business meeting.

Between the application hard buttons on most models, you find the Up and Down buttons, which you can use to scroll through lists of data.

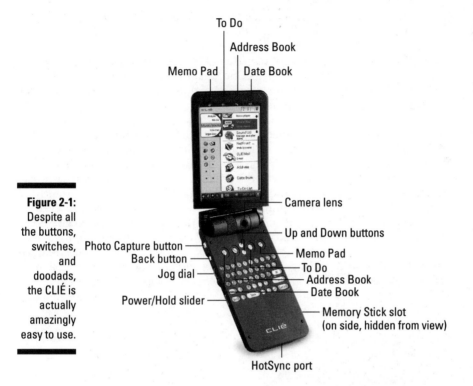

To Do

Address Book

Memo Pad   Date Book

Figure 2-1:
Despite all
the buttons,
switches,
and
doodads,
the CLIÉ is
actually
amazingly
easy to use.

Camera lens

Up and Down buttons

Photo Capture button ———   Memo Pad
Back button ———   To Do
Jog dial ———   Address Book
          Date Book
Power/Hold slider ———

Memory Stick slot
(on side, hidden from view)

HotSync port

On most CLIÉ models, you also find a slider labeled Hold. On older models, it's an individual slider; on newer units, it's integrated with the power button. Moving this slider up toward the top of the unit puts the device in the Hold mode. (Which, ironically, is designed for when you're *not* holding the CLIÉ. Go figure!) When in Hold mode, the CLIÉ doesn't turn on if you press one of the application hard buttons — in fact, on units with a separate power switch, even the power switch doesn't turn it on when Hold is engaged!

The Hold slider serves two purposes. First, it keeps your CLIÉ from accidentally getting turned on when it's being carried in your pocket or briefcase. Also, if your CLIÉ is equipped with an MP3 music player, you can start a tune playing and then move the Hold slider to disable both the application buttons and the screen. The display turns off, but your tunes keep playing, dramatically increasing your battery life. And if your CLIÉ includes a wired headphone extension that features music playback controls, you can continue to use that to control playback even in Hold mode.

If your CLIÉ has a separate power switch, and you can't get it to turn on, check the Hold slider before you panic.

The CLIÉ pioneered the concept of including a jog dial on the side of a PDA to allow one-handed scrolling and selection. Just turn the jog dial to scroll through lists or page up and down through a document, and press it to select an item.

Apparently, jog dials aren't sedentary creatures. In some models, such as the PEG-TG50 and PEG-NX80V, the jog dial rests in its traditional side-mounted, thumb-controlled spot, but it started wandering on the UX series, where it dropped below the keyboard. Now the jog dial sits below the screen on some models and is even found on the back of the PEG-TH55. And it's apparently talked other buttons into adopting its nomad ways. The newest CLIÉs (see Figure 2-2) feature the jog dial surrounded by the former Up and Down buttons, which are now Left and Right. (Though *Left* is actually *Up,* and *Right* is *Down.* Makes perfect sense, down? Er, I mean, right?) Many CLIÉs also feature a Back button next to the jog dial, which lets you back up after making a selection. A few models, however, omit this useful switch.

Figure 2-2:
The
PEG-TJ25
model's jog
dial rests
between the
application
buttons.
Some CLIÉ
models
place it on
the side or
the back.

Jog dial

Rounding out the hard-button brigade are the Capture and Voice Rec buttons. Now that every new CLIÉ includes a built-in camera, you find the Capture hard button on every current unit. Pressing it once loads the CLIÉ Camera application if it's not already running; if it is, pressing the button takes a photo. The Voice Rec hard button works in a similar manner: Press it once to launch the Voice Recorder program and begin recording.

Silky Soft Buttons

Along with the physical buttons, CLIÉs also have a series of soft buttons that are designed to be pressed with the stylus, rather than your fingers. These soft buttons are sometimes referred to in program documentation as *silk-screen buttons* because they were preprinted next to the writing area below the screen. That's still the case on some CLIÉ models, such as the TJ series, but on high-end units with larger screens, these buttons are now displayed right on the screen. This virtual writing area gives you the benefit of being able to make the buttons go away when you're not using them and thus use that area to see more data. Despite the fact that the icons are merely graphics on these models, Sony still calls this the silk-screen area.

You can find four soft buttons on all CLIÉ models, either silk-screened or drawn on the liquid crystal display (LCD) screen. In Figure 2-3, clockwise from the top-right corner, they are:

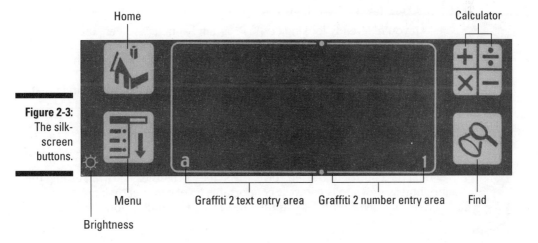

Figure 2-3:
The silk-screen buttons.

Home

Calculator

Menu

Brightness

Graffiti 2 text entry area   Graffiti 2 number entry area   Find

✔ **Calculator:** As you may guess, this button launches the Calculator application — either the built-in simple calculator or the souped-up powerOne Personal calculator that's included on your CLIÉ's install CD. I cover the calculator in Chapter 12, along with a bunch of other useful business tools.

✔ **Find:** Tapping this button pops open a window so that you can search for data such as names, addresses, and phone numbers. Just enter the information that you're looking for (capitalization doesn't matter), and the Find application searches for it first within the program that you're running, then in the built-in applications, and finally in third-party programs. This simple feature is amazingly useful for finding important information quickly. Check out Chapter 3 for some searching tips.

✔ **Menu:** Tapping this button activates any drop-down menus available in the program that you're currently running. These work just like the menus that you're probably familiar with on your desktop computer, and you can use them to access program settings and make adjustments. Note that some programs also have *tap-down menus,* typically on the right side of the screen. These have a small, black, downward-pointing arrow next to them and are activated by tapping the arrow, rather than by using the Menu icon.

The Menu button is a toggle. If you inadvertently tapped it and didn't really intend to choose a menu option, just tap it again, and it goes away.

✔ **Home:** The button with the picture of the house takes you to the CLIÉ's Program Launcher application, which is the home from which you set out on all your CLIÉ explorations. Whatever program you happen to be using, just tap the Home button to return the Program Launcher.

If you're already looking at the Program Launcher screen, tapping the Home button switches between program categories — more on those in the sidebar "I'll take the games category, Alex," later in this chapter.

One other tiny button lurks next to the Menu button. It's a small circle that looks like a sunburst. Fear not — this button doesn't cause your CLIÉ to engage a fusion reaction and transform into a small, handheld star. Rather, tapping this causes a slider to appear that lets you adjust your screen's brightness level.

Sliding the control to the left turns the screen brightness down. Turning the brightness down to the lowest comfortable level can greatly increase your battery life. See Figure 2-4 and then head to Chapter 20 if you want more details.

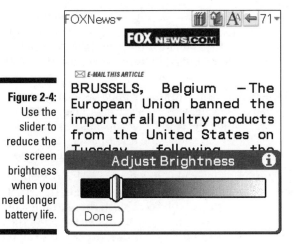

Figure 2-4:
Use the
slider to
reduce the
screen
brightness
when you
need longer
battery life.

Belly Up to the Status Bar

An additional set of icons on the Status Bar appears at the bottom of the
screen on large-screen Hi-Res+ (high-resolution) models such as the PEG-
NX73V and PEG-TH55. These models lack a preprinted silk-screen text entry
area, but instead use screen graphics to represent a virtual writing area.
(If you have a square-screen CLIÉ, you can skip to the next section.) In
Figure 2-5, from left to right, the icons are:

Figure 2-5:
The Status
Bar appears
at the
bottom of
the screen
on Hi-Res+
CLIÉs.

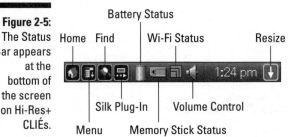

- ✔ **Home, Menu, and Find:** These three icons duplicate the functionality of
  their larger soft-button counterparts. They're useful when you're running an application with the full screen and the Graffiti writing area isn't
  visible.

- ✔ **Silk Plug-In:** You can use this icon to select a replacement for the standard Graffiti writing area. A plug-in for Decuma, an alternative handwriting recognition application, is included with the newest CLIÉ models.

Numerous third-party plug-ins are also available. You can even download applications that let you put pictures of your favorite people in the Graffiti writing area. Or for stress relief, upload pictures of your least favorite people and pretend that you're stabbing at them with the blunt end of your stylus as you write.

✔ **Battery Status:** This little meter visibly drains as your battery starts to run down, giving you a visual warning when it's getting to be time to recharge. On newer CLIÉs, tapping the icon brings up a more detailed display (shown in Figure 2-6), which shows the exact battery percentage remaining, as well as whether the battery is recharging or draining.

✔ **Memory Stick Status:** This icon glows blue if you have a Memory Stick inserted, a particularly useful feature on models like the PEG-TH55 that have an enclosed Memory Stick slot. If you see a slash through the icon, no Memory Stick is installed. If a small key appears above the icon, the Memory Stick is write-protected — that is, the little write-protect tab on the card has been moved so you can read from the Stick, but not delete or alter its contents.

Figure 2-6:
The Battery Status meter tells you how much juice is remaining and whether the battery is currently charging.

- **Wi-Fi Status:** This icon glows blue if you have a Wi-Fi Internet connection active or gray if you're offline. It's made up of three boxes, and the more boxes you see in blue, the stronger your Wi-Fi signal. Tapping the icon when you're online brings up a status window showing which access point you're connected to and how strong the signal is.

- **Volume Control:** Tap this icon to bring up the CLIÉ's volume controls.

- **Resize:** This is why you bought a big-screen CLIÉ! Tapping the rightmost icon causes the Graffiti writing area to slide off the bottom of the screen, giving you 50 percent more vertical screen real estate. If you're using a CLIÉ model with a built-in keyboard, such as the PEG-UX50, you can actually leave the writing area hidden all the time, of course. On models like the PEG-TH55, just tap the Resize icon when you need to enter text to bring up the writing area, and tap it again when you're finished. (See Figure 2-7.)

Odd CLIÉ out: The PEG-TG50

Sony's PEG-TG50 is like that kid in your class who always did things differently, yet still managed to do a great job. This is the only keyboard-equipped CLIÉ without a Hi-Res+ screen and a virtual Graffiti area. The PEG-TG50 also includes a pair of dual-function buttons that you can't find on any other CLIÉ model.

As you see in the following figure, to the left of the Date Book button is the Home/Menu button. Press it quickly to bring up the CLIÉ Program Launcher, or hold it down to activate the CLIÉ's drop-down menus. To the right of the Memo Pad icon is the Graffiti/Find button. Give it a quick press when the CLIÉ is waiting for text input, and a full-screen Graffiti writing area appears. (You probably bought the PEG-TG50 because of its keyboard, but it's good to know that Graffiti is available if you need it.) Hold the button down, and the Find window opens.

Note that the PEG-TG50 was in the process of being phased out as this book was being completed. But you may still find them in stores, or you may have snatched up one of these versatile devices before they were gone. And given that Sony releases new CLIÉ models so frequently that it could offer a CLIÉ of the Month Club, I wouldn't be surprised to see a similar configuration appear before long.

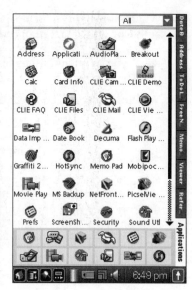

Figure 2-7:
Tap the
Resize icon
when you're
not using
the writing
area, and
your screen
gains 50%
more useful
space.

Stylus 101

Your CLIÉ's stylus does double duty as a replacement for both a keyboard
and a mouse. You can use it to write characters on the screen — just like
using a pen, but without the ink. You can also use it like a mouse to select
menus, icons, and other items on a screen. Unlike a mouse, though, no
double-clicking is involved — just tap the item to select it. Be gentle; the CLIÉ
needs only a light stylus tap. In fact, it recognizes your input better when you
don't press down too hard.

One unique stylus entry method is the *stroke*. Strokes are quick stylus motions
typically used as shortcuts for more involved procedures. For instance, a
stroke from the lower-left to the upper-right corner of the Graffiti writing area
brings up a shortcut bar on the bottom of the screen that offers options such
as Copy and Paste.

The styluses that come with many CLIÉs aren't the most comfortable input
tools around, particularly for those of us with hands so big that André the
Giant would look at them and go "Whoa!" Not to mention that the collapsi-
ble styluses included with some CLIÉs tend to, well, collapse when you're
trying to write. I've found that my own stylus precision goes up dramatically

Command strokes

Though unrelated to the popular band The Strokes, Command strokes are likely to rock your program usage. The Command stroke is basically a forward slash drawn in the writing area; its graphical representation can be seen at the left of the following figure. (This figure shows what pops up on the bottom of the screen when you enter the stroke.) The Command strokes give you quick access to the Cut, Copy, and Paste commands (the icons on the right side of the figure). Just make the Command stroke and then tap the respective icon to cut, copy, or paste data.

The Command stroke can also give quick access to menus without pulling them down. Shortcuts for various menu functions are listed on the right side of each drop-down menu. In the menu in the following figure, for instance, stroke-N — where you make the handy Command stroke and then write out N with the stylus or the keyboard — to create a new schedule event.

Like a demanding boss, the Command stroke lacks patience and wants information from you *now.* You have only a few seconds to tap an icon or enter a letter after making the stroke gesture. Otherwise, the Command window goes away, and you need to enter the stroke again.

Record	Edit Options
New Event	⁄N
Delete Event...	⁄D
Attach Note	⁄A
Delete Note...	⁄O
Purge...	⁄E
Beam Event	⁄B
2:00	
3:00	
4:00	
5:00	
6:00	

(New) (Details) (Go To)

when using a larger stylus, such as the Cross Matrix shown in Figure 2-8. You can often find full-size pen/stylus/pencil combos at your local office supply store. If you don't find one there that fits your needs, check out www.stylus central.com. You can find more styluses there than you can shake, well, a stylus at.

When using a combo pen/stylus, be *sure* that it's in Stylus mode before you write on the screen. The pen tip can leave a nasty gash on your screen. And even though you can use a fingernail to make a quick selection on the screen, for the most part you should stick with a real stylus to avoid screen damage.

Figure 2-8:
The upscale
Cross
Matrix
boasts
fountain and
ballpoint
pens that
also have a
stylus tip.

Charge and Go

The first half of this chapter covers the basics, but now I help you make sure that your CLIÉ is ready to rock and roll. After you unpack your brand-new CLIÉ, the first thing to do is plug it in to fully charge it. It very likely arrived with a dead (or at least nearly comatose) battery. Charging it takes three to four hours — a long time to wait before playing with a new toy. In the future, you'll usually just "top off the tank" on a partially charged CLIÉ, so typical recharges go much quicker.

Install the CD that comes with your CLIÉ on your desktop computer before you connect the HotSync cradle or cable that ships with your CLIÉ to your computer. (You can find more on installing software from the CD and on the whole HotSync process in Chapter 3.) Charge your CLIÉ and go through the initial setup first (more on that in just a few lines), and then you can insert the software CD and connect the cradle/cable when prompted to do so during the installation process. But first, here's how you set up the CLIÉ itself.

The first time you turn on your CLIÉ, you're greeted by the Setup screen, which takes you through a simple four-step process that lets you calibrate the screen digitizer — more on that later — and set the local time.

Tap the screen once to start the setup process. The CLIÉ then prompts you to tap the center of a series of targets to calibrate the digitizer, as shown in Figure 2-9. Do what to the what, you ask? The digitizer is the part of the glass covering the screen that detects where you're tapping with the stylus. Be *extremely* precise as you tap each target; if you're more than a little off, the CLIÉ may later have trouble figuring out what you're trying to tap. Don't worry, though. Your CLIÉ is as smart as it is snappy, and it figures out if you're too far off the mark and takes you through the process again.

```
Setup   2 of 4

In the following screen, you
will be asked to tap the
center of the target as shown
below. This ensures accurate
stylus entry.
```

```
Use the stylus to tap anywhere
to continue.
```

Figure 2-9:
Calibrating
the stylus.

If you later discover that your taps seem to be going a little off the mark — if you have to hit slightly above or below an icon for the tap to register — you can take another run through the calibration process. You do this by launching the CLIÉ's Preferences application and choosing Digitizer from the drop-down menu in the top-right corner of the screen. This re-launches the calibration process that you just completed.

The next stage of the setup procedure, shown in Figure 2-10, prompts you to set your country, time zone, and the current time and date. To set the country, just tap the drop-down menu arrow next to the word Region; do the same with the arrow next to Daylight Saving to tell your CLIÉ whether your region acknowledges Daylight Saving Time.

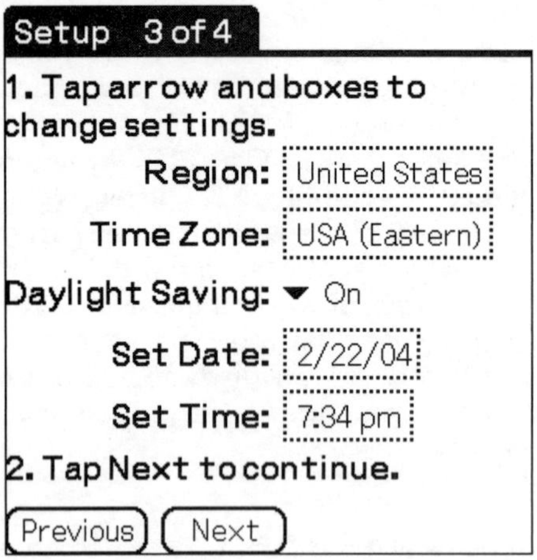

```
┌─────────────────────────────────────┐
│ Setup   3 of 4                       │
├─────────────────────────────────────┤
│ 1. Tap arrow and boxes to            │
│ change settings.                     │
│        Region:  United States        │
│     Time Zone:  USA (Eastern)        │
│ Daylight Saving: ▼ On                │
│      Set Date:  2/22/04              │
│      Set Time:  7:34 pm              │
│ 2. Tap Next to continue.             │
│ ( Previous ) ( Next )                │
└─────────────────────────────────────┘
```

Figure 2-10:
Setting the
clock and
time zone.

The default time zone is USA (Pacific). If that's not where you live, tap the text box next to the words Time Zone and select the correct zone. Tap the text box next to Set Date to — you guessed it — set the date. A small calendar pops up. Select the current year first, then the month, and finally the day. Finally, tap the text box next to Set Time. Use the up and down arrows to set each digit, and then select AM or PM.

Congratulations! Your CLIÉ is ready for use. The last step is to tap Done and dive in. Yes, you could tap Next, but if you do that, all it does is tell you to consult the documentation to find out how to use the Graffiti 2 or your computer keyboard to enter data. Real helpful, that!

Icon Do It!

Now that your CLIÉ is up and running, the launch programs can make themselves useful. The application hard buttons — the ones I discuss in the "Pushing the Right Buttons" section, earlier in the chapter — give instant access to the built-in organizer applications. (Or in the case of the PEG-UX50, the Web and e-mail programs.) For everything else, you use the Program Launcher.

The CLIÉ's Program Launcher comes in more varieties than gelatin flavors at a southern barbecue. The most popular launcher is the aptly named CLIÉ Launcher (Figure 2-11, left), which is used on most CLIÉ models. The UX series CLIÉs offer the somewhat gimmicky CLIÉ 3D Launcher (Figure 2-11, center), and the new PEG-TH55 integrates launcher functionality with its new CLIÉ Organizer program (Figure 2-11, right).

Figure 2-11: Sony currently ships three different versions of its Program Launcher with various CLIÉ models.

If you prefer the typical Palm OS Launcher (Figure 2-12), you can easily switch to it. Just tap the Menu icon to the left of the text entry area, and then choose Options⇨Go to Standard View.

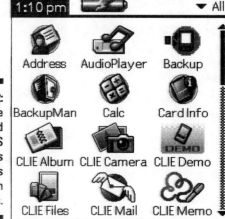

Figure 2-12: The standard Palm OS Launcher is available as an option on all CLIÉs.

Whichever launcher you're using, starting programs on the CLIÉ is as easy as tapping the appropriate icon with the stylus, which is the equivalent of double-clicking an icon on your desktop computer. (Just tap once, though.) You can also use the jog dial to scroll through the available programs, and then press it to select and launch an application — this method is great if you're using your CLIÉ one-handed.

To find a program quickly in the launcher, enter the first letter of its name with the stylus or keyboard. The launcher jumps to the first program whose name starts with that letter.

I'll take the games category, Alex

After you install a few third-party programs on your CLIÉ, your list of icons can start to get pretty darn crowded, making it harder to find and launch programs quickly. Like many CLIÉ programs, the launcher supports program categories, which make it easy to better organize your applications. You could put your most-used programs in the Main category, your Internet programs in the Web category, your games in Games, and so on. The CLIÉ ships with a number of predefined categories, and you can even create your own.

Sony calls categories *Launcher Groups* in its custom launcher. To categorize your programs in the CLIÉ Program Launcher, tap the Menu icon, and choose Edit CLIÉ Launcher Group from the first menu. (On UX series, the menu item is simply Edit Group.) In the window that appears (see the following figure), use the Up and Down buttons to rearrange group order, the Delete icon to remove a group, the Edit icon to change an existing group, or the New icon to create a new category. Tap Done when you're finished.

In the standard Palm OS Launcher, tap the drop-down menu arrow at the top-right corner of the screen, as shown in the following figure, to pop up the list of existing categories. Tap a category to choose it, or tap Edit Categories to create or edit existing categorizations.

To quickly switch between groups or categories, tap the Home icon.

The CLIÉ Program Launcher also lets you place your most-used icons in a Favorite Applications area, where they're always just a tap away. The Favorite Applications area has 12 slots. Tap the Menu icon and choose Edit Favorite Applications. When the screen shown in Figure 2-13 appears, simply tap any of the numbered slots, and a menu listing all your installed programs appears. Tap the name of the program that you want to put in that slot.

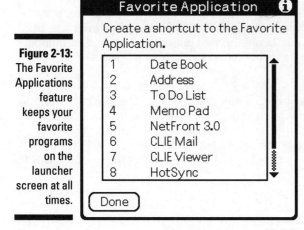

Figure 2-13:
The Favorite
Applications
feature
keeps your
favorite
programs
on the
launcher
screen at all
times.

Text Entry on Your CLIÉ

The CLIÉ is more accommodating than your average concierge at a $600-per-night hotel. Do you want to enter your text with a stylus by using tried-and-true PDA methods, one character at a time? Check. Do you want to try using your stylus to enter entire words at once? Roger. Tap an on-screen keyboard? Gotcha covered. Use your thumbs to type? Sure. Sony has CLIÉ models with mini-keyboards. Use the nice, big keyboard on your desktop system to enter handheld data? Yup. Beam data over *Star Trek* style with infrared light beams? You bet! Interact with your CLIÉ by using nothing but voice recognition? Well, if you're reading a tattered copy of this book in 2007, perhaps, but otherwise, you have to wait on that one. I show you the methods that work without the use of time travel.

Graffiti 2

The classic tried-and-true method for entering text on a CLIÉ, Graffiti 2 is the latest offspring of the Graffiti writing scheme pioneered on the original Palm Pilot. (The original Graffiti, ironically, was replaced by Graffiti 2 after Xerox accused Palm of copying the technology. Note to Alanis Morissette: Xerox getting mad about copying is ironic. Rain on your wedding day is not.)

If your interest in PDAs goes as far back as the ancient Apple Newton, you probably remember that its much-derided handwriting recognition was so quirky that even the *Doonesbury* comic strip took time out to make fun of it. So rather than try to adapt PDAs to human writing, the creators of the Palm OS decided it might be easier to ask humans to adapt their writing slightly for the PDAs. After all, humans are a fairly flexible species.

Thus was born Graffiti, a writing method that achieves admirable accuracy by recognizing printed letters one letter at a time. The writing area at the bottom of the screen is divided in half. The left side is used to write letters, and the right side to write numbers. The vast majority of letters and numbers are written just as you'd print them on paper, with just a few minor adjustments here and there.

Experienced PDA users take note: Graffiti 2 differs from the original Graffiti in a few minor but significant ways. If you've used Graffiti 1, take note of the differences, or you may find the letter *t* so frustrating to write that you'll just start trying to find words that don't use it. Considering I used it 23 times in the previous sentence, that's not easy. (Figure 2-14 shows the Graffiti 2 way to write the letter *t*.)

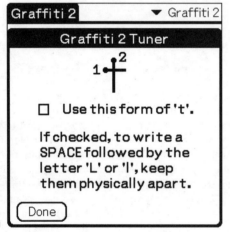

Figure 2-14: Most Graffiti 2 characters can be written with a single stroke of the stylus, but a few, such as *t,* require two strokes.

Graffiti 2 is actually very similar to the original. The main difference is that the use of two separate stylus strokes is required to make a few of the characters, such as *t* and *k*. This actually makes writing the characters more like writing on paper. However, it takes some getting used to if you're experienced in the original Graffiti.

What if you just can't get used to Graffiti 2? Install TealScript from TealPoint Software, and you can not only fine-tune your CLIÉ to recognize your own writing style, but also use classic original Graffiti strokes! (Check out the TealPoint Software Web site at www.tealpoint.com.)

Graffiti 2 has one new feature that makes the writing process much simpler: easy capital letters. If you want to write a lower-case letter, write it in the text area on the left. If you want to write a capital letter, center the letter on the line dividing the text and numeric writing areas. Note that you actually draw the letter the same way (see Figure 2-15) whether you're creating an upper- or lower-case letter. Where you draw it is the key.

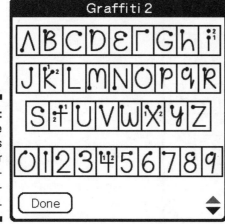

Figure 2-15:
The same alphabet is used for both upper- and lower-case.

Go ahead and get your hands dirty — practice entering a few characters.

1. **Press the Date Book hard button.**

   This turns on your CLIÉ and launches the Date Book application so that you have somewhere to write.

2. **Tap just above one of the lines next to a time.**

   This creates a new entry.

3. **Write your message in the text entry area by using Graffiti 2 strokes.**

That's all there is to it!

"Wait!" you say. "I don't know all the Graffiti 2 strokes!" Well, your CLIÉ box should have included a convenient, wallet-sized Graffiti 2 reference card. However, you can look up characters even more easily. Just take your stylus and do a quick stroke from the bottom center of the screen to the top center. This brings up an on-screen pop-up Graffiti 2 reference card. Tap the up and down arrows on the screen or press the Up and Down hard buttons to scroll through six pages of useful reference info that show you how to create letters, numbers, and symbols, as well as how to execute quick shortcut commands such as Cut and Paste. With the aid of this reference, you'll be scribbling words in no time.

Of course, words are a heck of a lot more readable when they're surrounded by spaces. Punctuation helps, too. To make a space, simply draw a dash centered across the letter or number input area. The opposite stroke (a backward, right-to-left dash) acts as a backspace. A period requires just a tap on the screen, and a comma is drawn like an *L* that's fallen on its back. See Figure 2-16 for more examples of how to create basic punctuation.

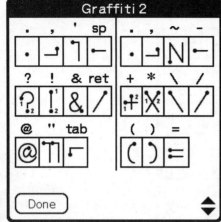

Figure 2-16:
The most
common
Graffiti 2
punctuation
characters.

Some punctuation marks and symbols require a *punctuation shift* — a line drawn from the bottom of the input area to the top — before you write them. This is typically because they're similar to other strokes. The beginning parenthesis, for instance, uses a stroke that's almost identical to writing a *C*. The pop-up Graffiti 2 reference lists an intimidating three pages of punctuation-shift strokes, but most of these are rarely needed for day-to-day use. Figure 2-17 shows you the ones you may actually end up using.

Figure 2-17:
The
Punctuation
Shift
characters
require you
to make a
vertical
stroke
before
entry.

If Graffiti 2 doesn't seem to have a very good grasp of what you're trying to tell it, don't give up. One very easy trick can improve the accuracy of Graffiti 2's character recognition dramatically: Just write *big*. Try to come as close as possible to filling the available space in the character entry box, and you may find that your Graffiti 2 entry accuracy is much, much better.

Decuma

If the idea of sitting down and rediscovering how to write the alphabet is as appealing to you as being told that you need to repeat kindergarten, fear not. Most CLIÉ models (except for entry-level units such as the PEG-TJ27) now include an alternative input system called Decuma. Decuma is designed to let you write entire words and correct them by using traditional writing strokes, such as writing over an incorrect character or crossing out a word that you want to delete.

To be honest, Decuma is so far only a little more popular with CLIÉ users than sidewalk snow-cone stands during a Vermont winter. But that's more reflective on its newness than its quality. It's a relatively recent addition to the CLIÉ line, so it may build an audience as time passes. And hey, if it's included with your CLIÉ, why not try it?

On the newest CLIÉ models, Decuma is built right into the device, so no installation is necessary. If your CLIÉ includes Decuma, but you don't see a Decuma icon in the Program Launcher, you need to install it by using the CD that came with your CLIÉ.

To activate Decuma on CLIÉs with a silk-screen writing area, tap the Decuma icon in the Program Launcher, and then choose Settings from the tap-down menu at the top-right corner of the screen. Finally, select the Enable Decuma Latin as Default Input Method check box. On these CLIÉs, the Decuma entry area obscures part of the screen as you write.

On Hi-Res+ CLIÉ units with virtual writing areas, just tap the Silk Plug-In icon on the Status Bar, and then select Decuma Latin Input, as shown in Figure 2-18. The Decuma input area replaces the usual Graffiti 2 writing area. If you decide to go back to Graffiti 2 later, just repeat the process and choose Standard Input.

Where Graffiti 2 has you print a character at a time, with Decuma you can enter entire words. However, Decuma still requires you to print, rather than handwrite. You use normal upper- and lower-case letters, and the program even lets you fine-tune characters to better reflect your own writing. The biggest quirk is that the entry line has room for only about eight to ten characters, so you have to tap the little green arrow to move to the next screen, and you must remember to include a hyphen if your word doesn't fit on the screen. Decuma is closer to typical writing than Graffiti 2 but still requires a bit of practice.

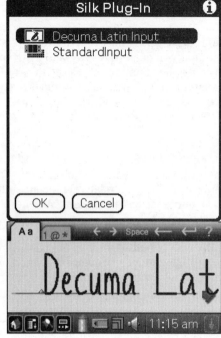

Figure 2-18:
Choosing
between
Graffiti 2
and
Decuma.

To enter numbers and symbols, tap the blue tab marked 1@* directly above the writing area. Tap the green Aa tab to return to character writing. (See Figure 2-19.)

Figure 2-19:
Decuma's
numeric
entry tab.

TIP

The software CDs that come with current CLIÉ models have fairly extensive electronic documentation in PDF format for using and tuning Decuma. (Some early Decuma-equipped units didn't include this manual.) You can also find it online by visiting www.decuma.com, clicking the Support button, and then selecting the correct manual to download.

Keyboards: The virtual variety

You can avoid the handwriting issue entirely by using the pop-up on-screen keyboard, which lets you use the stylus to tap out words. It's easier to use than Graffiti 2 or Decuma in that there's nothing to memorize. The CLIÉ replicates a miniature version of a computer keyboard on-screen, as shown in Figure 2-20. The downside is that the letters are very small, so you have to be very precise with the stylus.

Figure 2-20: The on-screen keyboard is an alternative to writing on the screen.

To activate the on-screen alphabet keyboard, just tap the Keyboard icon — the little *a* in the lower-left corner of the Graffiti area. (The *1* in the opposite corner brings up the numeric keyboard.) When either keyboard is showing, you can easily switch between the alphabetic, numeric, and international keyboards by tapping the appropriate selection at the bottom of the screen.

Note that the keyboard appears only when the screen displays an appropriate place to enter text. For instance, open Date Book and tap an appointment slot, and then you can bring up the on-screen keyboard. If you don't have an appointment slot selected, tapping the keyboard icon just results in an error beep because the program isn't expecting any text at the moment, just as entering Graffiti 2 text at this point would do nothing.

The following are few keyboard tips:

> ✔ **Shiftiness:** Because you can't hold down two on-screen keys at once, you enter an upper-case letter by first tapping the Shift key — it turns blue to indicate that it's selected — and then tapping the character you wish to enter as a capital letter. The Shift key then turns white again, and characters that follow are once again lower-cased.

✔ **Bustin' Some Caps:** The Cap key is used like Caps Lock on your keyboard; it's like holding down the Shift key. It's a toggle, so just tap it (it turns blue to show that it's engaged), enter all the characters you'd like to have capitalized, and then tap it again to return to lowercase text entry.

✔ **Legalized Graffiti:** You can still use Graffiti 2 when the on-screen keyboard is showing, as shown in Figure 2-21. If I'm writing something that I know will use uncommon symbols or punctuation, I often pop up the numeric keyboard, which is where most of the symbols are. I enter most of the text below the keyboard by using Graffiti 2, and then just tap the symbols as I need them.

Figure 2-21:
Even if you typically use Graffiti 2, the on-screen keyboard can be useful for entering rarely used characters.

On Hi-Res+ CLIÉ units with virtual writing areas, you can actually substitute a mini-keyboard for the usual writing area. Just tap the tiny keyboard icon below the Find icon on the right side of the text entry area. (Note that the UX series CLIÉs don't support the mini-keyboard due to the vertical orientation of their stylus writing areas.)

On the bright side, the mini-keyboard (shown in Figure 2-22) works just like the on-screen keyboard, but because it sits in the writing area, it doesn't obscure the program that you're running. Sony managed to fit the number row on the main keyboard, as well. On the downside, the mini-keyboard is slightly more cramped than the on-screen keyboard, so it requires even more stylus precision. It's good practice if your mother wants you to be a surgeon.

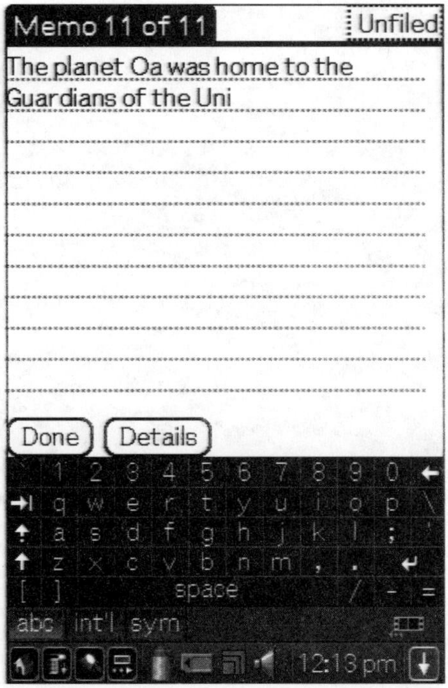
Memo 11 of 11
Unfiled
The planet Oa was home to the
Guardians of the Uni
Done
Details
1 2 3 4 5 6 7 8 9 0
q w e r t y u i o p \
a s d f g h j k l ; '
z x c v b n m , .
[ ] space / - =
abc int'l sym
12:13 pm

Figure 2-22: You can substitute a mini-keyboard for the virtual writing area.

TIP

Just as with the Graffiti 2 writing area, you can tap the Resize icon in the Status Bar to make the mini-keyboard go away when you're not entering text.

To return to Graffiti 2 entry, just tap the icon that looks like a miniature replica of the stylus text entry area, directly above the Resize icon.

Keyboards: The real thing

Many newer CLIÉ models offer an actual built-in keyboard. These aren't exactly like the keyboard on your computer. The small buttons are designed to be operated with your thumbs. Still, many users prefer thumb-typing to writing with the stylus.

These keyboards operate as you'd expect. The one thing to note is the inclusion of extra Function Shift keys. Some of these thumb keyboards lack numeric rows, so you have to hold down the Function Shift key (generally a key marked with either Fn or a blue dot, as shown in Figure 2-23) to enter numbers and many punctuation characters. Just press the Function Shift key, and then press the corresponding number or symbol key.

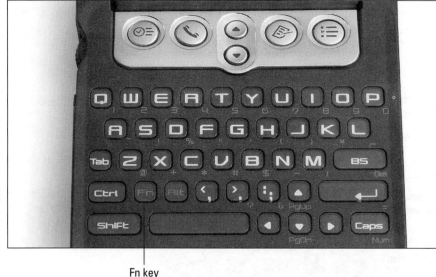

Figure 2-23:
Use the
Fn key to
access
numbers
and punctu-
ation.

Fn key

Note that all these CLIÉ models also let you enter text with the stylus. The NR, NX, and UX series CLIÉs all offer pop-up virtual text entry areas, and the PEG-TG50 model has a special pop-up Graffiti area that you can activate by pressing the Graffiti key at the top-right corner of the keyboard.

Other input alternatives

If all the choices in the previous sections aren't enough for you, well, I'd hate to be your waiter. But never let it be said that the CLIÉ isn't flexible! You can also enter text by using the following methods:

- ✔ **Using your computer keyboard and a program like CLIÉ Palm Desktop or Microsoft Outlook.** I take a look at how to do that in the following chapter.

- ✔ **Using third-party alternative text-entry utilities.** One of my favorites is Fitaly Virtual, available at www.fitaly.com. (See Figure 2-24.) Letters are optimized for minimal stylus movement, allowing you to rapidly tap words on the on-screen keyboard. It's a Silk Plug-In, so it appears in the virtual writing area and doesn't cover the screen.

- ✔ **Plugging your CLIÉ into a full-sized, folding keyboard.** About the same size as and with the same feel as a laptop keyboard, these pocket wonders let you touch type at full speed, yet they fold down to a size not much larger than your CLIÉ itself. See Chapter 17 for a look at my favorites.

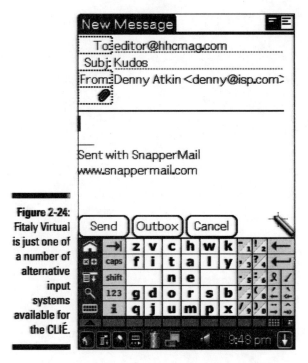

Figure 2-24:
Fitaly Virtual
is just one of
a number of
alternative
input
systems
available for
the CLIÉ.

Chapter 3

All That and the Kitchen (Hot)Sync

Congratulations. You've mastered the basics of using your CLIÉ, and you can enter data and launch programs like a natural. Unless, of course, you haven't yet checked out Chapter 2. In which case, it's probably a good thing that you bought a personal organizer device — it sounds like you need one.

With the basics out of the way, it's time for you to tackle a few slightly more advanced concepts. Don't worry, nothing intimidating — see *Relativistic Quantum Mechanics For Dummies* for that stuff. Rather, you're going to find out how to share information with your desktop system, how to tweak your CLIÉ to fit your preferences, and how a reset can make the CLIÉ listen when it stops responding to you.

Getting in (Hot)Sync with Your Desktop System

HotSyncing is one of the coolest and most useful tricks that you can do with your CLIÉ. As you might guess from the name, HotSyncing keeps your CLIÉ in sync with corresponding programs on your computer. This has all sorts of great benefits. First and foremost, after you HotSync, all the information that you've entered into your personal information management program is available on your CLIÉ — and vice versa! If you add a new phone number to your

CLIÉ, it is transferred to your desktop system the next time you HotSync. Create a To Do item on your desktop system, and it appears on your CLIÉ after you sync. And if you mark that item as done on the CLIÉ, the change is noted on your desktop system, as well. HotSync is even smart enough to recognize conflicts. If you modify an item on both your desktop system and your CLIÉ, HotSync keeps both versions and notifies you of the problem, allowing you to fix one entry and delete the other.

As a bonus, HotSyncing backs up the data on your CLIÉ to your desktop system, so if disaster strikes and you lose your data to a dead battery or crash, you can reinstall all your data simply by HotSyncing. I talk more about this safety net in Chapter 19.

Best of all, add-on programs can plug into the HotSync process; many such third-party programs take advantage of HotSync so that they can include their own desktop components. For instance, certain database programs, schedule programs, and even personal journals include both Windows and Palm versions and share data at synchronization.

Setting up for a HotSync

Even if you plan to HotSync with a different personal organizer program, you still need to install CLIÉ Palm Desktop because it contains the HotSync manager that's behind all the synchronization magic. If you haven't already done the Install routine yet, go ahead and dredge up the software CD that came with your CLIÉ and get ready to install Palm Desktop now.

After you get the CLIÉ installation CD fired up in your CD drive, you see that it includes loads of software, as shown in Figure 3-1. Throughout this book, I cover the important applications on the installation CD, but for now just install Palm Desktop, the heart of it all, by doing the following:

1. **Click the top button in the column on the left, labeled CLIÉ Desktop or CLIÉ Basic on most models.**

   Along with installing the Palm Desktop, your current task, you see a variety of options, depending on your CLIÉ model. These might include installing CLIÉ Organizer, Acrobat Reader, or CLIÉ Add-Ons.

2. **Click the Install button next to the Palm Desktop for CLIÉ entry.**

   The InstallShield Wizard appears. Click Next to begin and follow the prompts on the screen to begin copying the Palm Desktop program files.

3. **As the installation proceeds, you're asked to create a user account.**

   After the program files are copied to your computer's hard drive, the Create User Account screen of the Palm Desktop InstallShield Wizard appears, as shown in Figure 3-2.

4. Enter a name for your account in the User Name field and then click Next.

Choose the name wisely here. This is the name that the HotSync program and the Palm Desktop application use to identify your account. And more important, it's also the name that most third-party software producers will ask for to produce a registration code for you when you buy a program. So although you might think it's cute that your best friend calls you Sparkbuns, that might not be a good choice for a username. Your real name is always a safe bet. (Unless it really is Sparkbuns.)

Keep in mind that the HotSync username is supposed to be a unique identifier, and thus every PDA that you sync with your computer must have a different name. So if you call your first CLIÉ something creative like CLIÉ, and then you buy one for your spouse, you need to come up with a different moniker for the second handheld, or much electronic confusion and mixing of data will ensue.

5. Continue following the prompts to complete installation.

You're just a few clicks away from completing your installation. Just follow the InstallShield on-screen prompts. Depending on your CLIÉ model, you might be asked to perform your very first HotSync at the end of the process. See the next section for the full scoop on how to do that.

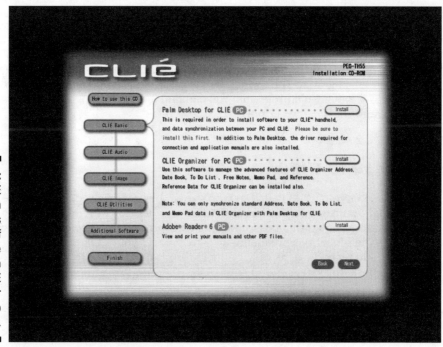

Figure 3-1: The CLIÉ installation CD includes a wealth of software for both your CLIÉ and your desktop system.

Figure 3-2:
Choose a
unique
HotSync
username
for your
CLIÉ.

Though Sony sometimes refers to this version of Palm Desktop as CLIÉ Palm Desktop or Palm Desktop for CLIÉ, it's really the same program that's included with all Palm OS handhelds. So if a third-party program is designed to work with Palm Desktop, it'll work fine with the version included with your CLIÉ.

What if you're upgrading from another CLIÉ or other Palm OS PDA? You still need to install the latest version of the Palm Desktop software because you need the program to allow your new CLIÉ to sync. When you're prompted for a username, enter the same HotSync username that you used on the older PDA if you want to transfer all your old data to your new PDA. But be aware that some programs that are designed for older Palm OS PDAs don't work properly on the newest generation of CLIÉs. I suggest downloading the free CLIÉ Migration Tool, which moves your information manager data over without moving old programs. You can find it at by visiting www.sony.com/clie and clicking the Support tab.

Sync time!

After you install Palm Desktop — see the previous section for more on that — it's time to introduce your CLIÉ to your desktop system. Depending on which model you own, your CLIÉ came with either a HotSync cradle or a cable. Their functions are identical — to connect your CLIÉ to your desktop system and recharge it, as well. Connect the cradle or cable to a USB port on your desktop system and to your CLIÉ.

After all this setup, you'll be happy to know that a HotSync is about the easiest thing you can do with your CLIÉ. If you have a cradle, just press the cradle's HotSync button, shown on the left in Figure 3-3. If you have a cable, you need to tap the HotSync icon in the Program Launcher to launch the HotSync application, and then press the HotSync icon in the center of the screen, as shown on the right in Figure 3-3.

Figure 3-3:
If you have a HotSync cradle, just press the button to sync. Otherwise, launch HotSync and tap the central icon.

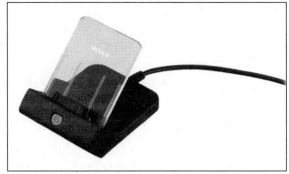 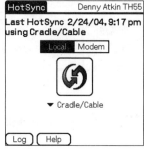

Your CLIÉ beeps, and the first time that you HotSync you see a dialog box on the Windows screen, asking you to confirm your username. Simply click the HotSync username that you just created and the sync starts. (See Figure 3-4 for a glimpse of what that exciting process looks like.) In the future, you can just press the button on the cradle — it asks for the username only on the first sync or if your CLIÉ has lost the contents of its memory.

 Speaking of lost memory, one of the most useful pieces of advice that I can give you is to make HotSyncing a habit. If you enter new contacts, press that HotSync button. If you download a new e-mail, press that HotSync button. If your cat hisses at you, press that HotSync button. HotSyncing ensures that the data on your CLIÉ is current and complete and that it's backed up on your desktop system in case your CLIÉ suffers any misfortunes.

Figure 3-4:
HotSyncing data often ensures that your data is backed up on your desktop system.

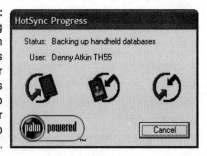

What about the Mac daddies?

The CLIÉ includes software for HotSyncing only with Windows systems. Despite this, the CLIÉ makes an excellent companion for the Mac, as well. You just need to buy a third-party program to allow the Mac and CLIÉ to communicate. Mark/Space offers just the ticket with The Missing Sync. Not only does it allow you to HotSync with the Macintosh version of Palm Desktop, but it also supports mounting your CLIÉ's Memory Stick as a drive icon on your Mac. It even transfers songs between your CLIÉ and iTunes, and photos between your CLIÉ and iPhoto. You can find more information at www. markspace.com/missingsync.html.

You don't need to limit yourself to HotSyncing with just one computer, either. You can install the Palm Desktop software on a second computer, connect your cradle or cable, and HotSync on it, as well. Your CLIÉ acts as a go-between, keeping all the data on both computers in sync. For example, add an appointment on your work laptop, and it's transferred to your CLIÉ during the HotSync. Then take the CLIÉ home and HotSync with your personal desktop system, and the appointment is saved there, as well. You'll be so organized that your biggest problem will be coming up with excuses to miss your appointments.

Connecting with Outlook

Some people love the Microsoft Outlook personal information manager. Others think the Magic 8 Ball said it best when it responded, "Outlook not so good." If you fall into the former camp and would prefer to use Outlook as your information organizer, you're in luck. The CLIÉ includes an application called Intellisync Lite right on its installation CD. This application allows you to HotSync the CLIÉ's personal information management applications with Outlook instead of Palm Desktop.

On the CDs included with most CLIÉ models, you find the Intellisync Lite application listed under CLIÉ Utilities. (Refer to Figure 3-1. You see the CLIÉ Utilities button on the left side of the screen.)You need to install Palm Desktop before you can install Intellisync Lite because it uses the Palm Desktop's HotSync conduit.

Advanced users can actually do a custom installation of Palm Desktop and just install HotSync manager, omitting the Palm Desktop application. However, I suggest that you go ahead and install Palm Desktop anyway. The program takes up little hard disk space, and some third-party programs incorporate Palm Desktop plug-ins that don't work with Outlook.

After installing Intellisync Lite, you need to configure it. A configuration
window automatically appears on your monitor after installation, as shown in
Figure 3-5. The window asks which CLIÉ applications you want to sync with
Outlook. Most users want to select all four applications, but if you choose,
you can leave an app unselected, and the application continues to sync with
Palm Desktop.

Figure 3-5:
Intellisync
Lite lets you
choose
which
organizer
applications
you want to
sync with
Outlook.

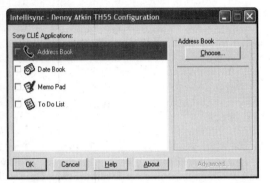

As you select each check box, a window appears, asking which application
you want to sync with. Select Outlook by clicking MS Outlook and then clicking the OK button. If you want a little more control over the HotSync process,
you can click the Advanced button on the Intellisync window — refer to
Figure 3-5 — to bring up a dialog box like the one shown in Figure 3-6. The
Conflict Resolution area lets you choose how to handle the situation when
records have been altered on both your Outlook and your CLIÉ between
HotSyncs. You can choose for Intellisync to add (duplicate) conflicting items,
ignore them, notify you, or just give automatic preference to the CLIÉ or
Outlook.

Figure 3-6:
The
advanced
Intellisync
Lite config-
uration
dialog box
for your
Date Book
settings.

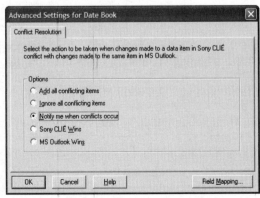

Take note also of the Field Mapping button in the lower-right corner of the advanced Intellisync Lite configuration dialog box. If you look at Figure 3-7, you notice that your standard Outlook contact screen has a number of extra information fields that aren't found in corresponding CLIÉ applications. If you need the information contained in one of these fields, you can alter the field mapping to transfer that info to one of the fields that is present.

If you typically utilize many Outlook fields that aren't represented in the standard CLIÉ organizer applications, a better option is to install a third-party application such as KeySuite from Chapura (www.chapura.com), which recreates all of Outlook's organizer functions on your CLIÉ. I take a look at the Chapura option in Chapter 13.

If you have both CLIÉs and Pocket PCs in your home, using Intellisync Lite keeps the organizer information in sync between both of them — which may or may not be a desired effect.

If you're upgrading to a CLIÉ from a PDA based on Microsoft's Pocket PC operating system, you can use Intellisync Lite to transfer all your organizer data from the old PDA. Just install Intellisync Lite and then HotSync your CLIÉ. All your Pocket PC data — which is stored in Outlook — syncs to your CLIÉ. After you've done this, you can leave Intellisync installed if you want to continue to use Outlook or remove it if you prefer to use the Palm Desktop.

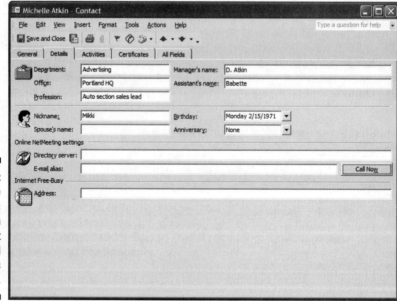

Figure 3-7:
The
Intellisync
Lite program
doesn't
support all
of Outlook's
fields.

HotSync 102: Advanced HotSync

This is an easy-A class. Even advanced HotSync adjustments are easy to handle. These are all tasks that you typically don't do on a day-to-day basis, but that could come in handy from time to time.

First, find the HotSync Manager menu, which is where you make adjustments to HotSync settings. Look in the Windows System Tray in the lower-right corner of your desktop system's screen. You see a small blue-and-red circle with arrows pointing inside it. That's the HotSync logo. Click this to bring up the menu shown in Figure 3-8.

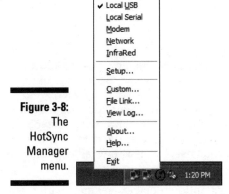

Figure 3-8:
The
HotSync
Manager
menu.

At the top of the menu are four or five HotSync options: Local USB, Local Serial, Modem, Network, and perhaps InfraRed if you're using a laptop. For the CLIÉ, you just need to make sure that Local USB is selected. The Local Serial option is used for older models of other PDA brands. The Modem option is designed to let you dial directly to your desktop system to sync, which is a bit dated in today's wireless Internet world. The Network option is mostly used in specialized business setups. The InfraRed option lets you HotSync with a laptop computer without using cables. It's handy in a pinch but very slow.

And now, a word about conduits. No, this isn't a commercial from the electric company. As you might guess from the name, a *conduit* is a connector. In this case, HotSync conduits connect a program on your CLIÉ with a program on your desktop computer — for instance, the conduit connects the Date Book application with either the Palm Desktop Date Book or the Outlook Calendar. The built-in Palm OS programs use conduits, and so do most third-party applications that transfer data to your desktop system. Because each program has its own conduit, rather than using one big pipe for all the data, you have lots of control over exactly what information goes where during a HotSync.

To adjust conduit settings, choose Custom from the HotSync Manager menu. A window like the one in Figure 3-9 appears, listing all the conduits currently installed on your system and their current settings. To alter a setting, either double-click a conduit or click it once and then click Change.

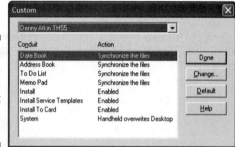

Figure 3-9: The Custom window lets you adjust HotSync settings.

Most conduits have four available settings, as shown in Figure 3-10. Here's what they do:

✔ **Synchronize the Files:** The default option for most conduits, this setting ensures that any new data entered on the CLIÉ is sent to your desktop system, and vice versa. After a HotSync is complete, the data on both devices should be identical. For normal usage, this is how all conduits should be set.

✔ **Desktop Overwrites Handheld:** This option replaces any information on the handheld with the information on your desktop system. Any information that's on your CLIÉ that's not already on your desktop system is lost. You might use this if you've, say, accidentally deleted some data on your handheld, and you want to copy the info from your desktop system's personal information manager back to the handheld. (Otherwise, the synchronization process results in the data being deleted from the desktop, as well.)

✔ **Handheld Overwrites Desktop:** As above, but this time the CLIÉ wins. The information on your CLIÉ replaces the information on your desktop computer.

✔ **Do Nothing:** This option deactivates this particular HotSync conduit. Suppose you have a conduit that takes a long time to execute, such as Mobipocket, which goes out to the Internet to gather data. You could set the conduit to Do Nothing by default and change it to Synchronize the Files when you want it to update its information.

Normally, if you alter a conduit's setting, the change takes effect only during the next HotSync, after which it returns to its default setting. If you'd like to change the default behavior, simply select the Set as Default check box after making the change.

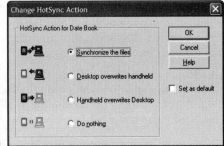

Figure 3-10:
Adjusting
conduit
settings.

Installing Programs

Along with synchronization, one other major task occurs during HotSync:
Installing add-on software. If you've purchased or downloaded a new program, HotSyncing transfers it to your CLIÉ.

Though a few programs arrive as EXE files and include step-by-step guided
setup programs like you find on your desktop system, most require a bit more
manual intervention from you. Typically, Palm programs are packaged in a ZIP
file on the PC or a SIT file on the Mac. To simplify unpacking and installing
these files, PC users can download a copy of WinZip from www.winzip.com.
Mac owners can use StuffIt, which is included with OS X.

When you open a downloaded ZIP file on your PC, it looks something like
Figure 3-11. The files in this example are the license agreement text file; three
versions of the program for various Palm OS devices; and most important,
the Read Me file. Here's a breakdown of typical file types that you find in a
Palm OS program distribution ZIP file, based on the last few letters of the end
of the filename:

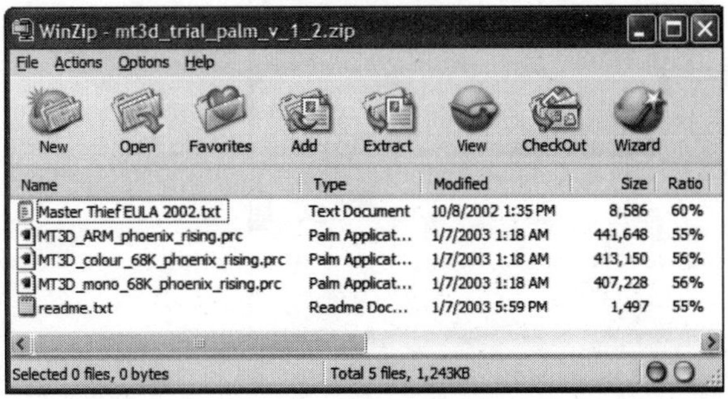

Figure 3-11:
A typical
Palm OS
download
viewed in
WinZip.

✔ **PRC:** These are program files. If the ZIP file just contains one PRC file, that's what you need to install. If you see multiple files, as in the example in Figure 3-11, consult the program's documentation to make sure that you install the correct file for your handheld.

✔ **PDB:** These are database files, in other words. These typically contain music, graphics, text, and other information needed by the Palm program that you're installing. If you see any PDB files in the WinZip window, chances are they need to be installed, but check the documentation to be sure.

✔ **TXT, HTML, or PDF:** This is the documentation that I keep telling you to check. Generally named something like ReadMe.txt or ProgramName.html, these files contain both installation instructions and the manuals for using the program.

After you figure out which files you want to install, just double-click them, and they appear in the Install Tool. You can also launch the Install Tool manually from your Windows Start menu. Choose Start⇨Program Files⇨Sony Handheld⇨Install Tool. Then you can drag and drop files into the Install Tool window. After you choose the files, the Install Tool window looks something like Figure 3-12.

If you want to install the files to a Memory Stick to save space in your CLIÉ's internal memory, click the Change Destination button in the Install Tool window. In the window that appears (see Figure 3-13), select any files from the left column that you'd like to move to the Memory Stick, and then click the >> button. (If you change your mind, select the unwanted file in the right column and click the << button to put it back.) Note that you must do this before you HotSync. If you want to move a file that's already in your CLIÉ's main memory to a Memory Stick, see Chapter 14 for the full scoop. You can also head to Chapter 14 for info on how to delete files that you no longer need.

Figure 3-12: Two Palm OS files are ready to install during the next HotSync.

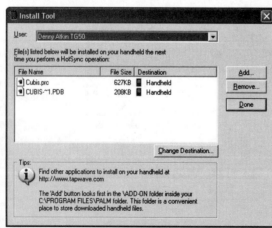

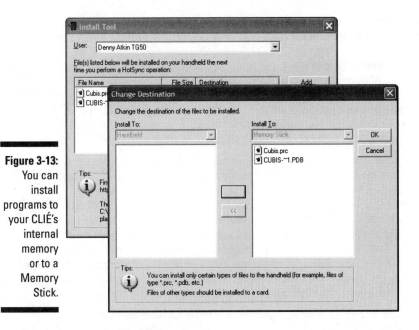

Figure 3-13:
You can
install
programs to
your CLIÉ's
internal
memory
or to a
Memory
Stick.

After you select the files that you want to transfer, initiate a HotSync application to install the files before the rest of your data is synchronized.

Want to automate the install process for your CLIÉ? Visit www.palmgear.com and download StreamLync. This automated installation program finds the right files for your CLIÉ and configures them for installation on HotSync — no dealing with WinZip or StuffIt.

Doing the Reset Shuffle

I spend a lot of time showing how to communicate with your CLIÉ. But what about those times when it just doesn't listen? Unfortunately, even handheld computers like the CLIÉ can crash or lock up occasionally. It's rare, but if it happens, your screen might freeze, or you might be presented with the rather frightening message Fatal Exception. The good news is that resets aren't fatal, and typically they're not even that big a hassle.

If a program crashes, the error screen might include a Reset button. Go ahead and tap it if you see it, but I've found that the button works only about half the time. Don't panic! Pressing the physical Reset button should get you back up and running.

Resets can be done in three ways. And the good news is that the first two ways leave all your data intact, and they do the job almost every time.

- **Soft reset:** This is the equivalent of pressing the Reset button or hitting Ctrl+Alt+Delete on your desktop computer. Just use the tip of your stylus to press the button inside the little hole next to the word Reset on the back or bottom of your CLIÉ. This reboots the CLIÉ. If a soft reset works, you see the CLIÉ startup screen, followed by the Preferences application, and everything is as good as new with no loss of data.

- **Warm reset:** Occasionally, a program that runs in the background, such as an application that replaces Graffiti 2, crashes your CLIÉ and then crashes it again whenever the CLIÉ starts up after a reset. If your CLIÉ crashes immediately after rebooting, hold down the Up button (or the Left button on CLIÉs with center-mounted jog dials; on the UX series, hold the PgUp key) and press the Reset switch, and then release the Up (or Left) button when you see the Palm Powered logo. This reboots your CLIÉ but disables any programs that run during startup. (It also disables any communications and wireless programs.) Then you can delete the offending application and try a soft reset.

- **Hard reset:** This is the reset of last resort. Use a hard reset only if the first two don't work. Fear not: Most users never have to do this. But if your CLIÉ remains locked up even after you've tried soft and warm resets, a hard reset gets things working by clearing out its memory completely. The downside is that you lose all the data in main memory. (Data in the Internal Media area on a UX series unit or on a Memory Stick isn't affected.) To perform a hard reset, hold down the power button, press the Reset switch, and continue to hold the power button until you see the Palm Powered logo on the screen. When you release the power button, the CLIÉ prompts you to press Up (or Left on the CLIÉs with center-mounted jog dials) to erase all data, or press any other key to abort. If the hard reset is successful, your CLIÉ returns to the same setup screen that you saw the first time you turned the unit on. Go through the setup procedure and then HotSync to restore all your data. If it doesn't respond after a few tries at a hard reset, it might be time to take it in for repair.

If your stylus tip doesn't fit in the Reset hole, try unscrewing the top of the stylus, where you may find a reset pin. If that doesn't work, or if you can't find your stylus, just unfold a paper clip, insert it into the Reset hole, and use it to gently press the button inside the hole.

Part II
Getting Organized

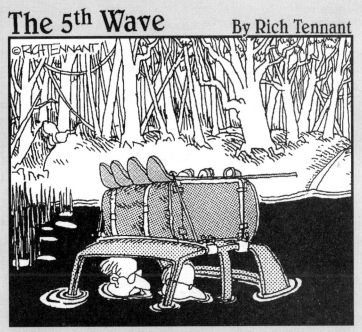

The 5th Wave

By Rich Tennant

"Okay, Darryl, I think it's time to admit we didn't load the onboard mapping software correctly."

In this part . . .

Personal Digital Assistants are best known for their organizer functions, and although the CLIÉ is a multitalented device, it doesn't skimp on the basics. It enhances them, as you see in these chapters. Making your way through Part II, you discover how to add photos to your contact list, drag notes and even movies onto your schedule, and more.

This part covers not only the standard Palm OS organizer applications — Date Book, Address book, Memo Pad, and To Do — but also the hot new integrated CLIÉ Organizer program.

Taking advantage of these organizer applications gives you plenty of free time to play with the really fun stuff that I cover in later chapters.

Chapter 4

Getting Street Smart with Address Book

I still remember the address book that my dad used to keep. If you looked at his entry for me, you could see my moves throughout my childhood, to college, from coast to coast, and back. It filled a couple pages of addresses, to the point that my listing had slipped to the *B* pages, and to the *third page* of the real *Bs*, at that. It had gotten to the point that the book was more useful as a historical record than as a reference tool. Of course, he could have gotten a new address book, but that would have required manually copying all the up-to-date addresses, as well. And that, of course, would be wasting time that could be better spent on golf!

I'm extremely glad to be living in the 21st century. I have electronic organizers to handle my addresses, TiVo to let me watch my favorite TV shows on demand, and a personal hovercraft to jet us to work. Well, two out of three ain't bad.

Obviously, an electronic address book like the CLIÉ's Address Book offers many advantages over the paper models. Some are obvious, but some might not have occurred to you.

- ✔ Updating is easy — no more crossing out old addresses.
- ✔ You have space for thousands of addresses.
- ✔ You always have current address info for all your contacts at home, at work, and on the road.
- ✔ The CLIÉ can keep your office and home address book programs in sync.
- ✔ You can create an electronic business card that you can beam to other Personal Digital Assistant (PDA) users.
- ✔ You can link addresses to appointments — a neat trick that I cover in Chapter 5.
- ✔ If something happens to your CLIÉ, you still have copies of your organizer information on your computer. If you lose a paper organizer, you're out of luck.
- ✔ On CLIÉs that are equipped with Bluetooth wireless communications, you can dial a Bluetooth cell phone directly from the Address Book.
- ✔ The Address Book can interface with add-on programs. For example, a Global Positioning System (GPS) mapping program can access your Address Book data to let you look up a destination without having to enter the entire address — just tap the contact name.

So toss that old paper address book on the pile of stuff to show the kids someday, along with the slide rule and the Commodore 64. Nothing beats the convenience of keeping your contact info on your CLIÉ.

Entering New Contacts

Despite its versatility as an address book, when you first take your CLIÉ out of the box, it's a clean slate. Entering addresses is a snap, though. If you don't currently have your contact information on a computer, it can be a bit time-consuming, but when the addresses are in electronic form, you never again have to reenter them — just update them as they change. And isn't that worth a little typing?

You can put addresses into your CLIÉ in three ways:

- ✔ Enter them directly on your CLIÉ.
- ✔ Enter them on your desktop system and HotSync them to the CLIÉ.
- ✔ Import them from Outlook or another address manager.

The last option is preferable if the info is already on your desktop system —
unless you just *really* want to practice your Graffiti 2 skills. But even if your
contact database is already on your desktop system, don't skip past the next
sections unless you plan to move to a South Sea Island and never make a new
contact again. (Can I come visit?)

Entering contacts on your CLIÉ

Begin by launching the Address Book program. On all CLIÉ models except
the UX series, you can do this simply by pressing the application hard button
that has a telephone on it. You can also tap the Address icon in the Program
Launcher.

After you open the Address Book program, creating a new entry is a snap.
Just do the following:

1. **Tap the New button at the bottom of the Address Book screen.**

   The Address Edit screen appears with the cursor flashing in the Last
   Name field.

2. **Enter the last name by using Graffiti 2 or the keyboard.**

   For more on Graffiti and other options for entering text, see Chapter 2.

3. **Tap the First Name field and enter the appropriate info by using
   Graffiti 2 or the keyboard.**

4. **Continue tapping and entering text until all the fields that you want
   covered are filled in.**

   To move to the next field, simply tap it. When you reach the bottom of
   the screen, tap the down-pointing arrow near the bottom-right corner of
   the screen (see Figure 4-1) or roll the jog dial down. The screen scrolls to
   the next set of fields.

Figure 4-1:
Creating
a new
Address
Book entry.

TIP

Although you can't add new fields to an Address Book listing, you can use multiple lines in a field. This can be handy for long addresses or for including a department along with a company name. (Refer to Figure 4-1.) After you finish the first line, just enter a Return Graffiti 2 stroke (a forward slash) or tap Enter on your CLIÉ's keyboard. When you're viewing the Address List screen, you see only the first line, but when you tap an address to display all its details, you see all the lines.

Adding additional contact info

In addition to the standard Last Name/First Name/Title lines, the Address Book includes four lines for storing various phone numbers, e-mail addresses, and similar contact information. The great thing about these lines is that you can customize them for each contact. A personal contact might list a home phone, a cell phone, an e-mail address, and an instant messenger name, but a business contact might list numbers for two different offices, a fax number, and a pager number. To change the description of a number, tap the down arrow to the left of the field name to make a pop-up list appear, as shown in Figure 4-2. Tap the description that's appropriate for your contact data.

Figure 4-2:
A variety of
labels are
available for
phone and
e-mail
entries.

TIP

Note that whatever name you choose for a phone number field, the first phone number in the list is the one that shows on the Address View screen by default, so listing the most-needed number first could be a time-saver. You can change which number is listed by tapping the Details button on the Address Edit screen (refer to Figure 4-2) and selecting the appropriate number from the Show in List pop-up menu.

When you scroll down to the very bottom of the Address Edit screen, you see four fields called Custom 1 through Custom 4. These can contain any data that you desire — extra e-mail addresses, spouse and kids' names, and so on. You can even choose custom field names, but note that unlike the phone fields, which you can customize for each entry, the custom field names show for all entries. To rename the fields, tap the Menu soft button and choose Rename Custom Fields from the Options menu. Tap OK when you're done.

If you're using Outlook to manage contacts on your desktop system, and you're using a few fields that aren't carried over to your CLIÉ's Address Book, you can use the Field Mapping feature in Intellisync Lite to map up to four fields to the Address Book's custom fields. (See Chapter 3 for more on the Intellisync Lite program.)

If you need to enter information about a contact that's not appropriate for one of the built-in fields or is too long to fit, tap the Note button at the bottom of the Address Edit screen. You can now enter up to 4,096 characters (roughly two printed pages) of additional information about your contact. Entries with notes gain a Note icon in the far-right column on the Address List screen; just tap this icon to view the note.

Finally, if you want to keep a contact's information private, tap the Details button at the bottom of the Address Edit screen, and then select the Private check box. You need to enable a password for your CLIÉ for the privacy to take effect — see Chapter 18 for details.

Adding a photo image

One field is unique to the CLIÉ's Address Book — the ability to associate a photo with an address. These pictures can be shots that you've taken with your CLIÉ's camera or JPEG photos transferred from your desktop system. Just tap the words No Image at the top-right of the Address Edit screen to bring up the CLIÉ's photo browser. Navigate through the browser, tap an image that you like, and — presto! — it appears at the top of your listing.

If you accidentally choose the wrong image — or you just don't want to look at that goofy picture of your ex anymore, but you can't erase her contact info because she still has your REO Speedwagon CD collection — just tap the image again, and a pop-up menu appears, giving you the option of choosing a new image or displaying no image.

Keep in mind that images use a *lot* more memory than text-only entries. I recommend associating images with only your most important contacts.

Assigning contacts to categories

Sorting contacts into categories makes finding entries much easier when your Address Book is heavily populated. Careful categorization can save you the hassle of scrolling through 19 screens of data in a crowded address book just to locate Renée Zellweger's number. With an entry open, tap the drop-down list box in the top-right corner of the Address Edit screen (it reads Unfiled by default) and choose a category for your entry from the pop-up list. If you don't see an appropriate category, tap Edit Categories; tap the New button on the screen that pops up; and enter a new category name, as shown in Figure 4-3. The Address Book supports up to 15 categories.

Figure 4-3: Create up to 15 categories to better organize your contacts.

Entering contacts by using Palm Desktop

To enter contacts on your desktop system, load the Palm Desktop by mousing to the Start menu and choosing Sony Handheld➪Palm Desktop for CLIÉ. When the program loads, you find a group of icons along the left side of the screen that correspond to the Organizer applications on your CLIÉ. Click the Address icon to get started.

To enter a new address — you guessed it — click the New Address button at the bottom of the Address Book screen. A list of the same fields that you see on your CLIÉ (except for the optional image) appears. Just enter the appropriate data in each field by using the mouse or the Tab key to move between fields.

When you finish an entry, click the OK button to return to the Address List screen or click New to place the current entry in the list and begin entering a new one.

When you finish entering your addresses, execute a HotSync to transfer them to your CLIÉ. (Chapter 3 gives you all the info that you need for performing HotSyncs.) Note that addresses are automatically saved when you exit Palm Desktop, so you don't have to save your file first.

Importing contacts from another program

If your addresses are in Microsoft Outlook or Lotus Organizer, and you'd like to import them to your CLIÉ, just install Intellisync Lite (see Chapter 3), and your PDA can sync with Outlook or Organizer instead of Palm Desktop. If you prefer to use Palm Desktop or the new CLIÉ Organizer program after transferring your contacts to your CLIÉ, just go to your Windows Control Panel, choose Add/Remove Programs, and remove Intellisync Lite after you HotSync your Outlook contacts to your CLIÉ.

If you're using a different third-party program, fear not. You don't have to retype all your contacts. The Palm Desktop's Import feature handles files in Address Book Archive (ABA), comma-separated value (CSV), tab-separated value (TAB), or VCard (VCF) formats. Consult your program's documentation to find out how to save a file in one of those formats.

When you have your contact info in a supported format, choose File➪Import from the Palm Desktop's main menu, and then locate the file that you created and double-click it. You see the Import Fields window, shown in Figure 4-4. Carefully match the field order, which likely differs at least slightly from the Palm Desktop's field order. You can use the Scan Records arrows to page through your entries, and then use your mouse to drag field names up and down the list to match the order of your address entries. When you're certain that everything's ordered properly, just click the OK button, and your contact list gets imported to Palm Desktop, ready to HotSync to your CLIÉ.

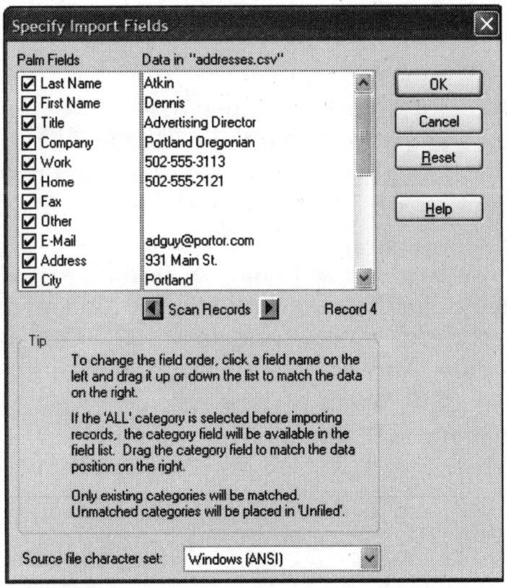

Figure 4-4:
When importing data from another program, make sure that the field names are arranged in the proper order.

Viewing and Finding Addresses

Now that you have your virtual black book installed in your CLIÉ, you can already see how it's more efficient than the paper variety. Tap the Address icon in the Program Launcher to bring up the Address Book. Finding information on a contact is as easy as scrolling through the Address List by using the Up and Down hard buttons or the jog dial. When you locate the contact you're seeking, just tap it or push the jog dial to bring it up on the Address View screen and view it in detail. Tap the Done button to return to the Address List view. If your CLIÉ is equipped with Bluetooth wireless communication, you can tap a phone number to dial it using your cell phone. (See Chapter 15 for the scoop on Bluetooth dialing.)

If you typically search for contacts not by name but by company association, tap the Menu soft button, and then choose Options⇨Preferences from the menu that appears. Here you can choose to list contacts by company name, and then last name, instead of last name, first name.

After you have more than a couple screens full of addresses, navigating the list can be a challenge. One way to pare down the number of entries is to use categories. When you first load Address Book, the category is set to All. Tap the down arrow next to the category box at the top-right of the Address List screen and choose a category to, for example, show only your business contacts.

To quickly switch between categories, just press the Address Book hard button. Each time you press it, the program switches to the next category. Note that entries in the Unfiled category don't appear if you use this method.

You can use a couple methods for quickly finding entries. At the bottom of the Address List screen, you see the words *Look Up* followed by a field. Just tap the field and enter the first couple of characters of the last name of the contact you're looking for.

To search through fields other than the last name or to find, say, all your contacts in the state of Mississippi, just tap the Find soft button and enter any piece of data — first name, state, area code, and so on. The CLIÉ searches the current application (in this case, Address Book) first, and then the rest of the applications installed in your CLIÉ. When you see the entry you were looking for in the results view, as in Figure 4-5, just tap the entry to bring up the detail view.

Figure 4-5:
The Find
feature
searches
the current
application
for matching
data and
then checks
other
programs.

Editing, Duplicating, and Deleting Entries

People are awfully nomadic in today's world, and the ability to easily update addresses is one reason to switch to the CLIÉ Address Book.

When Aunt Marge relocates from Canada to Florida, updating her address couldn't be easier. Just locate her Address Book entry and tap it to call up the Address View screen, and then tap the Edit button. Doing so brings up the by-now-familiar Address Edit screen. (Refer to Figure 4-1.) If you want to change the entry, just alter any field that has changed and tap the Done button when you're finished.

If you need to create a new listing that has similar information to an existing contact — say, people who work in the same company and share an address — you can duplicate an entry and just change the pertinent information. Tap the source entry on the main Address View screen, and then press the Menu soft button and choose Record⇨Duplicate Address from the menu that appears. An exact duplicate appears with the word *Copy* added after the first name. Now you can change just the name, phone, and other fields, and then save the new entry by tapping the Done button.

To delete a record, tap it to bring up the detailed Address View screen, and then tap the Menu soft button and choose Record⇨Delete Address from the menu that appears. If you already happen to be in the Address Edit screen when you decide to delete an entry, just tap the Details button and then tap the Delete button in the window that pops up.

Introducing CLIÉ Organizer for PC

Sony introduced yet another desktop synchronization application with the new PEG-TG55: the CLIÉ Organizer for PC. Though it truly changes the way you work on your handheld by putting all the major applications on one tabbed screen, the experience on your desktop computer isn't much different from that on the Palm Desktop. The biggest changes are support for the CLIÉ Organizer special functions that aren't available on other Palm OS handhelds, such as the Free Notes drawing pad, images in Address Book entries, and layered To Do items. For the most part, though, CLIÉ Organizer for PC works very much like Palm Desktop, so I focus on Palm Desktop for step-by-step instructions throughout the book. I cover any differences or

enhancements found in CLIÉ Organizer for PC in sidebars like this one.

As you can see in the following figure, the CLIÉ Organizer for PC Address Book works much the same way as the Palm OS version. The chief differences are the ability to display and choose pictures associated with Address Book entries (the Palm Desktop just ignores pictures) and the ability to associate Free Notes with an entry. (See Chapter 7 for more on Free Notes.)

Note that when you're choosing an Address Book image that's stored on a Memory Stick, you must use the Data Import program to mount that Memory Stick as a disk drive on your Windows system. I show you how to do that in Chapter 14.

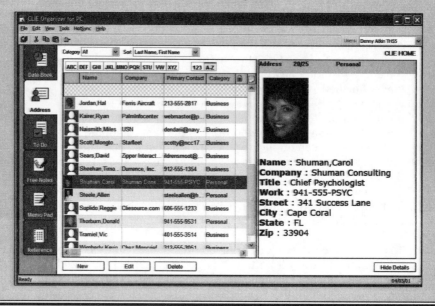

Creating and Beaming a Business Card

Even after working with PDAs for a decade, I still have a huge pile of business cards on my desk that I need to enter into my information manager as soon as I finish my quest to capture the mythical free time beast. Luckily, an alternative is available in today's widely wired world. (Try saying *that* three times fast.) By creating an electronic business card, you can easily beam your information to other handheld users — both Palm OS and recent Pocket PC devices can send and receive business cards to each other.

Creating a card couldn't be easier. Just bring up your own contact listing by tapping it in the Address List screen, and then tap the Menu soft button and choose Record⇨Select Business Card from the menu that appears, as shown in Figure 4-6. The CLIÉ asks for confirmation; tap Yes. A small icon with a tiny person next to an infrared beam appears at the top center of the screen to confirm that this is now your business card entry.

Figure 4-6: Setting a record as a business card lets you beam it by holding down the Address Book hard button.

On most CLIÉs, beaming your business card couldn't be simpler. Just hold down the Address Book hard button. (On the UX series, you need to tap the Menu soft button and choose Record⇨Beam Business Card because this series lacks the Address Book hard button.) The CLIÉ pops up a window asking you whether you want to beam your business card with or without an image. Tap Send to beam it. Make sure that your CLIÉ's infrared window is pointing at — and a few inches away from — your recipient's address window. When your recipient receives the card, her PDA asks her to confirm that it should be entered into the Address Book and which category it should be placed under.

You might want to create a couple listings for yourself — one with business information and another that stores the personal info that you prefer not to share with your business contacts, for example. Although Address Book lets you create only one business card, you can actually beam any entry (such as your personal record) in your Address Book. Just bring up the Address View screen, tap the Menu soft button, and choose Record⇨Beam Address from the menu that appears.

Address management using CLIÉ Organizer

The handheld version of the CLIÉ Organizer application included with the PEG-TH55 differs from the Address Book primarily in appearance. The main Address List screen has a couple significant enhancements — it shows the image associated with each entry and displays icons if notes are attached. It also includes a set of tabs across the top of the screen for quick access to entries starting with a particular letter.

You see three icons at the bottom-left corner of the screen in the following figure. The left icon toggles off the picture display so that you can see more entries at once. The middle icon opens a blank, new entry, and the right icon

brings up a screen designed to allow you to easily delete multiple entries.

The information contained in the entries is the same as in Address Book but with the addition of the ability to associate a Free Note with an entry by tapping the Free Note button on the Address Edit screen. See Chapter 7 for more on Free Notes.

Note that all the standard organizer applications, including Address Book, are also included on the PEG-TH55. So if you prefer the classic version, it's available from the Program Launcher. You can even use the Buttons function in the Preferences application to assign Address Book to the PEG-TH55's Address button in place of CLIÉ Organizer.

Chapter 5

An Appointment with the Date Book

*I*f you're having trouble finding the time to sit down and read this book, this is the chapter for you. The CLIÉ's Date Book application can do wonders for helping you manage your schedule. Daily, weekly, and monthly views let you know at a glance just how frantic life is about to get, and alarms can not only pop up to warn you of impending appointments, but they can also remind you days or even weeks before a project is due. Getting an alarm about your upcoming anniversary a week or so *before* the event is a lot more useful than getting it the morning of. Your CLIÉ can keep you from ever having to say, "Don't think of it as Red Lobster, honey. Think of it as *Lobster Rouge!*" when that's the only place where you can make a last-second reservation.

Looking at Your Schedule

Before I show you how to enter your business meetings, kids' soccer games, and manicure appointments, I want to take you on a quick tour of the Date Book program, concentrating first on the various views that it gives you of your schedule. To launch Date Book, press the Date Book hard button or tap the Date Book icon in the Program Launcher.

Date Book comes up in the Day View (see Figure 5-1), which shows you all your appointments for a single day. This view also makes use of teeny-tiny icons for showing you whether particular appointments have notes or alarms set. (Do you see the teeny-tiny alarm clock on the right in Figure 5-1? Guess what that one's for.) Small black lines in the left margin indicate the duration of an appointment; the line turns red to reflect appointments that overlap.

By default, Date Book compresses your entries to fit on a single screen — that is, if you have appointments that would normally scroll off the bottom of the screen, Date Book omits showing some blank appointments slots so that you can see all your appointments on a single screen.

Figure 5-1:
In this Day
View, thin
lines on the
left tip you
off that two
appoint-
ments
overlap;
thick lines
on the right
show the
duration.

If you have more appointments than can fit on one screen, simply scroll down to see the rest of your schedule by tapping the down arrow in the lower-left corner of the screen, by pressing the Down hard button, or by rolling the jog dial downward. You can view any other day of the week by tapping the appropriate day letter in the top-right corner of the screen. To move forward or back a week, use the left and right arrows surrounding the day letters Tapping the Go To button at the bottom of the screen brings up a calendar for quickly jumping to a specific day; you can find this handy button in all the different views.

To go instantly to today's appointments, press the Go To button at the bottom of the Date Book screen, and then tap the Today button at the bottom of the Calendar View that pops up.

You can find four small icons at the bottom-left corner of Day View. The first icon, Day View, should be highlighted. Tap the second icon or press the Date Book hard button to move to the second view, the Week View, as shown in Figure 5-2. This gives you an at-a-glance look at your schedule for the week — handy for figuring out which days are busy and which aren't. Appointments are represented by gray boxes, and you can tap any box to see what it represents.

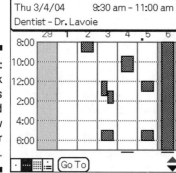

Figure 5-2: The Week View gives you a good overview of your schedule.

If you need to move an appointment to another day, the Week View makes it a snap. Just hold the stylus down on the gray box representing that appointment and drag it to a new day and/or time.

Tap the third icon at the bottom-left of the Week View screen or press the Date Book hard button again to see the Month View. Here, scheduled appointments are represented by dots in each day's box, as shown in Figure 5-3. The Month View can be made more useful by tapping the Menu soft button, choosing the Display Options item from the menu that appears, and then selecting all three options for the Month View. In addition to scheduled meetings, this shows repeating events and events that don't have a specific time associated with them.

Tap any date to jump to the Day View for that day. If you have a large-screen CLIÉ, you can tap the down arrow on the Status Bar to retract the Graffiti area and see the first few appointments for the day at the bottom of the screen. To scroll through days without leaving the Month View, use the jog dial.

Finally, tap the fourth icon at the bottom-left of the Month View screen or press the Date Book hard button one more time to go to the Agenda View, as shown in Figure 5-4. This extremely handy at-a-glance screen shows you your appointments for the day, as well as your pending To Do items.

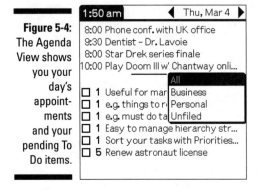

Figure 5-3:
The Month
View is
handy when
you're
setting
appoint-
ments more
than a few
days apart.

At the top-right corner of the Agenda View, you can see the current date as well as arrows that you can use to scroll forward and back through the calendar. Tapping any appointment takes you to that appointment in the Day View, and tapping a To Do item opens the To Do application (which I cover in the following chapter). At the top-right corner of the To Do section is a small drop-down menu arrow next to the word All. Tap this arrow to call up a pop-up menu that you can use to filter To Do entries by category.

Unfortunately, Date Book doesn't offer categories. If you want to categorize your appointments, a third-party replacement like Agendus or DateBk5 is for you. (See Chapter 22 for more info on these great third-party programs.)

Figure 5-4:
The Agenda
View shows
you your
day's
appoint-
ments
and your
pending To
Do items.

1:50 am	◀ Thu, Mar 4 ▶

8:00 Phone conf. with UK office
9:30 Dentist – Dr. Lavoie
8:00 Star Drek series finale
10:00 Play Doom III w' Chantway onli...

☐ 1 Useful for mar | Business
☐ 1 e.g. things to r | Personal
☐ 1 e.g. must do ta | Unfiled
☐ 1 Easy to manage hierarchy str...
☐ 1 Sort your tasks with Priorities...
☐ 5 Renew astronaut license

All

Making Appointments

In yet another example of how the CLIÉ can adapt to a variety of usage styles, you have four, count 'em, four different ways to start a new appointment entry:

✔ Tap the New button at the bottom of the screen in the Day View to call up the Set Time window, shown in Figure 5-5. Tap numbers in the hour and minute columns to set the Start Time value, and then tap the End Time text box and repeat the process. Tapping the All Day button assigns all available hours to the appointment, but tapping the No Time button is useful for creating what are referred to as *untimed appointments,* which are events like payday or a birthday, for which no specific time of day is associated with the event. After you set the time and duration, tap OK to return to the Day View screen. Now simply write the details of the event — the line corresponding to the time that you just set is highlighted.

✔ Start entering a time by using Graffiti 2 or the keyboard. The Set Time window appears, and the time that you wrote appears selected in the Start Time text box. To change from a.m. to p.m., just write a *P.*

✔ If your appointment starts on the hour, and you're in the Day View, you can tap in the blank line next to the time that your appointment starts and begin writing. The appointment is set to last one hour by default.

✔ Tap a time slot in the Week View to select a time. This is useful for getting an overview of how busy your week is before choosing a time for the appointment. After you choose a time, you're taken to the Day View, and the cursor is in the appropriate appointment slot, ready for input. This works only with appointments that start on the hour, but when you're in the Day View, you can adjust the start time if necessary.

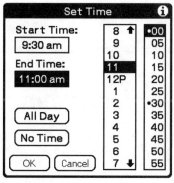

Figure 5-5:
The Set Time window lets you choose an appointment's start time and duration.

Are you trying to slip an appointment in for later today, but you don't know what the current time is? Just hold the stylus down on the date at the top-left corner of any of the views, and the tab changes to show the current time.

The Address Book link

Suppose you're making an appointment with Jessica Jones, and you plan to call her the morning of the meeting to confirm that it's still on. Sure, you could look up the appointment and then go to the Address Book to look up Joan, but the CLIÉ makes it easier than that. You can easily paste a contact's name and phone number into an appointment directly from the Address Book.

Just create an appointment normally, and then tap the Menu soft button and choose Options⇨

Phone Lookup from the menu that appears. A list of your contacts appears. You can scroll through them to find Joan's name or enter the first couple of characters of her last name in the Look Up text line at the bottom of the screen, as in the following figure. Tap her number and then tap Add to paste her name and phone number at the end of your appointment entry. If you enter a Return character (a forward slash in Graffiti 2) before performing the phone lookup, the contact name appears on its own line, making it easy to read.

Changing or Deleting Appointments

To alter an appointment, open the Event Details window by tapping the appointment entry in the Day View and then tapping the Details button at the bottom of the screen. As you see in Figure 5-6, you can easily alter the appointment time or date, set an alarm, make the appointment repeat, or flag the appointment as Private. (For more on private records, see Chapter 18.) You can also create a note to attach to the appointment in case you need to include additional information.

To delete an appointment, first select it. Then you can tap the Menu soft button and choose Record⇨Delete Event from the menu that appears, or tap the Details button and then tap the Delete button in the Event Details window when it pops up. A windows appears, asking for confirmation. Selecting the Save Archive Copy on PC option in this window saves deleted appointments in a text file in your Palm Desktop directory in case you need to reference them later.

Figure 5-6: The Event Details window lets you set alarms, change times, and more.

To delete several outdated appointments at once, tap the Menu soft button and choose Record⇨Purge from the menu that appears. The command defaults to deleting events more than a week old, but you can tap the arrow next to the time period and change this to as much as one month.

Repeating appointments

The Repeat feature is useful when an event recurs regularly or if an event lasts a number of days. After tapping the Details button, tap the text box next to Repeat in the Event Details window to make the Change Repeat window appear, as shown in Figure 5-7. Now you need to determine which time period to use. You can repeat by days, weeks, months, or years.

Here's what to do if you want to block off a span of time for an event (for this example, a vacation) in Date Book:

1. **With Date Book open, tap the New button at the bottom of the screen in the Day View.**

   The Set Time window appears. (Refer to Figure 5-5.)

2. **Tap the No Time button to create an untimed appointment, and then tap the OK button.**

   Your CLIÉ returns to Day View, where you can enter **Vacation** in the entry line that you just created.

Figure 5-7:
Setting up a
repeating
appointment.

3. **With the Vacation entry selected in Day View, tap the Details button at the bottom of the screen.**

   The Event Details window appears. (Refer to Figure 5-6.)

4. **Tap the text box next to Repeat in the Event Details window.**

   The Change Repeat window appears. (Refer to Figure 5-7.)

5. **Tap the Day button at the top of the Change Repeat window and enter 1 in the Every . . . Day(s) field.**

6. **Tap the drop-down menu arrow next to the End On field, and then select Choose Date from the menu that appears.**

   A calendar appears, and from it you can select the last day on which your appointment should repeat.

7. **Tap the last day of your vacation.**

   The Change Repeat window reappears with your selected end date entered in the End On field.

8. **Click OK to accept your settings and close the Change Repeat window**

   You now have an untimed appointment marking each day of your vacation.

You can use the Week or Month options in the Change Repeat window to set less frequent events, such as flagging your payday for every two weeks on Friday. Options abound — you can even set up an appointment to occur, say, on the third Thursday of each month. And of course, the Every 1 Year(s) setting is very useful for events like birthdays and anniversaries.

Note that if you edit or delete a recurring appointment, a window appears, offering the choice of deleting only the current occurrence (if, say, you know you're going to miss a regular weekly meeting), future occurrences (if an event is going to stop repeating after a particular date), or all occurrences.

Setting alarms

Sure, having your schedule in one place is great — when you remember to check it. But what about those events that sneak up on you? Getting an alarm the day of your mom's birthday isn't very helpful when you still need to buy her a present and mail it to her in Bermuda. Luckily, Date Book has a very versatile alarm feature.

After you tap the Details button to call up the Event Details window (refer to Figure 5-6) for an appointment, you see a check box next to Alarm. Select this check box, and on the line to the right of it, set how far before the event you want the alarm to go off. If you want the alarm to sound right at the beginning of a scheduled event, choose zero minutes. If you need to drive to the appointment, you might want to have the alarm go off two hours before it begins. If the event requires a lot of planning — say, you need to buy a gift or a plane ticket beforehand — you can even set the alarm to go off 30 days before the event.

When an alarm goes off, a window appears with the appointment time and description. Tap the OK button to dismiss the alarm, the Snooze button to have the alarm remind you again in five minutes, or the Go To button to jump to viewing the appointment in Date Book.

If you want every appointment to have an alarm by default, tap the Menu soft button and choose Options➪Preferences from the menu that appears. In the Preferences window — shown in Figure 5-8 — select the check box next to Alarm Preset. With this check box selected, every new appointment you create automatically has an alarm. The Alarm Preset feature defaults to five minutes before the appointment, but you can alter the default and still change the value for individual appointments, as well. You can also choose a default alarm sound and set how many times the alarm plays if you don't cancel it. I suggest setting the Remind Me feature to at least 5 Times just in case you happen to be away from your CLIÉ when it goes off. It doesn't repeat if you acknowledge it, so there's no harm in a high repeat value.

Figure 5-8: You can customize the default alarm time and sound.

The CLIÉ Organizer Date Book

The Date Book application included as part of the CLIÉ Organizer software suite, which first appeared on the PEG-TH55, is perhaps the most enhanced of all the updated applications. It has all the features of the standard Date Book — and can share data with the standard Date Book — but it also features a number of very useful new features.

The first time you run the CLIÉ Organizer Date Book, a window appears, allowing you to install the program's built-in holidays. The program prompts you to tap the country that you live in, and you can optionally import all the major national holidays. You can also add your own holidays — useful for permanently adding birthdays, anniversaries, and so on — or delete holidays that you don't celebrate.

In the visuals department, the CLIÉ Organizer Date Book adds a new six-month view and the ability to associate colors with specific dates. But most dramatic are the changes to the Day View. You can drag and drop pictures, movies, voice recordings, free notes, and icons (called Stickers) right onto your schedule, making this the most multimedia-oriented data manager yet. Play with these features to discover just how useful they are. Suppose you remember an item that you need to pick up at the grocery store on the way home. Jot down a Free Note or make a voice recording, and then drag it to the time slot for when you're heading home and set an alarm.

Another slick feature is the ability to write and draw freehand directly on any of the Date Book pages, as shown in the following figure. Text that you write in freehand can't be found in a search, but this feature is extremely useful for highlighting items so that you notice them at a quick glance.

Dates on the Desktop

The Palm Desktop application for Windows includes the same basic Date Book views as the CLIÉ version, except that a Year View replaces the Agenda View. With the Date Book application open, click the New Event button at the bottom-left corner of the screen and enter the information in the same way and with the same options as the handheld version, as shown in Figure 5-9.

The column to the right of your schedule can display either Address Book or To Do items. What's really slick is that you can drag either of these over to a time slot to instantly create an appointment containing either the Address Book contact information or the To Do information. You can then double-click the item to add further info, set an alarm or repeat value, or change the duration.

You can also create a new appointment by clicking in an appointment slot and typing. One nice enhancement is the ability to tap an appointment and drag it to a different time to quickly reschedule it not only in the Week View, but in the Day View as well. If you want to shorten or lengthen an appointment, click it, and a small arrow appears at the bottom of the appointment box. You can grab the arrow with the mouse and stretch or reduce the duration of the appointment.

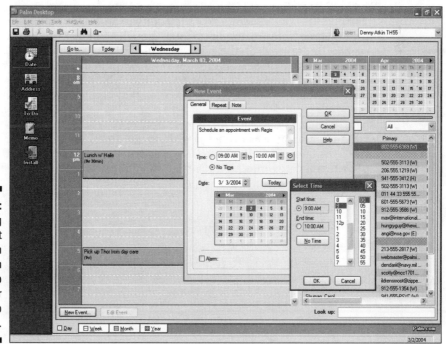

Figure 5-9:
Entering
appointment
data with
Palm
Desktop
on your
desktop
system.

Note that the Palm Desktop doesn't play alarms by default. If you want alarms to register on your desktop system as well as on your CLIÉ, choose Tools⇨Options from the Palm Desktop main menu, and then click the Alarms tab, as shown in Figure 5-10. Select the Always Available (Put in Startup Folder) radio button to have the Alarm Manager application start up automatically every time you turn on your desktop system. You can also choose what happens when an alarm goes off — whether an alarm window pops up, a sound plays, or a custom WAV sound file of your choice plays.

Figure 5-10:
Activating
the Palm
Desktop
Alarm
feature.

The CLIÉ Organizer for PC application works much the same way as the Palm Desktop but with the addition of the ability to add color coding, icons, and attached Free Notes to appointments. Though you must use your CLIÉ to add graphics or drawings on the schedule, the desktop version displays these elements in the CLIÉ Screen Preview window to the right of your schedule, as shown in Figure 5-11. You need to use the CLIÉ to modify or delete multimedia elements, however.

If you're using Intellisync Lite to synchronize your schedule with Outlook, everything transfers as expected with no unwanted surprises. (For more on Intellisync Lite and Outlook, see Chapter 3.) The one exception is that appointment categories aren't carried over, because the CLIÉ Date Book doesn't support them.

Figure 5-11:
The CLIÉ Organizer for PC Date Book lets you view attached images, drawings, and so on.

Chapter 6

So Much To Do

• •

• •

The CLIÉ's To Do application is a like a cute bunny rabbit. A rabid cute bunny rabbit, that is. At first glance, it looks like a little, unassuming thing, but start playing with it, and it's darn scary. After all, seeing your entire To Do list — all your work deadlines, all your Honey-Do list items from home, and the various and sundry other looming tasks — in one place can be intimidating. One look at all those items together could send you into a nervous breakdown. You have to write the work report before you can clean the yard, which needs to be done before you can take the kids to the museum, after which you can update your calendar, which you have to do before writing the work report. It's enough to make you wipe the whole list and replace it with a single entry: Run screaming from the house.

Don't do it. Putting all your To Dos in one place is the best possible way to make sure that the important stuff gets done, and it helps you put the unimportant stuff in perspective. In a way, the To Do list is one of the most challenging games available for the CLIÉ. The goal is to fill it up and then get it back to the way it looked when you first started using it.

Creating To Dos

To launch the To Do list, press the To Do hard button (note that this button is absent on the UX and TH series) or tap the To Do icon in the Program Launcher. The list is mercifully free of To Do items, except perhaps a few sample tasks, but you'll soon fix that.

To enter a new To Do item, you can tap the New button at the bottom of the main To Do screen, but you don't even have to do that. Just start writing with the stylus or your keyboard, and the text appears in a new To Do entry.

Creating a To Do is simple, but to get the most out of the application, you want to add a few details to your entries, such as priority and due dates. To do that — you guessed it — just select a To Do item and tap the Details button at the bottom of the screen. The To Do Item Details window appears. (See Figure 6-1.)

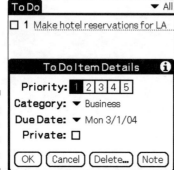

Figure 6-1:
Setting a
To Do item's
details.

The first setting on the To Do Item Details window is the Priority number, with 1 being the highest priority and 5 the lowest. Just tap the number of your choice. Choose wisely, grasshopper: This setting is key to efficiently using the list. When you first start using the To Do list, you'll probably have lots of 1 and 2 items because, after all, *everything* is important. However, you can actually make better use of the application if you save Priority 1 for *extremely* urgent items. On the other side of the coin, reserve the 5 for items that you want to address if you have time but that aren't critical.

You can actually change the Priority listing right on the main To Do screen. Just tap the number next to a To Do entry, and a menu pops up. Tap your priority of choice.

Next in the To Do Item Details window is the Category setting, which is perhaps more useful here than in any of the other applications. Tap the drop-down menu arrow and choose a category, or choose Edit Categories to create a new one. The two initial categories — Business and Personal — are useful, but the application works best if you create several categories for various social, business, and personal tasks. Figure 6-2 illustrates setting up custom categories; I explain how to do that later in this chapter in the "Using the Category menu" section. By setting up numerous categories, you can quickly and easily find the appropriate list when you have a free moment. You also avoid the temptation to always prioritize work tasks to the exclusion of others.

Figure 6-2:
Creating
multiple
categories
is a great
way to keep
personal,
family,
and work
tasks from
jumbling.

The Due Date setting is next in the To Do Item Details window. You can ignore this field if the task doesn't have an associated deadline. Otherwise, tap the down arrow to access the menu for setting the due date. Choices include the convenient Today, Tomorrow, and One Week Later. If none of those fits, tap Choose Date and select a due date from the calendar that pop ups.

Although you can set due dates, you can't set an alarm to go with them, so you have to remember to check your To Do list periodically to ensure that you don't miss a task deadline. If you want to set alarms for your To Do items, consider purchasing ToDo PLUS from Hands High Software (www.handshigh.com), which adds alarms and other fun features to the To Do application.

Finally, you can select the Private check box to hide or mask a To Do entry. See Chapter 18 for more on privacy options.

Notice the Note button in the lower-right corner of the To Do Item Details window? To Do entries can end up filling multiple lines, and you can use the Return character (a forward slash in Graffiti 2) to add a line break for easier readability. However, for lengthy items, consider attaching a note instead because having a number of multi-line items on the screen means that you see only a small portion of your list without scrolling. Tapping the Note button lets you add lengthy descriptions — up to 4,096 characters — of a To Do item. When an entry has a note, a small Note icon appears next it; you can tap that from the main To Do screen to read the note.

Adding a phone number to a To Do item is easy. Just select the item, tap the Menu soft button, and choose Options⇨Phone Lookup from the menu that appears. Tap the phone number that you want to show in your To Do item, and then tap the Add button to paste the name and number into the current To Do item.

Viewing Your Priorities

Much of the To Do application's versatility comes from all the different views that it gives you, allowing you to view your impending tasks by category, due date, or priority.

Setting preferences

To customize your main To Do screen, tap the Show button at the bottom of the main To Do screen. The To Do Preferences window appears, as shown in Figure 6-3. Tap the drop-down menu arrow at the top of the screen to choose the sorting order. You can sort by

✔ Priority, Due Date

✔ Due Date, Priority

✔ Category, Priority

✔ Category, Due Date

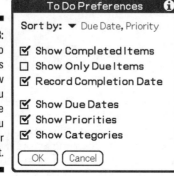

Figure 6-3:
The To Do Preferences window lets you customize how you view your task list.

If your To Do items are often deadline-oriented, the Due Date, Priority option is probably best. The Priority, Due Date option is a good choice if task priority is king and due dates aren't as important to you. Because you can easily toggle the category view from the main screen, the final two selections are the least useful.

If you deselect the Show Completed Items check box, your To Do items disappear from the main To Do screen when you check them off as completed. This helps keep your screen from getting cluttered with completed tasks. You can always re-enable the feature if you need to see the finished items.

Selecting the Show Only Due Items check box displays only tasks due today, overdue tasks, and tasks without a due date. This might be a good item to enable if you fall way behind and need to address only urgent deadline issues, but be careful. With this option enabled, major tasks can sneak up on you because you can't see them until the day they're due.

The Record Completion Date option replaces the Due Date value with the date that you marked an item as completed. This option is handy for tracking your progress in completing various tasks, but be aware that after the Due Date value has been overwritten by the completion date, you can't get the original Due Date information back.

If you use Due Dates for tasks, you definitely want to select the Show Due Dates check box, which adds a column on the main To Do screen containing the due date. (Figure 6-4 shows this handy option in use.) Otherwise, you have to select an item and tap the Details button to see when it's due, which might allow major tasks to sneak up on you.

Figure 6-4:
Change
a date
by tapping
it and
selecting a
new value
from the
pop-up
menu.

The Show Priorities option, which is selected by default, displays the priority to the left of each item. Turn this off only if you don't prioritize your tasks.

Finally, the Show Categories option adds a column displaying the category for each item. This can be useful, but it takes away space from the item description column. With Categories and Due Dates both displayed, most of your To Dos end up taking up two lines of screen space. Because you can check categories by displaying all items in a category together, you might want to leave this one off.

REMEMBER

You can also view your To Do items from the Agenda View in Date Book, which I discuss in Chapter 5. This is handy for trying to find time between scheduled tasks to address items on your To Do list.

Using the Category menu

By default, the To Do list mixes all your pending tasks together on the same screen. Categorizing To Dos is a great way to keep from getting overwhelmed. At the office, view just the Business category. When you're at home on Saturday morning feeling guilty about watching *Speed Racer* reruns, check the Around the House category. Are you planning an overseas trip? Put all the preparatory tasks in a Vacation category.

But you say that your To Do application doesn't have an Around the House category? That it has only Business and Personal? You can fix that by doing the following:

1. **From the main To Do screen, tap the drop-down menu arrow in the top-right corner of the screen and choose the final option, Edit Categories.**

   You see a list of your current categories, along with New, Rename, Delete, and OK buttons.

2. **Tap New.**

   The Edit Categories Enter screen appears. (Refer to Figure 6-2.)

3. **Enter your new category name, tap OK, and then tap OK on the main Edit Categories window to return to the main To Do screen.**

To view a specific category, tap the drop-down menu arrow in the top-right corner of the main To Do screen. The category list appears, as shown in Figure 6-5. Choose the category that you want to view or select Edit Categories if you need to add or delete categories.

If your CLIÉ has a To Do hard button, pressing it while viewing the To Do application switches the display to the next category. Press it multiple times to cycle through the category list.

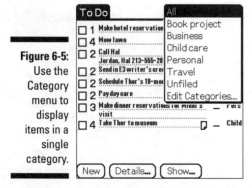

Figure 6-5: Use the Category menu to display items in a single category.

Checking Off and Deleting To Dos

The best kind of To Do item is the completed one. When you finish a task, marking it as completed couldn't be easier: Just tap the check box to the left of the item description. If you have the Show Completed Items option enabled in the To Do Preferences window, a check mark appears in the box. (For the scoop on preferences, see the "Setting preferences" section earlier in this chapter.)

If the Show Completed Items option is disabled, your item disappears from the screen when you check it off. It's not actually gone, just hidden from view.

If you want that To Do item to be really, really gone — not just conveniently hidden away — you have to delete it. You can rub out your To Dos one by one or all at once. To delete a single To Do, first tap the description. You can then delete it by tapping the Menu soft button and choosing Record⇨Delete Item from the menu that appears, or by tapping the Details button at the bottom of the main To Do screen and then tapping Delete in the To Do Item Details window.

To delete all your completed To Do items, tap the Menu soft button and choose Record⇨Purge from the menu that appears. The Purge window appears, as shown in Figure 6-6. Tap OK to clear all your checked-off items from memory. If you select the Save Archive Copy on PC check box, purged items remain available in an archive file that you can view in Palm Desktop for later reference.

Figure 6-6:
Purge your
CLIÉ of
all your
completed
To Do items.

The CLIÉ Organizer supercharged To Do list

The To Do list in the CLIÉ Organizer application that was introduced on the TH series offers all the features of the Palm version and a number of useful new features, such as outline-like hierarchies and new views of your data.

The most noticeable difference is the addition of *hierarchies,* which turn your list into an outline, as shown in the following figure. You can set up tasks as subtasks of other items by moving them to a lower hierarchy. For example, you might create an item at the top level called Work on Job Search with the Update Resume task listed below it at a lower hierarchy level, and the Rewrite Resume and Photocopy Resume tasks might fall below that at the third level. By tapping the Collapse/Expand icon to the right of an entry, you can hide or display its subtasks so that you see only the major project. Just tap it again to see the individual subtasks. When an item is hiding subtasks, the Collapse/Expand icon has a plus sign (+) in the circle. If all tasks are showing, the icon shows a minus sign (–) in the circle.

The four icons at the bottom-right corner of the screen give you complete manual control over sorting your To Do items. These icons move an item up or down in the list and up and down the hierarchy. Although you can't sort by priority or due date, two new view controls let you easily alter the screen to show items based on those settings. The View by Priority icon lets you view items by priority ranges, from showing just Priority 1 tasks to showing Priorities 1 through 5. The View by Task Status icons (labeled Term) let you toggle on or off overdue tasks, current tasks, and tasks that haven't yet started. As with the standard To Do application, you can view tasks by category, as well. However, the real power comes from combining all these options. For instance, you can choose to view only the overdue Business tasks of Priorities 1 through 3.

To accommodate the Task Status display, the CLIÉ Organizer To Do list adds a new Start Date field. Items that aren't due to be started yet show up in a light gray font.

Finally, in addition to attaching standard text notes, you can attach handwritten Free Notes, which I cover in Chapter 7, to To Do items.

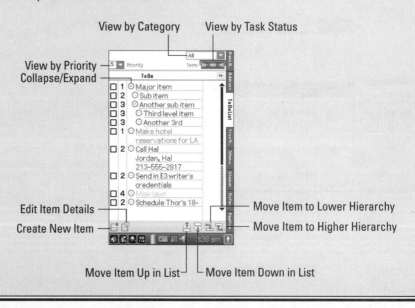

View by Category   View by Task Status

View by Priority
Collapse/Expand

Edit Item Details   Move Item to Lower Hierarchy
Create New Item   Move Item to Higher Hierarchy

Move Item Up in List   Move Item Down in List

To Do on the Desktop

The Palm Desktop version of the To Do list is very straightforward because it has the same options as the CLIÉ version.

Load the Palm Desktop on your computer by choosing Start⇨Sony Handheld⇨ Palm Desktop for CLIÉ. When the program loads, you find a group of icons along the left side of the screen that correspond to the organizer applications on your CLIÉ. Click the To Do icon to get started.

To alter a task's details, simply click the New To Do button on the bottom of the screen to create a new task, or highlight an existing task and click Edit To Do.

The one significant enhancement is the ability to turn tasks into appointments — handy if you want them to show up on a day's schedule or you want to associate an alarm with them. Just click the Date icon on the left side of the Palm Desktop screen, and then click the To Do button to the right of your appointment list. Then you can drag a To Do item to a Date Book appointment time slot. Note that the To Do item and the new Date Book appointment remain separate entities — deleting the To Do task doesn't affect the Date Book appointment that you created from it, and vice versa.

The CLIÉ Organizer for PC version of the To Do list is absolutely identical to the handheld version. After you master the application on your CLIÉ, you'll have no problems using the desktop version.

Outlook users can find their To Do items in Outlook's Task List view. Outlook handles tasks quite a bit differently than the CLIÉ. The CLIÉ ignores the Start Date, % Complete, Alarm, and Owner fields in Outlook, as well as the fields on the Details tab. Also, Outlook handles priorities differently. CLIÉ items with Priority 5 sync to Outlook with a Priority setting of Low. Items that are Priority 2 through4 sync with Normal Priority. Priority 1 items show High Priority in Outlook.

To HotSync with Outlook, you need to install Intellisync Lite. You can find out all about this in Chapter 3.

Chapter 7

Notes from a Small PDA: Memo Pad, CLIÉ Memo, and Free Notes

*T*he programs that I show you in previous chapters excel at organizing your data. But for many people, the most-used pages in their paper organizers are the blank ones at the back where you make quick scribbles when you're in a hurry. You might jot down a grocery list or copy a phone number that you'll transfer to your address book later. Some people substitute sticky notes for the organizer pages, decorating the edges of their computer monitors with rings of lovely yellow paper squares.

Your CLIÉ includes a couple of programs that are perfect for this sort of note-taking, as well as for creating or copying short documents that you might want to bring along for reference.

All Palm OS Personal Digital Assistants (PDAs) include the classic Memo Pad program, which is essentially a basic word processor that's limited to documents of about two printed pages in length. Most CLIÉs also include CLIÉ Memo, which is a basic sketchpad application that's designed to allow you to quickly jot down basic notes and drawings. Finally, the new CLIÉ Organizer suite included with the PEG-TH55 replaces CLIÉ Memo with a much-enhanced note-taking program called Free Notes. So whether you want to write something for later transfer to another organizer application or your word processor, or you just want to jot a quick note for later reference, the CLIÉ has you covered.

Flip Open the Memo Pad

Memo Pad is a simple text editor that's designed to allow you to take notes or write short documents with Graffiti 2 or your CLIÉ's keyboard. It's a very open-ended program, and the types of information that you can keep with it are limited only by your imagination. Here are a few things that I use Memo Pad for:

- ✔ Grocery lists
- ✔ Want lists for individual stores, such as books that I want to pick up next time I'm at the bookstore
- ✔ Meeting notes
- ✔ Registration codes for software I've purchased
- ✔ My secret macaroni and cheese recipe
- ✔ Driving directions
- ✔ DVDs to rent
- ✔ A list of useful info for business trips in new towns, such as good restaurants
- ✔ Dial-up modem access numbers for cities that I visit
- ✔ A quick-reference of useful phrases when visiting a foreign country
- ✔ Fantastic ideas and amazing inspirations that I don't want to forget

Creating memos

To launch the Memo Pad program, just press the Memo hard button (if your CLIÉ has one) or tap the Memo Pad icon in the Program Launcher.

Entering a new memo couldn't be easier. When you launch Memo Pad, the program opens to the Memo List view, which is your embarking point to the wonderful world of memo writing. The official method is to tap the New button at the bottom of this screen to start a new memo. You don't even have to do that, however. If you just start writing or typing, a new memo automatically opens.

The first line in your memo is displayed as a title in Memo List view, so you can think of this as the title or filename for your memo. You can start by entering something like Shopping List or Places to Visit in Cannes.

Memos can be up to 4,096 characters, which is about 800 words. If you typically need to create longer documents than that, I suggest looking into some of the full-featured handheld word processors such as Documents To Go, which I cover in Chapters 12.

Memo Pad includes some basic text-editing capabilities. You can highlight a sentence or paragraph by tapping the stylus on the screen and dragging it across the text just as you would do with a mouse on your desktop computer. (See Figure 7-1.) You can also highlight a single word by quickly double-tapping it or highlight an entire line by triple-tapping. When it's highlighted, you can tap the Menu soft button and use the Cut and Paste commands on the Edit menu to delete or move text in your document.

Figure 7-1:
You can highlight text in Memo Pad by dragging your stylus tip across it.

If you've used the Notes features in the other organizer applications, such as Address Book, Date Book, and To Do, you know how to use the Memo Pad because it works the same way. In fact, if you want to take notes during a meeting, for instance, you could just create a note attached to the meeting appointment in Date Book to associate it with the entry. However, this has the disadvantage that you'll eventually lose access to that note when your old meetings are purged from memory. By using Memo Pad, the notes stick around until you manually delete them.

If you tap the Details button at the bottom of the Memo Entry screen, a window pops up, giving you the opportunity to set a category for your memo and to mark an entry as Private. (For more on private records, see Chapter 18.)

If you don't see an appropriate category for your memo, you can create a new one by doing the following:

1. **Tap the drop-down menu arrow in the Details window and select the final option, Edit Categories.**

You see a list of your current categories, along with New, Rename, Delete, and OK buttons.

2. **Tap New and enter your new category name, and then tap OK to return to the Details window.**

When you finish entering a memo, either tap the Done button at the bottom of the screen or press the Memo Pad hard button to return to Memo List view.

Organizing and deleting memos

When you start accumulating memos, Memo List view can start to become a bit overwhelming. Memo Pad offers a few different methods for organizing your data.

Like the To Do list and Address Book, Memo Pad supports categories. Just define a category for each new entry (see the previous section), and you can easily switch between business, personal, and other memos by pressing the Memo Pad hard button repeatedly or by selecting a new category from the drop-down list box in the top-right corner of the screen.

Memo Pad offers two options for sorting your memos. By default, the program is set to sort entries alphabetically. As I discuss in the previous section, the first line of your memo is used as the title, so be sure to include appropriate info on the top line if you plan to use this option.

You can also manually sort memos. To activate manual sorting, tap the Menu soft button and choose Options⇨Preferences from the menu that appears. The Memo Preferences window opens, as shown in Figure 7-2. Tap the drop-down menu arrow next to the Sort By option and choose Manual. (To go back to alphabetic sorting, follow the same steps, but choose Alphabetic from the drop-down menu.) With Manual Sorting active, you can move items in the memo list by holding the stylus down on them and dragging them up or down the list.

If you're sorting memos alphabetically, and you want to put an important memo at the top, just start the first line with a number. Those memos appear at the top of the list.

To delete a memo, tap it in the memo list to open it. Then either tap the Menu soft button and choose Record⇨Delete Memo from the menu that appears or first tap the Details button at the bottom of the screen and then tap the Delete button in the window that pops up. Whichever method you choose, a confirmation dialog asks you to verify your decision. Tap OK to delete the memo. If you want to keep a backup of the deleted memo in Palm Desktop on your desktop system, make sure to select the Save Archive Copy on PC check box.

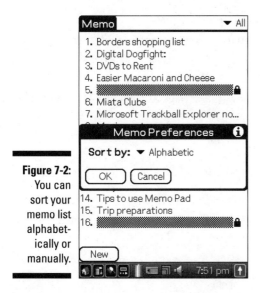

Figure 7-2:
You can
sort your
memo list
alphabet-
ically or
manually.

Sketching in CLIÉ Memo

CLIÉ Memo is a very simple application that's designed to allow you to quickly jot notes without having to worry about character recognition or typing skills. It literally acts like a piece of paper. On the upside, this means that you can also use it to create quick sketches, such as maps or diagrams. On the downside, the pages don't take much advantage of their digital format. You can search only titles, not information contained in the memos, and you can't turn your scribbled text into standard computer text.

TIP

For anything more sophisticated than a quick sketch, check out the Photo Editor application, which is included with most CLIÉ models. (Chapter 8 has more on Photo Editor.)

Creating a sketch

When you start CLIÉ Memo, it opens on a blank page where you can start sketching immediately. To create something more advanced than a simple black-and-white sketch, check out the toolbar across the top of the screen. In Figure 7-3, from left to right, are the following tools:

✔ **Pen Weight:** Three line thicknesses are available.

✔ **Pen Color:** The program defaults to just three colors, but you can use up to 256 colors. I tell you how in the following section.

- ✔ **Undo:** This removes the most recent pen stroke.

- ✔ **Redo:** This places a pen stroke back where it was if you decide to undo the undo.

- ✔ **Delete Page:** This deletes the current page.

- ✔ **Add New Page:** This inserts a new, blank page at the end of the document and takes you to it.

- ✔ **Create New Document:** This closes the current sketch and creates an entirely new document.

- ✔ **Return to Memo List:** This takes you to Memo List view.

Above the toolbar, you find a memo title and drop-down list box. If you don't enter a memo title, the CLIÉ uses the current date and time as the title.

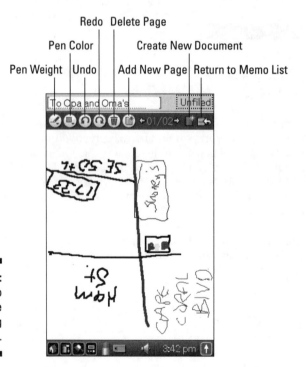

Redo Delete Page

Pen Color   Create New Document

Pen Weight Undo   Add New Page Return to Memo List

Figure 7-3:
CLIÉ Memo
is a simple
sketching
program.

Organizing memos

Memos can have multiple pages, and on some CLIÉ models, you can even shuffle pages between documents. (Not all CLIÉs offer this feature.) To find out whether your CLIÉ can manage the pages shuffle, tap the Return to Memo

List icon. If, when you're back at Memo List view, you see a third icon with a pair of scissors on it to the right of the Delete Page icon, you can use it to delete or move pages. Just highlight a memo, tap the Scissors icon, and choose Delete Pages or Move Pages from the menu that appears. Select the page that you want to move or delete. If you're deleting a page, tap the Delete button at the bottom of the screen to remove the selected pages. If you're moving a page, tap Move Pages and then tap the memo that you want to move the page to. Finally, tap a page in the existing memo (see Figure 7-4) to place the new page before that page.

You can change the memo sorting order by tapping Date or Title at the top of the screen. Tapping Date once sorts by date with the most recent memos first; tapping it a second time sorts with the oldest memos first. Tapping Title once sorts the memos in alphabetical order; tap it again to sort in reverse alphabetical order.

Figure 7-4:
Newer
versions of
CLIÉ Memo
let you
shuffle
pages
around
between
documents.

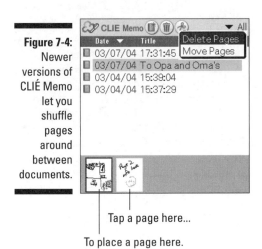

Tap a page here...

To place a page here.

Just like Memo Pad, CLIÉ Memo supports categories, so you can choose to view, say, just your business-related memos by tapping the drop-down list box in the top-right corner of the screen and choosing Business — or whatever category you created for your memo.

CLIÉ Memos also show up in the CLIÉ Viewer application, which I cover in the following chapter. CLIÉ Viewer lets you visually select memos from thumbnails. You can view the memos but not edit them in this application.

To delete a memo from the memo list, just highlight it and tap the Delete Page icon at the top of the memo list screen. (Refer to Figure 7-4.)

Versatile Free Notes

Free Notes is part of the CLIÉ Organizer application that's included with the PEG-TH55. It's similar to CLIÉ Memo (which is omitted on units that include CLIÉ Organizer) in that it lets you scribble text or make drawings with the stylus. It's much more versatile, however, in that it allows you to include standard CLIÉ text in addition to handwritten notes; to drag and drop photos, stills, movies, and voice memos onto your notes; and to attach Free Notes to entries in the other CLIÉ Organizer modules, such as Address and Date Book.

Sometimes a picture really is worth a thousand words, so take a look at the Free Notes module in the following figure to see exactly what Free Notes can do for you.

Directly below the page viewing area is the Stickers/Contents area. Here you can scroll through all the photos, movies, and voice memos in your CLIÉ and drag them onto the page. When they're on the page, tapping them launches the original file, playing the video or audio file or displaying the photo on the full

screen. You can use this to, for instance, gather photos and videos from a trip into one central location where you can easily access them and show them off.

You can use the text box in the lower-left corner to toggle the Stickers/Contents area to display stickers instead of your CLIÉ's multimedia content. You can drag the tiny icons onto your sketch to spruce it up or categorize it.

Unlike CLIÉ Memo, the Free Notes module lets you enter text with Graffiti 2 or a keyboard, in addition to scrawling with your stylus. Note that even though this text is editable, it doesn't show up in a Find operation.

Free Notes is the only note-taking module on the CLIÉ that lets you associate an alarm with a memo. This is really handy for making sure you don't forget to revisit that note you jotted down. Just tap the Information icon, which opens the Page Details screen, and then tap the Alarm check box and choose a date and time for the alarm.

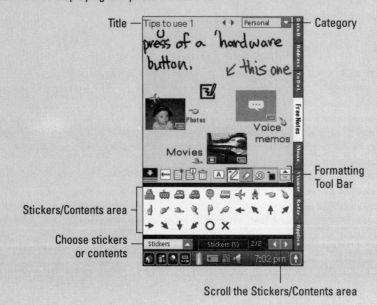

Customizing CLIÉ Memo

To tweak your CLIÉ Memo settings, tap the Menu soft button and choose Options⇨Preferences from the menu that appears. You find the following four choices, as shown in Figure 7-5:

- ✔ **Launch Screen:** Every time you start the program, it opens by default to a new, blank page. If you change the setting from New Note to Latest, it instead opens to the most recent memo.

- ✔ **Date:** This option controls the date setting for the memo's filename. By default, CLIÉ Memo records the date that the memo was created. If you change the setting to Modification, the date changes every time you modify a memo.

- ✔ **Pen Color:** This is the most useful of the settings. By default, the program offers you just three colors to use — that's fewer than you'd get from a 1978 Apple II! Change the setting to 256 Colors to get a more useful palette to work with.

- ✔ **Edit Mode:** Standard mode is a 1X magnification of your document. Detail mode zooms in and lets you edit the screen at a higher magnification, allowing for better detail.

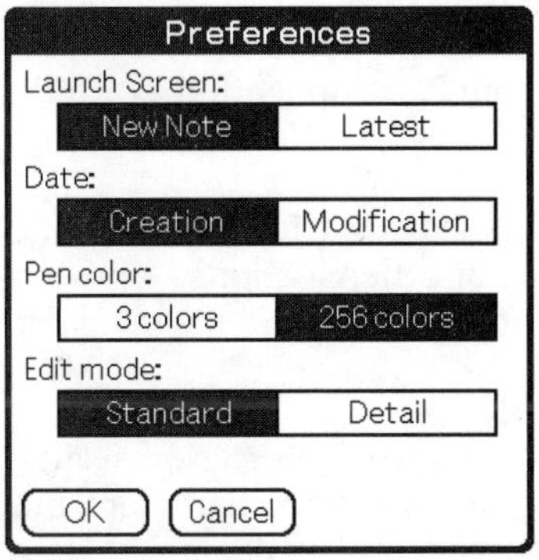

Figure 7-5: Setting CLIÉ Memo to 256 Colors gives you much more sketching flexibility.

Preferences
Launch Screen:
New Note / Latest
Date:
Creation / Modification
Pen color:
3 colors / 256 colors
Edit mode:
Standard / Detail
OK / Cancel

Notes on Your Desktop System

Support for the CLIÉ's various memo functions on the desktop system is a mixed bag. Memo Pad is duplicated exactly, CLIÉ Memo is missing entirely, and Free Notes has desktop support that's a bit quirky.

Syncing with Palm Desktop

Palm Desktop includes a Memo module that parrots the CLIÉ Memo Pad's functions. To enter or edit on your desktop system, load the Palm Desktop by choosing Start⇨Sony Handheld⇨Palm Desktop for CLIÉ. When the program loads, you notice a group of icons along the left side of the screen that correspond to the organizer applications on your CLIÉ. Click the Memo icon to get things started.

To create a new memo, just click the New Memo icon or start typing. You can do quick edits on a memo by clicking it in the memo list, and then altering the text on the right side of the screen. To open the memo in its own window, select it from the memo list and click the Edit Memo button.

At the top of the screen, you find drop-down menus that let you choose which categories to display, as well as whether to sort alphabetically or by using the order of memos on the handheld.

Note that CLIÉ Memo drawings can be viewed only on your handheld. There's no provision for transferring them to your desktop system.

Syncing with Outlook

Intellisync Lite supports only the Memo Pad application, so Outlook users can't synchronize data from CLIÉ Memo or Free Notes.

Memos are synchronized with the Notes module in Outlook. This module uses a simple paradigm with no fields or other sections — just an on-screen window that looks just like a sticky note — so no data is lost in moving memos back and forth to the CLIÉ.

Just two minor caveats go with transferring to Outlook Notes. First, the Memo Pad application doesn't allow files larger than 4,096 characters, but the Outlook Notes module allows much longer documents. Any documents that are longer than the CLIÉ's limit can transfer, but they get cut off at 4,096 characters.

Also, Intellisync Lite doesn't transfer categories. That means your Outlook memos will appear in the Unfiled category on your CLIÉ, and vice versa.

Syncing Free Notes

CLIÉ Organizer for PC supports the Free Notes module in a surprisingly full-featured manner. When you click the Edit button on the right side of the CLIÉ Organizer for PC screen with a Free Note selected, you're essentially presented with a duplicate of your CLIÉ's screen. You can draw on it with the mouse, create text with the keyboard, and drag and drop graphics and icons onto it.

Unfortunately, you can't directly drag pictures, movies, or recordings from your desktop system to a Free Note. Also, the support for these files on your CLIÉ is a bit quirky if they're stored on a Memory Stick. Just viewing notes isn't a problem — you see the small icon versions of these files on the desktop system. If you want to add new media files to a Free Note, display the full-screen versions of photos on the page, or play linked voice recordings or movies, your CLIÉ's Memory Stick must be mounted as a disk drive on your desktop system by using the Data Import feature (see Chapter 14 for details), and the Memory Stick drive must be assigned by using the Tools/Options menu item. Also, you need to run the Data Import program on your CLIÉ before you begin editing a note. After you master this procedure, it all works fine, but the whole process is convoluted enough that you're likely to just grab your CLIÉ and make the changes there.

Part III

Multimedia and Entertainment

The 5th Wave   By Rich Tennant

@RICHTENNANT

It's an e-mail from my mother. She wants me to know how happy she is for us.

In this part . . .

The CLIÉ is a bigger attention hound than a politician at a fund-raiser. It's always showing off. Even the most basic CLIÉs run around displaying high-resolution photos and showing how they can run games that used to take a six-foot-tall arcade machine to play. The audio-equipped units dazzle you with their ability to play movies or act as a handheld jukebox. They're shameless.

This part covers all the fun stuff that you can do with your CLIÉ. You find out how to view and shoot photos and movies on the go and how to transfer your favorite music files to the CLIÉ. I give a rundown on the very best games for any kind of gamer, and the entertainment extravaganza wraps up with a look at eBooks and audiobooks.

Chapter 8

Picturing the World with Your CLIÉ

● ●

In This Chapter

▶ Keeping an eye on CLIÉ Viewer

▶ Getting the shot with CLIÉ Camera

▶ Moving shots to and from your desktop system

▶ Making slideshows with PhotoStand

▶ Touching up with Photo Editor

● ●

*I*f the CLIÉ were a superhero, it would be Captain Multimedia. (And it would probably hire a PR agent to come up with a better name.) With its high-resolution screen, brilliant color, and speedy processor, the CLIÉ is an excellent tool for viewing pictures and even movies (more on movies in the following chapter) anywhere you go.

The included photo software differs by CLIÉ model. All CLIÉs include the CLIÉ Viewer application, and because all currently available models now feature built-in cameras, they also feature the CLIÉ Camera application.

The wild-card applications are included with older CLIÉ models, as well as the high-end UX series units. These include the PhotoStand slideshow program and the Photo Editor paint program.

All these applications are built in, so the easiest way to determine whether your CLIÉ is equipped with them is to check the Program Launcher for their icons. And don't forget that if you have a TH-series device, you can also view images directly from the CLIÉ Organizer.

An Eye on CLIÉ Viewer

CLIÉ Viewer is an all-purpose multimedia manager. It not only lets you view photos, movies, and CLIÉ Memo files, but also lets you move media between handheld memory and a Memory Stick, rotate images, select them for printing, and more. It even plays back Voice Recorder audio files.

Tap the CLIÉ Viewer icon in the Program Launcher to get started. The program pops up and displays all the supported media files on your CLIÉ whether they're in main memory or on a Memory Stick. Files that are stored on your Memory Stick have a small Memory Stick icon overlaid on their thumbnail.

Note that CLIÉ Viewer offers different options on each unit, depending on which other applications are installed, so you may not see some of the icons depicted in Figure 8-1.

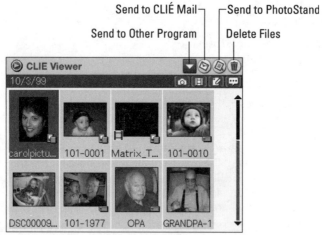

Figure 8-1: CLIE Viewer uses an icon-based interface.

Going from left to right, the top row of icons that you see in the upper-right corner of the screen offer you the following functions:

- ✔ **Send to Other Program:** Typically, pressing the icon with the drop-down menu arrow gives you a choice of Photo Editor or CLIÉ Album. After you select which program you want to send files to, select the photos that you want to transfer.

- ✔ **Send to CLIÉ Mail:** Select a file to attach to a new CLIÉ Mail e-mail message.

- ✔ **Send to PhotoStand:** Select this, and then select the images that you want to send to PhotoStand, the CLIÉ's slideshow program.

- ✔ **Delete Files:** Tap the trash can and select the files that you want to remove.

The lower row of icons in the upper-right corner of the screen is used to filter out what gets displayed in the main part of the screen. From left to right, the icons represent photos, movies, memos, and audio recordings. To remove any of those types of files from the display, just tap the icon, which changes it from blue (selected) to gray (unselected); tap it again to add them back to the list. If you want to see everything, just keep all the icons in this row selected.

The CLIÉ Viewer program also offers a number of functions on its Data drop-down menu. Just tap the Menu soft button to bring up the menu choices that are illustrated in Figure 8-2.

Figure 8-2:
Many CLIÉ
Viewer
commands
are
accessed
through a
drop-down
menu.

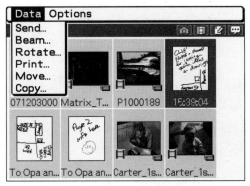

The commands are

- ✔ **Send:** Available only on the CLIÉs that are equipped with Bluetooth wireless capabilities, this option lets you send a file via Bluetooth to another PDA or computer, or via Short Messaging System (SMS) to a cell phone.

- ✔ **Beam:** Send a file via an infrared beam.

- ✔ **Rotate:** Rotate an image to better fit it on the CLIÉ's screen. Note that this command works only with photos.

- ✔ **Print:** This doesn't actually print a photo, but marks it for printing next time you place your CLIÉ's Memory Stick in a printer that's equipped with a Memory Stick slot.

- ✔ **Move:** Move a file to main memory, a Memory Stick, or (on the UX series) to Internal Media memory.

- ✔ **Copy:** Copy a file to main memory, a Memory Stick, or (on the UX series) to Internal Media memory, but without deleting the original.

One other menu choice is tucked away on the Options menu. The Preferences of CLIÉ Viewer command, though oddly translated, lets you sort images by either the date that they were taken or by the date that the file was created.

To view or play a file, tap it with your stylus or use the jog dial to scroll through the thumbnails and press the jog dial when the image you want is highlighted.

Viewing still images

When viewing still images, you see a row of icons across the bottom of the screen, as shown in Figure 8-3.

Figure 8-3:
Displaying a
photo in
CLIÉ Viewer.

Return to Thumbnail View   Zoom In   Show File Information

Display Full Screen   Zoom Out

Left to right, the icons perform the following functions:

- ✓ **Display Full Screen:** This removes all the icons and borders. Tap the image to get the icons back.

- ✓ **Return to Thumbnail View:** This exits the file-viewing mode and returns you to the thumbnail file list.

- ✓ **Zoom In:** Each time you tap the icon, the image is further magnified.

- ✓ **Zoom Out:** Zoom out to reduce the size of the image on the screen. Each tap zooms out further.

- ✓ **Show File Information:** This displays the filename, the date that the file was created, the dimensions of the image, and how large the file is in bytes.

You can also use the jog dial to zoom in and out on an image. Drag the stylus around a zoomed image to scroll it.

The CLIÉ Organizer built-in Viewer

Although units with built-in CLIÉ Organizer software include CLIÉ Viewer, you don't need it for basic viewing. CLIÉ Organizer includes a Viewer tab that duplicates most of the functionality of the standalone CLIÉ Viewer program.

On the main screen, you can find an additional icon at the bottom-left corner, evident in the following figure. You can use this icon to toggle between the thumbnail view and a text-only list view.

Click here to toggle between views.

Viewing or listening to the other stuff

When you tap a sound file, you see typical home-audio-style playback and volume controls. Tapping a CLIÉ Memo sketch brings up a full-screen display of the memo in a read-only mode, where it can't be altered.

See the following chapter for explanations of the Movie Viewer controls.

Getting the Shot with CLIÉ Camera

By early 2004, all the Sony CLIÉ models were equipped with built-in cameras. However, don't toss out your five-megapixel optical zoom camera now that you have your CLIÉ. The CLIÉ cameras offer low resolution (all current models are one-third-megapixel VGA cameras, though some earlier models have had high-resolution cameras), no flash, and a basic digital zoom that I recommend you ignore.

That said, the camera is still a wonderful perk because the most useful camera is the one you have with you. You probably don't carry a digital camera with you 24/7, but you likely do carry your CLIÉ quite often, and you'll be glad for even low-resolution photos when unexpected opportunities come up: the kids doing something cute; somebody denting your car; or Gina Gershon saying, "Sure, I'll take a picture with you." The camera works well outdoors or in bright light, and the low resolution is fine for e-mail, Web pages, and 4 x 6 and smaller prints.

To launch CLIÉ Camera, tap the CLIÉ Camera icon in the Program Launcher or just press the Capture button on your CLIÉ. When the program is running, press the Capture hard button or its on-screen counterpart to take a photo.

The CLIÉ Camera controls, shown in Figure 8-4, are relatively simple. Along the thin bar in the middle of the screen is the word *Still.* If your CLIÉ includes the Movie Recorder application, tapping this switches the mode from Still to Movie Recording; otherwise, it does nothing.

Figure 8-4:
The CLIÉ
Camera
interface.

To the right of Still is the Zoom control. The best advice here is to pretend that it doesn't exist. The CLIÉ features a digital zoom, which simulates zooming by doubling the size of the pixels in the center of the screen. That means the already-low-resolution image is going to get extremely blocky at 2X zoom and is going to turn into a fuzzy mess at 3X zoom.

To the right of the Zoom control is the brightness reading, represented by ±0. I cover how to adjust that in just a moment.

On the wide bar in the middle of the screen is the Wrench icon, which takes you to the Camera Preferences screen. To the right of the Wrench icon is a status display, showing, among other things, the File Number counter, resolution (640 x 480, for example), and an icon representing whether the image will be stored in main memory or on a Memory Stick when you save. The Play arrow takes you to CLIÉ Viewer to see your handiwork, and the next icon — the one that looks kind of like a clock with just one hand — sets the next shot to be taken on a ten-second delay. Finally, the Capture button takes a photo.

To tweak how your CLIÉ captures images, tap the Wrench icon. This takes you to the Camera Preferences screen, as shown in Figure 8-5. However, some options may vary slightly on different CLIÉ models.

Figure 8-5:
The CLIÉ
Camera
Preferences
screen.

The various options are as follows:

- **Save To:** This option has three settings. You probably want to leave it set to PriorityMS, which saves to a Memory Stick (if one is present) or to the handheld's memory if not. You could also set this option to Memory Stick, Handheld, or (on the UX series only) Internal Media memory.

- **Size:** This option controls the resolution of the image. If you plan to use the image on a computer or print it, leave Size at its highest setting, which is 640 x 480 on most models. If you're going to be displaying the image only on your CLIÉ, you can save memory by dropping the resolution to 320 x 480 (which is the full screen on large-screen models) or lower.

- **File Numbering:** Series is the default setting. If you change the setting to Reset, the File Number counter is reset to 1.

- **Shutter Sound:** Here you get a choice of three different shutter sounds.

- **Shutter Sound Vol:** This option lets you adjust the volume of the shutter sound.

- **Flicker Control:** You can set this to 60 Hz (the default for North America) or 50 Hz to eliminate screen flicker. In some countries, lights are powered at 50 Hz frequencies, so your liquid crystal display (LCD) camera screen might flicker if you take your CLIÉ with you on a trip. Setting the CLIÉ screen to 50 Hz solves that problem.

- **Brightness:** You can use this option to adjust the brightness of the current shot.

- **White Balance:** This option controls how the camera handles adjusting for different lighting types. Normally, it works fine on Auto, but if you're seeing whites with a bluish or greenish tone, try using one of the other settings. Two indoor settings are available, as well as an outdoor setting.

- **Effect:** With this option, you can apply special effects to your image. All CLIÉs offer B&W and Sepia (which gives an old-photo, brownish look) settings. Some models also offer Neg. Art (which makes it look like a photo negative) and Solarize (a vivid, surreal look). If you have a photo editing program on your desktop system, you're probably better off ignoring these options and adding effects later.

After you make your settings, just tap OK to return to the Camera screen.

To get the best shots with your CLIÉ, shoot with as much light as possible. With a couple of exceptions (the PEG-NX80V's assist light and the PEG-NZ90's flash), CLIÉ cameras don't include any type of illumination. Shots in the dark generally turn out grainy. I recommend shooting outdoors or with your subjects facing a bright light. Also, be careful of backlighting, which can flare in the background and also cause your subjects to be dark.

Transferring CLIÉ Photos

To move images to and from your desktop system, you need to mount your Memory Stick as a disk drive. You can do this in two ways. The fastest is to purchase an inexpensive Universal Serial Bus (USB) Memory Stick card reader for your computer. Plug one of these in and pop in your Memory Stick, and it acts just like a small hard drive. You access the files on your Memory Stick by double-clicking the icon in My Computer, the same way you would if the files were on a hard drive or CD-ROM. If you don't have a USB reader, you can actually convert your CLIÉ into one by running the Data Import application.

I cover Data Import and copying files in more detail in Chapter 14. In a capsule, though, you simply run the Data Import application on your CLIÉ, connect your CLIÉ's data cable or cradle to your computer, and tap the Connect icon on the Data Import screen. Your CLIÉ's Memory Stick now appears as a drive on your computer.

If possible, always save photos that you take with CLIÉ camera on a Memory Stick because the CLIÉ doesn't include software for transferring images from handheld memory to your computer. If you do have an image in handheld memory but no available Memory Stick, one way to transfer the image is to send it as an attachment in CLIÉ Mail.

If you're running an older version of Windows, you may need to manually copy files to and from the Memory Stick drive by browsing the drive in My Computer or by using an add-on application such as Photoshop Album 2.0.

If you're using Windows XP, inserting the Memory Stick into the drive or launching Data Import brings up the Removable Disk dialog window, which gives you a number of choices. (See Figure 8-6.) You can choose the Open Folder to View Files option if you want to manually copy the files to your desktop system, or choose the Copy Pictures To a Folder on My Computer option if you want to use the XP built-in Image File Transfer wizard.

To copy images from your desktop system to your CLIÉ, Sony includes an easy-to-use application called Image Converter. This application supports all the major graphic formats and can also convert movie files to formats that are playable on your CLIÉ.

Copying pictures with Image Converter is a snap. Just start up the program on your desktop system, wait for the application window to come up on screen, and then drag and drop the pictures that you want copied to the window. (You can also click the window's Add to List button to call up an Open dialog box for selecting the files that you want copied.) After you build a list of files to convert, click the Output to Memory Stick button to copy the files to your Memory Stick card.

Figure 8-6:
Windows
XP offers
several
options for
viewing or
copying
your CLIÉ
images.

If you're working within Image Converter, and you want to visually select images to copy — handy when your photos have helpful names like DSC03521.jpg — click the Add to List button, and then click the View Menu icon in the Open dialog box's toolbar. Choose Thumbnails from the drop-down list, and the view changes from a text list to a set of thumbnail images. See Figure 8-7 for an illustration.

Figure 8-7:
The
Thumbnail
view makes
selecting
images
much
easier.

Note that you don't need to use Image Converter. If your shots are in JPEG format already, you can simply drag them to the DCIM folder on your Memory Stick. The advantage of using Image Converter is that it can shrink photos for CLIÉ display purposes, so they take up less space and load faster.

If you choose File⇨Settings from the Image Converter main menu, you see the Settings window that's shown in Figure 8-8. This window lets you choose a size and quality level for your image and rotate them for proper orientation for when you transfer them to your CLIÉ. For large-screen CLIÉs, consider setting a width of 480 pixels. For square-screen units, set the width to 320 pixels unless you want to be able to zoom in on the image.

Figure 8-8:
The Settings window for Image Converter.

The Rest of the Toolbox

Although the applications that I describe in this section are missing on the newest models, some photo-related tools are included with the UX series and older CLIÉs, and they're worth a look. If your CLIÉ doesn't include PhotoStand and Photo Editor, don't despair. With over 20,000 Palm OS add-on programs available, you can easily find third-party replacements that are even more full-featured.

PhotoStand

This is a slick slideshow program that's good for showing off sets of images or for setting up a slideshow to run on your CLIÉ while it sits in its cradle.

1. **Tap the PhotoStand icon in the Program Launcher.**

   The main screen of the PhotoStand application appears.

2. **Tap the New button at the bottom of the PhotoStand main screen.**

   A group of thumbnail images appears in a new screen.

3. **Tap the check boxes next to the images that you want to include in your show, and then tap OK.**

   The PhotoStand Settings screen appears, as shown in Figure 8-9.

4. **Enter a title for your Slideshow.**

   This can be anything you want, but it should be easily recognizable to you when you're showing off pictures a year or two down the road.

5. **Choose a transition effect.**

   Tap the Effect drop-down menu arrow to choose whether to set a wipe or transition between photos, or choose to overlay your images with a clock, turning your CLIÉ into perhaps the coolest (and perhaps most expensive) desk clock ever, as shown in Figure 8-10.

Figure 8-9: You can use the PhotoStand Settings screen to configure your slideshow.

PhotoStand Settings

Title: Vermont vacation

Sort By: ▼ Random

Effect: ▼ Clock & Calendar

Display Interval: ▼ 1 minute

☑ Loop   ☐ Autorun

☐ Image Info

☑ BGM

Selected Images: 13   [Select]

(Preview) (Save) (Cancel)

6. **Set the Display Interval.**

   Tap the Display Interval drop-down menu arrow to choose how long you want each image to appear on the screen.

7. **Finish creating your slideshow by setting the miscellaneous options.**

   Below the Display Interval setting, you find the following settings, which you can adjust to your preference:

   • **Loop:** Check this if you want the slideshow to repeat automatically.

   • **Autorun:** The slideshow will launch automatically when you insert this Memory Stick into your CLIÉ.

- **Image Info:** This will scroll the title, date of creation, and comments for each image across the screen.

- **BGM:** Play the current background music (MP3 audio files) playlist while viewing the slideshow.

8. **Tap the Preview button to make sure that your slideshow works as you expected, or tap the Save button to save your file and exit the PhotoStand settings screen.**

   You're returned to the main screen.

Figure 8-10:
You can overlay a clock or a clock and calendar on your slideshow.

9. **To view your slideshow, simply tap the slideshow name and tap the Play button to launch the show.**

   Alas, I'm still waiting on Sony to release a Memory Stick that pops popcorn.

Photo Editor

Replacing the fancier CLIÉ Paint program, which was included on early CLIÉ models, Photo Editor is an extremely simple image touch-up program. It features just a few editing tools, as shown in Figure 8-11, but it's fun for doing goofy stuff like adding a beard to a picture of your grandfather.

For more sophisticated photo-editing operations, such as fixing red-eye, sharpening images, and so on, you need to use a desktop editing application. But for quick doodles and fun retouching, Photo Editor fits the bill.

Magnification

Brightness and contrast filters   Color selection eyedropper

Shrink toolbar   Pen type   Pen weight

Send photo to   Redo   Eraser   Color palette   Image title
another program   Move   and resolution
            Undo   image   Current color

Open file menu

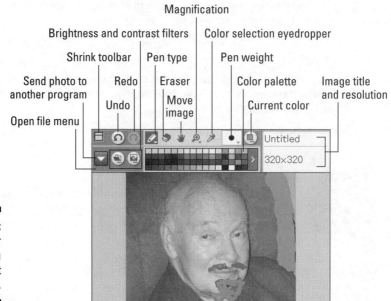

Figure 8-11:
Photo Editor
includes a
basic set
of tools.

Chapter 9

Hollywood on the Go

*I*f you thought viewing still photos on your CLIÉ was impressive, imagine carrying a copy of *The Lord of the Rings* or the latest episode of *The Simpsons* with you to watch next time you're on a plane or stuck in a waiting room. Better still, some CLIÉ models don't just allow you to watch movies — they let you make your own, as well.

Pocket Spielberg: Movie Recorder

Some camera-equipped CLIÉ models can shoot not only stills, but movies as well. Would-be cinematographers can find movie capabilities in the UX series and in the older NX series CLIÉs. Unfortunately, the TH and TJ series models omit the Movie Recorder application, although I wouldn't be surprised to see third-party alternatives available soon, such as an updated version of the excellent Vivid video capture program currently available for the older PEG-NR70V from www.clievideo.com.

Although the CLIÉ can play back movies at full-screen 320 x 480 resolution, capture is limited to a postage-stamp-sized 160 x 112 pixels. These little flicks are fine for playback on the CLIÉ or even on your desktop system, but this isn't a feature that you want to use to record priceless memories with or to create flicks for TV playback.

The Movie Recorder interface, shown in Figure 9-1, is very similar to the CLIÉ Camera interface, which I cover in Chapter 8. The same tips apply for using this application: Make sure that your subjects are well-lit and avoid the digital zoom feature because it makes your subjects blurry.

Unless you're using a UX-series CLIÉ, which includes special additional Internal Media memory that acts just like a Memory Stick (see Chapter 14 for the full scoop on various memory types), you must have a Memory Stick in your CLIÉ to use the Movie Recorder program. The CLIÉ can't save movies in the CLIÉ's standard internal memory.

Figure 9-1: Movie Recorder in action.

You use the Wrench to access the Preferences screen. To the right of the little wrench is the status display, which tells you the elapsed time, whether your movie file is being saved to Memory Stick or to the Internal Media memory found on the UX series, and how much time is left for your recording. Pressing the icon to the right of the status display takes you to the Movie Player — where you can view the rushes for your blockbuster epic — and the Record icon is there to punch when you want to begin filming.

You can also press the Capture hard button to begin recording.

The Preferences screen, shown in Figure 9-2, offers the following options:

✔ **Save To:** This option is present only on the UX series, which includes Internal Media memory. You probably want to leave it set to PriorityMS, which saves to Memory Stick, if one is present, or to Internal Media memory otherwise. You can also specify Memory Stick or Internal Media memory.

✔ **Bit Rate:** This option lets you adjust the *bit rate* of your recording, which is basically how much data is stored for each second of recording. Setting to a lower value gives you additional recording time, but given the general low resolution of CLIÉ video recordings, I recommend leaving it set to its highest setting (V:256), if possible.

✔ **Time Limit:** You can limit the recording time to a variety of values ranging from 3 seconds to 60 minutes.

✔ **File Number:** Series is the default setting. If you change the setting to Reset, the File Number counter is reset to 1.

✔ **Capture Sound Vol:** This sets the microphone sensitivity. For most purposes, you want to leave it set to High.

✔ **Brightness:** This option allows you to adjust the brightness of the current shot. Turning it up can help brighten the footage in a dark situation, but it causes your recording to be somewhat grainy.

✔ **White Balance:** This option controls how the camera handles adjusting for different lighting types. Normally, it works fine on Auto, but if you're seeing whites with a bluish or greenish tone, try one of the other settings. Two indoor settings are available, as well as an outdoor setting.

✔ **Effect:** This option applies special effects to your image. All CLIÉs offer B&W and Sepia (which gives an old-West, brownish look) settings. Some models also offer Neg. Art (which makes it look like a photo negative) and Solarize (a vivid, surreal look). If you have a video editing program on your desktop system, you're probably better off ignoring these options and adding effects later.

After you make your settings, just tap OK to return to the Movie Recorder main screen.

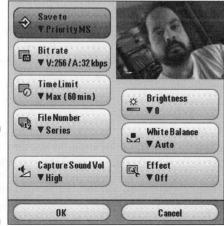

Figure 9-2:
The Movie
Recorder
Preferences
screen.

You can transfer movies from Memory Stick to your desktop system by using a Universal Serial Bus (USB) Memory Stick reader or via the Data Import utility. (See Chapter 14 for details.) You can find the files saved to your Memory Stick in the `\MQ_ROOT\100MQV01` folder. Although they have an `MQV` file extension, they're actually QuickTime files. After you move them to your desktop system, you can change the extension from `MQV` to `MOV`, which gives you the ability to play the files by double-clicking them. Otherwise, you can use the Open command in the QuickTime Player File menu to open the files.

Although a version of the QuickTime Player is included on your CLIÉ's Installation CD, I'd suggest visiting `www.quicktime.com` to download and install the latest version. Apple frequently updates the player with new features and bug fixes.

In addition to recording movies, you can turn your CLIÉ into a Webcam. A slick new application called Vivid Webcam from the folks at `www.clievideo.com` lets you use your CLIÉ's camera for video chats in conjunction with your Windows system. See Chapter 22 for more details.

Viewing Movies on Your CLIÉ

All current CLIÉ models ship with CLIÉ Viewer, which I cover in Chapter 8. This multimedia hub lets you select movies for playback with a single tap. The UX series also ships with the older Movie Player application, but it duplicates the same functionality that's also found in CLIÉ Viewer.

Chapter 8 shows you how to get CLIÉ Viewer up and running. (Okay, if you don't want to flip back to that chapter, here's the scoop: Tap the CLIÉ Viewer icon in the Program Launcher, and voilà, you're there.) To start a movie in CLIÉ Viewer, simply find it in the display of the CLIÉ Viewer main screen, and then tap it with your stylus or use the jog dial to scroll to the movie, and then press it to start playback.

When viewing movies, as shown in Figure 9-3, the controls from top to bottom are

✔ **Play:** Starts the movie.

✔ **Stop:** Stops the movie.

✔ **Use Full Screen for Playback:** This eliminates the distracting icons and gray borders on the screen.

✔ **Stretch Movie to Fill Screen:** Stretches smaller movie files so they fill the screen instead of being surrounded by black letterbox bars.

✔ **Volume Control:** Turns the volume up and down.

✔ **Return to Movie List:** Exits the movie viewing screen and returns you to your list of movies.

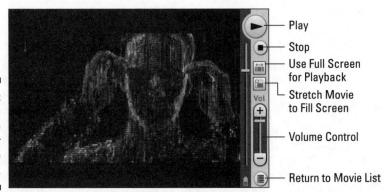

— Play
— Stop
— Use Full Screen for Playback
— Stretch Movie to Fill Screen
— Volume Control
— Return to Movie List

Figure 9-3:
Watching a
film in the
CLIÉ Viewer
movie
player.

Note that the position of these controls varies depending on the screen size and the orientation of the CLIÉ that you're using. Also note the tiny Battery icon to the left of the Movie List icon on some units, which is handy for making sure that you don't completely run down your battery while watching *The Matrix.*

To convert a movie on your desktop system for playback with CLIÉ Viewer, you use the Image Converter application, which I cover in Chapter 8. Image Converter can convert and transfer QuickTime, AVI, and MPEG-1 format files to CLIÉ format. (Unfortunately, it can't convert MPEG-2 format, which is the format used by DVDs.) Image Converter offers four quality levels for converted films, ranging from Long Mode, which stores 130 minutes on a 128MB Memory Stick, through High Quality, which stores about a half-hour in the same space. A High Plus Quality mode is also available, but it creates huge files, offers little noticeable improvement on the CLIÉ screen, and isn't compatible with all CLIÉ units. Standard mode — 60 minutes per 128MB — is a good choice if you have a large Memory Stick.

Add-On Movie Utilities

The CLIÉ Viewer does a great job of offering smooth playback and compact movies. But at times, you might want to play other movie formats or convert files from formats that aren't supported directly by the CLIÉ. Here are some of the top third-party utilities to consider:

- ✔ **MMPlayer:** This full-featured video playback program lets your CLIÉ play files in the popular DivX and MPEG-4 file formats directly on your CLIÉ with no conversion necessary. For more info, go to www.mmplayer.com.

- ✔ **Kinoma:** The most popular movie player for the Palm OS, Kinoma offers excellent performance, fantastic image quality, and small file sizes. The player is free, but you need to buy the converter to create your own movies. The player and converter are both available at www.kinoma.com.

- ✔ **TealMovie:** Although this is an older program, TealMovie offers some of the fastest, smoothest playback that you can get on the CLIÉ, and numerous movies are available online in TealMovie format. TealMovie is available at www.tealpoint.com.

- ✔ **Movie2MemCard:** This movie converter supports a wider variety of formats than Image Converter and offers you excellent control over the final size of your video files. Although it's aimed at Pocket PC users, the DivX files that it creates can be played by MMPlayer. You can find it at www.kvmd.com.

Sources for Movies

Okay, so your CLIÉ is a great video player. But a visit to your local video store in search of videos to watch on a CLIÉ is going to be about as fruitful as trying to find a copy of *Spider-Man* on a Betamax tape. With a little ingenuity, though, you can use a variety of methods for getting movies onto your CLIÉ:

- ✔ **Record movies yourself.** Add a TV tuner card to your desktop system and record movies right on your computer, and then convert them for playback on your desktop system. The best package that I've found for this is the SnapStream Beyond TV 3, which offers TiVo-like recording functionality and the unique ShowSqueeze feature, which automatically converts movies into a format and size compatible with your CLIÉ. You can find information on Beyond TV 3 at www.snapstream.com. And if you have a Sony computer with a video recording card, a plug-in is available on your CLIÉ Installation CD for the GigaPocket video recording software that allows you to create files in CLIÉ–compatible format.

✔ **Download movies online.** You can find movie trailers, music videos, noncommercial films, and many other movies online. Sites to check out include `www.sonypictures.com/mobile/handheld` for CLIÉ–format movies, `www.tealpoint.com/movies.htm` for TealMovie flicks, and `pocketmovies.net` and `www.divx.com` for movies that can be converted with Image Converter.

✔ **Convert home movies.** If you have a digital camcorder and video-editing software, you can take the home movies that you've created on your desktop system and use Image Converter to transfer them to your CLIÉ.

✔ **Record movies directly to Memory Stick.** The Sony PEGA-VR100K, shown in Figure 9-4, is a small, solid-state video recorder that records TV programs or videos directly to a Memory Stick in a CLIÉ–compatible format. Just like a VCR, you can set it to record your favorite programs at a particular time.

Figure 9-4:
The PEGA-VR100K records TV shows directly to a Memory Stick.

Chapter 10

Audio Excellence: Music and Voice Recording

• •

In This Chapter

▶ Playing tunes with AudioPlayer and AeroPlayer

▶ Getting music for your CLIÉ

▶ Setting enhanced alarms with Sound Utility

▶ Using the CLIÉ Voice Recorder

• •

Don't tell anyone I said this, but I admit that watching a mime can actually be amusing . . . for about five minutes. However, listening to a good band puts silent entertainment in perspective. A four-hour concert can fly by in no time at all. Thus, it's no great surprise that most CLIÉ models don't rely on their visual prowess but also pack impressive audio capabilities.

CLIÉ: The Musical Muse

As the cost of adding MP3 support to Personal Digital Assistants (PDAs) has dropped, musical capabilities have trickled down into less expensive CLIÉs. Today, only the least expensive CLIÉ model still makes do with old-style Palm beep-and-buzz sounds.

Figuring out whether your CLIÉ has MP3 audio support is a snap — just look for a headphone jack like the one on the unit in Figure 10-1. If your CLIÉ has one, roll up for the magical (musical) mystery tour. If not, well, hey, you got your CLIÉ at a great price, right? And there're always the eBooks that I discuss in the following chapter . . .

High-end CLIÉ models also include a digital voice recorder, and most of these have a switch marked Voice Rec. However, because some models (such as the UX-series models) omit this switch, the surest way to check is to look for the Voice Rec application in the CLIÉ Program Launcher.

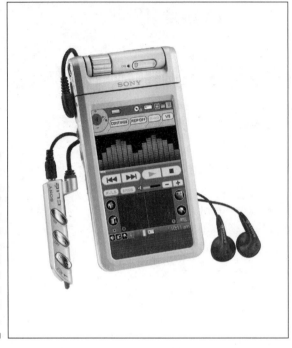

Figure 10-1:
Some CLIÉs
include not
just a
headphone
jack, but an
external
audio
remote
control, as
well.

MP3 Mania

In case you missed the whole Napster issue and the multibillion-dollar-industry-suing-teenagers fiasco, a quick introduction to MP3 is in order. MP3 stands for MPEG-1 Audio Layer-3, a format that compresses music files to a size that's on average about a tenth of the amount of space that they occupy on an audio CD but with little noticeable reduction in sound quality.

Why is MP3 popular? Because without it, a typical album would take up about 600MB of space, requiring you to purchase a 1GB Memory Stick just to bring along an hour of tunes. When this book was written, a 1GB Memory Stick cost about $400 — more than a midrange CLIÉ. MP3 compression shrinks music files to the point where you can fit an hour of music on a 64MB Memory Stick — which at this writing went for under $30.

Of course, another reason for the popularity — and notoriety — of MP3s is that smaller files are feasible to download online. This had several results: the skyrocketing popularity of online file-sharing programs like Napster and Kazaa, hundreds of lawsuits against people sharing their music online, and much public grumbling from aging band members who depend on the royalties on their '80s albums for their boat payments.

Although digital music has gained an outlaw reputation, it's also a very useful tool for legitimate music distribution and listening. Up-and-coming bands often release sample tunes online in hopes of bringing in new fans. Services like iTunes, Musicmatch, and the new "legit" Napster make it possible to buy thousands of songs from the comfort of your own desk. And you can legally *rip* (that is, copy and convert) your own CD collection to MP3 files, allowing you to listen to your tunes on your CLIÉ.

Depending on your CLIÉ model, a quick check of your Program Launcher screen shows either Sony's homegrown Audio Player or Aerodrome Software's AeroPlayer. (The use of two different players is due to some differences in how various CLIÉs handle music.) They're both excellent programs, although AeroPlayer is a bit more powerful. In the following sections, I take you on a tour of both programs.

Audio Player

Audio Player plays MP3 files, as well as tunes recorded in Sony's proprietary ATRAC3 format. It has the classic Sony-designed look and feel with a heavy emphasis on icons and buttons for control, as shown in Figure 10-2.

The most-used controls are arrayed across the bottom of the screen. The symbols should be familiar to anyone who has used any piece of home audio equipment manufactured in the past couple of decades. From left to right, the buttons are Play, Stop, Previous Track, Next Track, as well as a Volume Control slider bar. To rewind, tap and hold the Previous Track button, and to fast-forward, tap and hold the Next Track button. You can adjust the Volume Control slider bar by dragging the Volume slider with the stylus, tapping the plus sign (+) or minus sign (–), or by scrolling the jog dial up and down. Directly above the primary controls is the Progress slider bar, which shows you the progress of the song playback. You can grab the slider with the stylus and drag it to jump to another part of the audio file.

Above the Progress slider are three buttons. Tapping the music note gives you information about the current song, including the length, artist, title, and album name. The AVLS button toggles the Automatic Volume Limiting System, which is designed to prevent your CLIÉ from generating ear-damaging volumes through headphones. Finally, tapping the BASS button cycles the Mega Bass feature from Bass (off) to Bass 1 (low bass boost), Bass 2 (medium), and Bass 3 (high).

Current Album Info

Edit Playlist   Choose a Card to Search

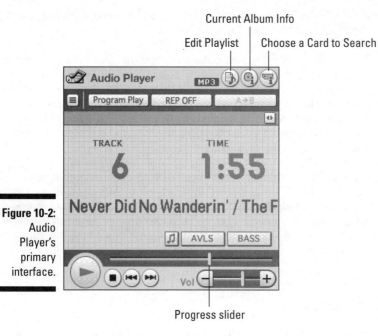

Figure 10-2:
Audio
Player's
primary
interface.

Progress slider

Moving to the top-right corner of the screen, you see MP3 followed by three icons. Tapping the first icon brings up the Edit Playlist screen, shown in Figure 10-3.

Figure 10-3:
The Audio
Player
playlist
screen.

Simply select the songs that you want to include in your playlist. Tapping the Select All button automatically selects all the songs, and pressing the Invert button selects all the unselected tunes and deselects the selected tunes. Pressing the Clear All button deselects all tunes, and pressing the Default button moves the songs back to their original order. You can change a song's position in the playback order by tapping it to select it, and then using the buttons in the top-right corner of the screen to move it up or down in the list.

After you choose your song order, tap OK to return to the main interface. Note that Audio Player doesn't support multiple playlists, which wasn't a big issue when Memory Sticks topped out at 128MB (about two hours of tunes) but might be annoying now that 1GB cards capable of holding 16 hours of music are available.

Note that your CLIÉ can utilize third-party MP3 player applications, such as the AeroPlayer program, which is included with some models. If you're seeking a missing feature, such as multiple playlist support, you can always use an add-on program instead of the built-in player.

The middle icon in the top-right corner of the Audio Player main interface provides information on the current album (that is, all the songs on your Memory Stick). The final button on the top row lets you choose which card the program should look for music on. This option is available only on units with multiple expansion areas, such as the UX, which includes special Internal Media memory, and NX-series units, which come equipped with CompactFlash memory cards.

Moving down to the second row of buttons (refer to Figure 10-2), the first button switches between the normal display (which shows just the name of the current song playing) and a song list (which shows you a list of all the songs in your current playlist). The second button toggles through the following play modes:

- **Continue:** Plays songs in the order on the Memory Stick, ignoring the playlist.
- **Shuffle:** Plays songs in random order.
- **Reverse:** Plays songs in reverse of their order on the Memory Stick.
- **Program Play:** Plays songs in the order specified in the playlist.

The button to the right of the Play Mode button controls the Repeat setting:

- **Rep Off:** Play each song once, and then stop.
- **Rep All:** Play each song once, and then start again at the first song.
- **Rep 1:** Continuously repeat the current song.

The last button in the row, labeled A→B, lets you repeat a portion of a song over and over. Just tap it once at the spot where you want the repeat to begin, and then tap it again at the end of the clip. That section will play over and over again until you tap the Stop button or tap A→B again. (This feature is great for those times when, for example, you just have to figure out what John is *really* singing in the fourth verse of "I Am the Walrus.")

By default, switching to another application shuts down the Audio Player and ends your music, leaving you to face the task of entering your expense report without the soothing sounds of The B-52's to accompany the process. Luckily, an easy fix does exist — just enable the Background Play mode, which lets you listen to music while using other Palm OS programs. Tap the Menu soft button, and then choose Options⇨Preferences from the menu that appears. When the Preferences screen comes up, select the Enable Background Play check box.

If you're not planning on doing other things with your CLIÉ while listening to music, you can significantly extend your battery life by turning off the screen display. Just move the Hold slider on your CLIÉ to the Hold position. The screen turns off, but the music plays on.

Overall, the Audio Player does a good job with the most common MP3 files. If you're an audiophile, though, you may be chagrined to discover that it doesn't support MP3 recordings that are made in Variable Bit Rate (VBR) format, which allows higher-quality music without ballooning the file size. So if you have VBR recordings in your music library, or you're looking for multiple playlist support or a graphic equalizer, don't skip the following section. You may want to purchase a copy of the standalone version of AeroPlayer.

AeroPlayer

The PEG-TJ35 and PEG-TJ37 CLIÉs include AeroPlayer for MP3 playback instead of Audio Player. Developed by Aerodrome software, this slick little application offers several features that aren't found in Audio Player, including support for Variable Bit Rate (VBR) MP3 songs, multiple playlists, the ability to play Ogg Vorbis–format music files, and support for playing files in multiple directories on your Memory Stick.

For a peek at the default interface of the CLIÉ version of AeroPlayer, check out Figure 10-4.

Directly below the song list is a Progress slider, which you can drag with your stylus to jump to any point in a song. The program uses standard stereo-style playback controls. From left to right, they represent Play, Pause, Stop, Previous Track, and Next Track. To rewind, tap and hold the Previous Track button, and to fast-forward, tap and hold the Next Track button. Next to the controls are the Volume Control slider bar and the View button. Tapping View swaps the song list between song names, filenames, and filenames showing the full directory path.

Along the bottom of the screen, you find buttons to toggle between Repeat and Shuffle modes. The final button takes you to the Playlist screen, shown in Figure 10-5.

Figure 10-4:
The
standard
AeroPlayer
interface
included
with the
CLIÉ PEG-
TJ37 model.

Figure 10-5:
The
AeroPlayer
playlist
selection
screen.

Here you can choose among any playlists that are stored on your Memory Stick. Note that AeroPlayer also supports the standard M3U playlist files used by desktop system applications. The Lemonheads playlist shown in Figure 10-5 was actually generated by the freeware Winamp 5 on a Windows computer and copied along with the MP3 files to Memory Stick.

To create a new playlist, do the following:

1. **Tap the New button at the bottom of the Playlists screen.**

   A blank Playlist Editor screen appears.

2. **Tap the Add Tracks button at the top-left corner of the screen.**

   The Add Tracks screen appears with a list of the songs available on your Memory Stick.

3. **Tap each track that you want to add to your playlist.**

   If you want to add all the songs to the list, tap the All button at the bottom of the screen.

4. **Tap the Add to Playlist button at the bottom of the screen to add the selected songs to the playlist.**

   You're then returned to the Playlist Editor screen.

5. **If you want to change the song order, just tap a song to select it, and then tap the up and down arrows in the top-right corner of the screen to move the song up or down in the playlist.**

   Repeat this process for each song that you want to move until you're happy with the playlist.

6. **Enter a name for the playlist in the Name field near the top of the screen, and then tap Use Playlist to save the list.**

   You're returned to the main screen, where you can tap the Play button to start listening to your new musical mix.

7. **To change to another playlist or edit an existing playlist, tap the Playlist button on the main screen, and then tap the name of the playlist of your choice.**

   After tapping the playlist name, you're taken to the Edit Playlist screen (see Figure 10-6), where you can make adjustments in song order, if you like. Now tap Use Playlist to return to the main AeroPlayer screen.

Figure 10-6: AeroPlayer playlist creation screen.

What about the SonicStage program on the CD?

If your CLIÉ shipped with Audio Player, the Installation CD that came with your unit has a program called SonicStage that promises to allow you to manage your music collection and transfer songs in ATRAC3 format. "ATRAC3? What's that?" you might ask. And that question is why I'm not delving into SonicStage in this book. ATRAC3 is a music format that employs Digital Rights Management to limit the copying of music files that you create. It offers no benefits to the *end user* (you, that is) but does create plenty of hassles.

For instance, you have to *check out* a song (like checking a book out of a library) to transfer it to Memory Stick, and then you have to check it back in before you can play or transfer it elsewhere.

Also, you can't copy ATRAC3 songs to standard purple Memory Sticks. You have to use a Memory Stick that's equipped with MagicGate copy-protection technology. (See Chapter 14 for more on the different types of Memory Sticks.) And if you decide to replace Audio Player with a more powerful music player, you'll find that none of them supports ATRAC3 format.

SonicStage isn't even a rocking music library manager because of its rather dated interface. Just leave it on the CD and download a free copy of Apple's iTunes for Windows from www.itunes.com to manage your music collection. Follow the instructions elsewhere in this chapter to find out how to transfer audio files manually.

You can create dozens of playlists on a single Memory Stick, and you can use the same songs in multiple playlists.

To customize how AeroPlayer works, tap the Menu soft button, and then choose Options⇨Settings from the menu that appears. You see the Settings screen opened to the General tab by default, as shown in Figure 10-7.

Figure 10-7:
The
AeroPlayer
Settings
window.

Select the Background Playback check box so that AeroPlayer can work in the background while you're using other programs on your CLIÉ.

TIP

If you're not using other programs while listening to AeroPlayer, you can significantly extend your battery life by turning off the display screen. Just move the Hold slider on your CLIÉ to the Hold position. The screen turns off, but AeroPlayer continues to crank out tunes.

Selecting the Start Playing on Launch check box on the Preferences screen does just what it says. It's useful if you typically just use one playlist or the default song order for each Memory Stick.

Music is a personal thing, as is style. If the AeroPlayer default gray interface doesn't fit your metro-sensibilities, don't despair. The program supports *skins,* graphic files that can give the program a whole new interface. You can find a selection of free skins to download at `www.aerodrome.us/aeroplayer/skins.html`, as well as instructions for creating your own if you have an artistic bent. Downloadable skins range from the cool to the geeky, as illustrated in Figure 10-8.

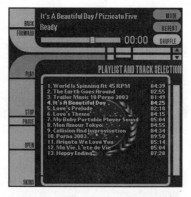
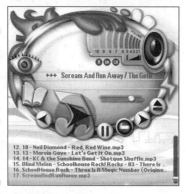

Figure 10-8:
These are just a few of Aero-Player's many available add-on skins.

When you're using another application while music is playing, making a shortcut stroke (a forward slash) in the Graffiti 2 writing area brings up the usual shortcut window with a couple of useful additions: Play and Stop buttons, as well as an *AE* button that pops up a miniature set of playback and volume controls.

Transferring MP3 Songs to Memory Stick

Unfortunately, the CLIÉ doesn't include an application for automatically downloading MP3 audio files, so you need a little basic understanding of how to copy files using Windows. Because this isn't *Windows For Dummies,* I assume that you've got the whole copying-files process down. (If I'm following the classic definition of *assume* here, you can find some basic help on the process by pressing F1 when viewing your Windows desktop to bring up Windows Help, and then searching for *move files.* Alternatively, buying a copy of the fine book *Windows XP For Dummies,* by Andy Rathbone, published by Wiley, is always a good option.)

AeroPlayer for everyone!

Although it's included on only some models, AeroPlayer actually works with all headphone-jack-equipped Palm OS 5 CLIÉ units. You can download a trial copy at www.aerodrome.us and use it for a couple weeks to decide whether you like it. The downloadable version includes a few features not found in the built-in version, such as the graphic equalizer shown in the following figure, so it may be worth checking out even if you did get the program with your CLIÉ. Aerodrome Software offers a discount to PEG-TJ35 and PEG-TJ37 owners.

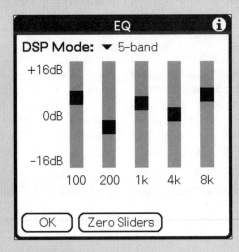

Where do I get MP3s?

The best place to find MP3 songs to play on your CLIÉ is in your own CD collection. You already own the music, and you know you like it, so all you have to do is get the song into MP3 format. This is done by *ripping* the music, which involves copying the digital music data from your CD to your desktop system and then compressing it to a smaller MP3 format file. The CLIÉ doesn't include an MP3 ripper application, but many free applications can rip CDs to MP3 format.

You can't beat the price of Apple's iTunes for Windows (free!), and it not only rips CDs to MP3 or AAC (used by the iPod, but not compatible with the CLIÉ) formats, but it's also a stellar music manager. If you choose to use iTunes, be sure that it's set to rip in MP3 format. Choose Edit⇨Preferences from the main menu, and then when the Preferences dialog box appears, go ahead and click the Importing tab. Then select the Import Using MP3 Encoder option. You can also set the *bit rate* (the quality of the MP3 files) here. If space is a big issue, choose 128 Kbps. Otherwise, choosing 160 or even 192 Kbps gives a bit clearer sound quality at the expense of larger files. The quality gain is very noticeable if you're listening to Bach or Pink Floyd, but that's perhaps not as big a deal if Eminem or Britney Spears is in high rotation. You can download iTunes from www.itunes.com.

Other good choices are Musicmatch Jukebox ($19.99 to buy, but you can use it at reduced speed for free) from www.musicmatch.com, or for those who value pure audio quality over ripping speed and ease of use, the freeware Exact Audio Copy from www.exactaudiocopy.org might be right up your alley.

As you've probably heard, you can now buy songs online for about a buck apiece from services such as iTunes, Musicmatch Downloads, and the new Napster 2.0. Unfortunately, none of these music services supports the CLIÉ. iTunes saves songs in AAC format, and Musicmatch Downloads and Napster 2.0 both use Microsoft's Windows Media format for their music. None of the add-on CLIÉ music players support these formats due to high licensing costs and other restrictions. So you're out of luck, right?

Wrong! Assuming you have a CD burner, there's actually a slightly convoluted way that you can convert the songs that you've purchased from one of these services into an MP3 file that you can play with your CLIÉ. All these services allow you to use your desktop system to copy the songs you've purchased to a CD. You can them turn right around and use your desktop system to rip that CD, converting the songs back into MP3 format. Presto! You now have the songs in a format that can be played on your CLIÉ. If you don't want to keep a CD copy for playback on your home stereo or in your car, just use a CD-RW (a rewriteable disc), erase it when you're through, and use it again next time you buy new songs.

Although you can occasionally find free MP3s from your favorite artists on their Web sites or on sites run by their record labels, legal free downloads of popular tunes are few and far between. If you don't mind giving up-and-coming artists a try, you can find some great (and a lot of not-so-great) free music at the Internet Underground Music Archive at www.iuma.com. Despite the *underground* in the name, the site hosts everything from rock and hip-hop to kids' music and the blues.

To copy the files, you need to place your Memory Stick in a Memory Stick reader drive on your desktop system, or you need to connect your CLIÉ to your desktop system and use the Data Import program to mount the Memory Stick as a drive on your desktop system that way. To do this, tap the Data Import icon in the Program Launcher, and then tap the Connect button at the bottom of the screen. Your Memory Stick is given a drive letter in My Computer on your desktop system. (For more Memory Stick usage basics, see Chapter 14.)

When you have your Memory Stick mounted, all you have to do to transfer your files is copy them to the \Palm\Programs\MSAudio directory, as shown in Figure 10-9. If you're using AeroPlayer, you can also copy M3U playlists and folders containing MP3 files to this directory; Audio Player recognizes only MP3 files in the main MSAUDIO directory.

When your files are copied, just put the Memory Stick back in your CLIÉ — if you went the Memory Stick reader route — or, if you went driveless, just close out of the Data Import program, and you're literally ready to rock.

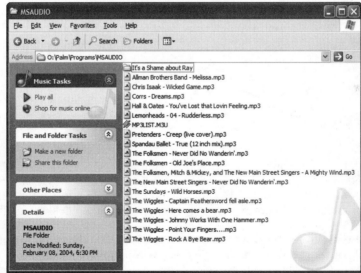

Figure 10-9:
The MP3 directory on a Memory Stick mounted as drive O: on a Windows system.

Alarmingly Cool Alarms

When you were in high school, your car horn did its best impression of the *Dukes of Hazzard* car, General Lee. Now your cell phone blasts "Copacabana" whenever someone calls. Don't you wish that you could personalize your CLIÉ to the same degree?

Okay, I hope neither of the first two things is true. But you can indeed personalize your CLIÉ's alarms. Depending on my mood, my CLIÉ might play a nice Bach minuet to get my attention or play Homer Simpson shouting "D'oh!" If your CLIÉ is equipped with advanced audio, you can use a program like Sound Converter on your desktop system to add alarms by copying MIDI music files or short WAV digital audio files to your CLIÉ's built-in sound database.

If your CLIÉ is equipped with enhanced audio, you can find Sound Converter 2 on the CD that accompanied the unit, typically under the heading CLIÉ Utilities. When the program is installed on your desktop system, you can find Sound Converter 2 listed on your Start menu. Launch the program to see the screen in Figure 10-10.

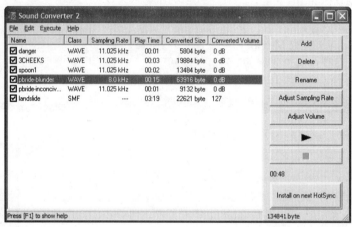

Figure 10-10:
Sound
Converter 2
can convert
MIDI music
and short
WAV audio
files into
CLIÉ alarm
sounds.

To add files to Sound Converter, drag and drop them onto the program's window by using the mouse, or click the Add button to open a file requester window and use it to locate and select files. You can add multiple files at one time and preview them by clicking each file and then clicking the Play arrow.

Note that converted WAV files are limited to 64MB (about ten seconds, typically) in length. If you have a file that goes slightly over that in size, you can reduce the quality a bit by clicking the Adjust Sampling rate and then choosing 8 kHz. This might give you the extra few seconds that you need to get the entire sample in.

When you're satisfied with your new alarm selection, click the Install on Next HotSync button, and the files are set to transfer next time you sync your handheld.

After you move the files over, you can check out how they sound by tapping the Sound Utl icon in the Program Launcher to run the Sound Utility application. This simple application, shown in Figure 10-11, allows you to play, delete, and rename alarm sound files. Although WAV files typically transfer to the CLIÉ unharmed, many MIDI files sound terrible after the conversion process, so give them a listen before choosing them as alarms.

Figure 10-11:
Sound Utility
lets you
preview
sounds on
your CLIÉ.

To actually use your new alarm, you need to load the Date Book application by tapping its icon in the Program Launcher or by pressing the Date Book hard button. Then tap the Menu soft button and choose Options⇨Preferences from the menu that appears. Tap the pop-up menu next to the words *Alarm Sound,* as shown in Figure 10-12, and your new alarms appear in the list.

When you select an alarm, it plays back so you can confirm that it's the one you want to use. Tap OK, and you're now set to be alerted by anything from the opening riff from your favorite song to your kid saying, "I love you!"

If you have a microphone on your desktop system and want to create your own alarm sounds, look for the program called Sound Recorder on your Start menu. (Under Windows XP, it's typically under Accessories/Entertainment.) You can use this program to record new WAV files for conversion with Sound Converter. After you make a recording, pull down the File menu, and select Properties to make sure that the size is less than about 60K. If it's larger than 60K, transferring the WAV file with Sound Converter cuts the sound off after the 60K point.

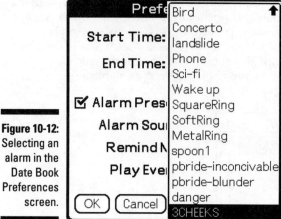

Figure 10-12:
Selecting an
alarm in the
Date Book
Preferences
screen.

Its Master's Voice: CLIÉ Voice Recorder

Many high-end CLIÉ models include a built-in digital voice recorder, which comes in handy for recording everything from short audio notes to yourself to interviews and speeches.

To launch Voice Recorder, tap the Voice Rec icon in the CLIÉ Program Launcher, and then tap the on-screen Rec button to start recording. If your CLIÉ is equipped with a Voice Rec switch, toggling it both launches Voice Recorder and starts a recording.

The interface, shown in Figure 10-13, is fairly straightforward — it actually looks a lot like Audio Player with the addition of a Record button. You find typical home-stereo-style Play, Stop, Previous Track, and Next Track buttons, as well as a Volume Control slider bar.

The A→B repeat button works during playback just as it does in Audio Player: Press it once at the beginning of the section that you want to hear repeated, and then press it again at the end. The section repeats over and over until you press the A→B button again. When listening to voice recordings, this is very useful because you can set a hard-to-hear section to repeat until you understand what was said. Tap the Rep button, located above the Volume Control slider bar, so that it reads Rep 1, which makes it repeat the entire sound continuously.

Move a Voice Recording

Mail a Voice Recording   Delete a Voice Recording

Figure 10-13:
The CLIÉ
Voice
Recorder
in action.

Tapping the SP/LP button to toggle between standard-play (SP) and long-play (LP) recording modes. LP mode reduces audio quality noticeably but triples the available recording time. You can use the Low/High button to set recording sensitivity. If the person speaking is near the microphone, set it to Low. If the speaker is farther away (or is what Kramer from *Seinfeld* called a *low talker*), set it to High.

At the top of the screen are three icons. The first lets you attach a voice recording (as a WAV file) to a CLIÉ Mail message. The second lets you move recordings between the handheld's memory and a Memory Stick, and the last is for deleting files.

Tapping the Wrench icon in the lower-left corner brings up the Voice Recorder Preferences screen, as shown in Figure 10-14.

If you don't want the program to play a confirming beep when you start and stop recording, deselect the first check box. Selecting the Enable Continuous Play check box causes Voice Recorder to play all recordings in succession when you press the Play button.

The List/Rec. Media option lets you choose whether to use handheld memory or your Memory Stick for voice recordings. If you set it to Priority MS, the program uses the Memory Stick, if it's present, or handheld memory if it's not.

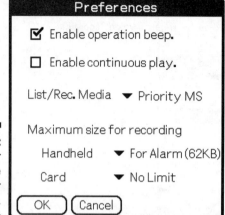

Preferences

☑ Enable operation beep.

☐ Enable continuous play.

List/Rec. Media ▼ Priority MS

Maximum size for recording

Handheld ▼ For Alarm (62KB)

Card ▼ No Limit

[OK] [Cancel]

Figure 10-14:
Adjust your
Voice
Recorder
Preferences.

Finally, you can set a maximum size for voice recordings. If you plan to use your recordings as alarms — or you want to get over your habit of filling all your CLIÉ's memory with lengthy monologues — set the maximum size to 62K, which is the largest size possible for an alarm, for both the Handheld and Card settings.

To convert a voice recording to an alarm, tap it in the Voice Recorder main screen (refer to Figure 10-13), and then tap the Menu soft button and choose Date⇨Convert to Alarm from the menu that appears. If the recording is too long, a window pops up, warning you that the file will be cut off after 62K. This window actually has a little Play button that lets you hear how much of your recording will be used for the alarm before you make a final decision. Handy, that! Note that converting a recording to an alarm doesn't delete the original file.

Chapter 11

Games, Books, and More!

• •

• •

Now that Frank Sinatra is playing the Big Vegas in the Sky, the Sony CLIÉ can quite possibly lay claim to being one of the most versatile entertainers around. In previous chapters, I show you how your CLIÉ can handle TV, movies, and music with panache. But it doesn't stop there. The CLIÉ is also a handheld video game system, an entertainment and education system for the kids, a pocket-sized library, an audiobook narrator, and a portable radio player.

The best news about all this versatility is that you can bring your CLIÉ everywhere, so you *need never be bored again!* Stuck in a long line at the grocery store? Read a short story. Trapped in the waiting room at the dentist's? Play backgammon. Are your kids going crazy during the a traffic jam? Let them draw, do puzzles, and more. Are *you* going crazy during a traffic jam? Plug your CLIÉ into your car stereo and listen to the latest John Grisham novel.

And to think you told your spouse that you bought the CLIÉ to get better organized. . . .

Goodbye, Game Boy

With its brilliant graphics, superb sound support, and beefy memory capabilities, the CLIÉ is an excellent game platform. Although early CLIÉ games were fairly simple, tending to be more of the puzzles-and-cards variety, the faster processors and larger screens of the models available today have allowed game developers to create titles that are comparable to the games that you were playing on your desktop system just a few years ago.

Games for the CLIÉ are available just like any other program that you might buy — either on a CD that you buy in the store (a fairly rare animal) or more frequently, as a download. Some downloadable games are free, but others are commercial. Almost all the commercial games offer time-limited demo versions that you can try and then buy if you like them. (You can find a couple of these on your CLIÉ Installation CD.) After paying for the game at the site where you initially downloaded it, you'll receive an e-mail with a code to fully unlock the game. Games are relatively inexpensive — most fall in the $5-to-$20 range.

Games of virtually all types are available for the CLIÉ. Puzzle games are the most common — and among the best suited for playing with a stylus — but you can also find trivia, card, action, and strategy games. Even a few DOOM-style first-person shooters are available. Just about everyone can find a game that they like that's available for the CLIÉ.

For a look at some of the best games available for the CLIÉ, organized by game type, check out the following couple sections. (And be sure to check out the illustrations. I selflessly spent umpteen hours trying out these games just so that I could find representative shots for this book.)

Action games

Action games are the ones that test your reflexes and reactions: 3D shooters, arcade games, racing games, and so on. Because many CLIÉs have awkward button designs for gaming (see the sidebar "The CLIÉ Game Controller"), action games that are designed to be played with the stylus tend to work best.

Insaniquarium

```
www.astraware.com
```

Insaniquarium is the first of many games in this chapter from Astraware, the king of Palm OS gaming. Your job is to keep your fish alive, earn money to buy new fish, and occasionally fight off scary alien invaders. (Hey, it does have *insane* in the name.) It delivers fast-tapping action thrills. (See Figure 11-1.)

Agent Z 2

```
www.ellams-software.co.uk
```

Reminiscent of the classic Commodore 64 game Impossible Mission, this action title has you working your way through a multilevel, evil-agent head-quarters, using stairs and elevators to avoid evil agents while planting cameras and microphones and occasionally defusing bombs. The graphics are simple, as is readily apparent in Figure 11-2, but the action is nonstop. Finish all 20 levels and you can get the original Agent Z for free!

Figure 11-1:
Insani-
quarium can
sometimes
get a bit
fishy.

Figure 11-2:
Agent Z 2
might look
primitive,
but the
action
makes it
worthwhile.

GTS Racing Challenge

www.astraware.com

GTS Racing Challenge is a 3D car racing game. You drive a car from the outside view, as shown in Figure 11-3, in this simple but fun game. It's a snap to
get the basics down, but mastering how to take the curves without sliding off
the track can be tricky. You have three cars to choose among and a whopping
32 tracks to race on.

Figure 11-3:
GTS Racing
Challenge's
driving
action will
have you
searching
for an
airbag add-
on for your
CLIÉ.

Siberian Strike

www.gameloft.com

This World War II shoot-'em-up game puts you in the cockpits of a series of planes from a top-down view as you fly over Russia blasting all manner of bad guys. The five levels of arcade action look as good as anything you'd have dropped a quarter into in the late 1980s. (See Figure 11-4 for a bird's-eye view.)

Figure 11-4:
Siberian
Strike offers
high-soaring
action.

Kickoo's Breakout

www.kickoo.com

This is not the slow, mind-numbing Breakout game where you tediously bat the ball back and forth, trying to knock down a wall of boring bricks. Rather, this is the extremely fast-paced Breakout game where you excitedly bat the ball at high speed toward a wall full of power-ups, traps, and other glowing miscellany. Catch the right power-up and you might get three balls, a set of lasers, or a wide paddle. Catch the wrong one and you might get a tiny paddle or a super-speedup. Simple, thrilling action. (Okay, Figure 11-5 doesn't exactly convey the thrills and chills, but use your imagination.)

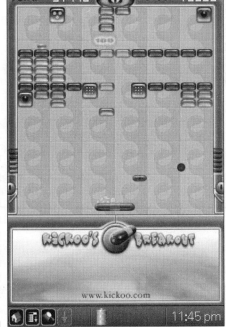

Figure 11-5:
Kickoo's
Breakout
gives you a
chance to
break down
some walls
without
years of
therapy.

Midway Arcade Classics

www.handmark.com

If you have a CLIÉ that supports the PEGA-GC10 add-on Game Controller, buy the controller immediately and get Midway Arcade Classics to go with it. This collection of authentic arcade games offers the classic Spy Hunter, Joust,

Defender II, Sinistar, and Root Beer Tapper. (Root Beer Tapper is shown in all its retro glory in Figure 11-6.) They're a bit too hard to play with the standard CLIÉ application hard buttons, however.

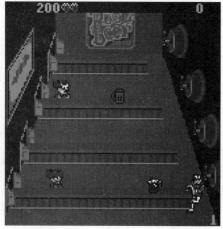

Figure 11-6:
Root Beer Tapper, part of Midway Arcade Classics, might bring back some memories.

Zap!2016

www.astraware.com

This classic arcade shooter is your basic "shoot the aliens that come from the top of the screen while picking up power-ups and avoiding the lasers" game. Although the graphics are low-resolution — see Figure 11-7 — the action is good enough to make up for it. Note that the game isn't playable on the UX series.

Figure 11-7:
Asteroids, enemy ships, and powerful boss aliens are some of the things that can ruin your day in Zap!2016.

The CLIÉ Game Controller

For the most part, Sony's engineering of the CLIÉ is nothing short of brilliant. But somewhere deep within the bowels of a design lab in Japan, there sits a very angry engineer who must believe that games are beneath the CLIÉ's station in life. With each successive series, this person designs button shapes and jog dial placements that make action gaming more difficult. For instance, the movement of the jog dial to the center of the new TH and TJ models prevents up-and-down directional control in an action game. And the UX series includes only three application hard buttons, which are commonly used for game control.

What's a gamer to do? Well, the good news is that the vast majority of today's Palm OS games play just fine using only a stylus, with no need for more than one or two application hard buttons. I recommend trying the demo version of any game to ensure that you're comfortable with the control scheme on your CLIÉ.

If you have an older CLIÉ model, though, a fantastic solution is available to you: Sony's PEGA-GC10 Game Controller, shown in the following figure. This PlayStation-quality game pad clips onto the bottom of NR-, T-, and SL/SJ-series CLIÉs, interfacing via the HotSync port. It boasts a four-way game pad, two fire buttons, and four additional control buttons. For compatibility with older games, the driver lets you program the buttons to emulate the standard Palm OS application buttons. Button feel and responsiveness are superb. With the Game Controller, I was able to make it to the end of Zap!2016 without losing a single ship.

Unfortunately, the PEGA-GC10 doesn't fit the newest CLIÉ models, and Sony doesn't appear to be developing a new version for these units. If you have a CLIÉ that it fits and you enjoy action games, though, it's a must-have peripheral.

Although it's out of production, you might still be able to find the PEGA-GC10 at your local CLIÉ provider; if not, you can order one from www. sonystyle.com. They're usually available on eBay, as well.

Puzzle games

Puzzle games exercise the mind as much as they do the reflexes, and the CLIÉ excels at offering them. Break out the stylus and the cerebellum and prepare to be challenged.

Bejeweled

www.astraware.com

Warning: This is the most addictive game since Tetris. It's also amazingly simple. Swap adjacent jewels around the board by tapping with the stylus to get three matching jewels in a row. But something in that simplicity makes it very, very hard to stop playing. One of the first enhancements that the developers made to the original version of the game was to add the optional clock and battery meter that you see at the top of Figure 11-8. (Bejeweled players tend to lose track of both time and battery juice.) The latest version offers high-resolution graphics and enhanced music when run on the CLIÉ. If you buy only one game on your CLIÉ, buy this one. Your CLIÉ might have come with a demo version on its CD, but skip that and download the latest release to be sure that you have the newest bells and whistles. You'll want to explore Astraware's site anyway if you enjoy puzzle games. The site is chock full of other fantastic puzzle titles, such as Alchemy, Atomica, Dynomite, Cubis, and Rocket Mania.

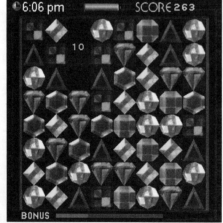

Figure 11-8:
Bejeweled
isn't just a
game. It's an
obsession.

Lemmings

www.ardiri.com

Lemmings is a classic game. Your job is to save the lemmings before they head off to the great lemming beyond. You're given a variety of special powers that you can bestow on lemmings to help them save their brethren.

Turn them into diggers, blockers, and so on to create a safe path. The game itself is free, and expansion levels are available at a low price. (Figure 11-9 gives you a taste of what you can expect.)

Figure 11-9: Don't throw your lives away, lemmings!

Tetris

www.handmark.com

Tetris is the Russian falling-block puzzle game shown in Figure 11-10. If Bejeweled is addictive, Tetris should be regulated by the government. Back in the early '90s, I actually had Tetris *dreams*. Over 15 years after its release, this game remains disturbingly entertaining despite the fact that all you have to do is create solid rows out of falling blocks. Although the Palm OS port features low-resolution graphics, you'll be so mesmerized that you'll hardly notice.

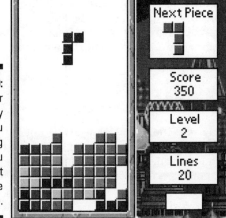

Figure 11-10: You'd better get comfy before you start playing Tetris. You could be at it for quite a while.

Vexed

vexed.sourceforge.net

Shown in Figure 11-11, Vexed is perhaps the best free game, oh, ever. In this simple game, you slide tiles around the board, utilizing virtual gravity to get them into the right spot so that they match. Match two tiles, and they disappear. Get to the end of the game with any tiles left, and you lose. The original game was so good that a team of fans enhanced it and added dozens of new levels. Be careful, though: This game can easily nullify any added productivity that your CLIÉ might afford you by absorbing your time.

Figure 11-11:
Who knew
that mere
boxes could
be so
vexing?

Bookworm

www.astraware.com

Crossword fans, bibliophiles, and anyone who enjoys word puzzles will find Bookworm to be a fantastic time-killer. The objective is to build words by connecting adjacent tiles, as shown in Figure 11-12. The longer the word is, the better your score. As the game progresses, you get bonus tiles, as well as special tiles that can help or hinder your game. Fantastic word fun.

Board and card games

Ah, the games that you can play with the whole family. Well, not in this case, right, because you're playing on your CLIÉ? Nope. Some board and card games for the CLIÉ actually offer multiplayer support, making them just as social as the real thing! And of course, solitaire is always an option for those times when you just want to be alone.

Figure 11-12:
Play
Bookworm
and
exercise
your
vocabulary
muscles.

AcidSolitaire

www.red-mercury.com

Red Mercury's AcidSolitaire is fully enhanced for the CLIÉ, with support for large-screen models, beautiful full-color backgrounds, animation, sound, and an amazingly intuitive interface, as shown in Figure 11-13 The company also offers a version of Freecell Solitaire called, you guessed it, AcidFreecell.

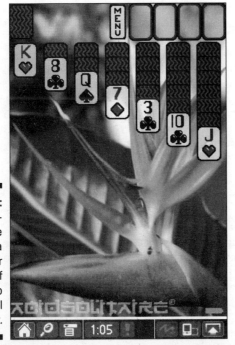

Figure 11-13:
Acid-
Solitaire
changes a
regular
game of
Solitaire into
a graphical
delight.

Aggression

www.blitgames.com

If you enjoyed playing Risk as a kid, you'll love Aggression, shown in Figure 11-14. This game of world conquest plays much like a cyber version of the board game classic, but it's packed with modifiable rules, devious artificially intelligent opponents, and a variety of other enhancements to spruce up the game play. And the board is far more beautiful than anything you ever put on your kitchen table.

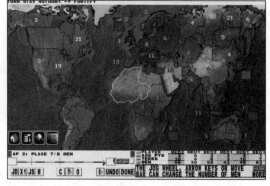

Figure 11-14:
Aggression might give you a taste for conquest.

Scrabble, Monopoly, and Trivial Pursuit

www.handmark.com

I'm grouping these three games together because they share common characteristics: They're true to the original games, they're enhanced to take advantage of all the CLIÉ's features, and they all support multiple human players. All three games can be played by passing a single CLIÉ around, and Scrabble and Trivial Pursuit also support playing with multiple PDAs — even of different brands — by using infrared or Bluetooth communication. (Figure 11-15 shows you what Scrabble on a CLIÉ looks like.)

Strategy games

The Strategy category covers a wide variety of games, from cerebral games like chess to combat in Warfare Incorporated to snail artillery combat. Fess up: When you bought your CLIÉ, you never imagined that you'd use it to drop anvils on the heads of virtual snails, did you?

Figure 11-15:
You can't cheat at Scrabble on a PDA.

Snails

www.snailsgame.com

At first, Snails looks like your basic mortar mollusk mayhem, another case of gory gastropod genocide. But this cartoonish snail-against-snail artillery game, shown in Figure 11-16, is chock-full of fun, strategy, and laughs. And it's not just action — there's a wacky storyline behind each mission. The game boasts excellent audio, amusing animation, lots of levels, and tons of wacky weapons — including an anvil that you can drop on your enemy's head. The game is amazingly inexpensive (under $10) given its level of quality and fun.

Figure 11-16:
The Snails game really shells out the fun.

Warfare Incorporated

www.handmark.com/warfare

A full-blown, real-time strategy game, Warfare Incorporated sends you on a 14-mission campaign to gather interstellar artifacts and keep them away from the bad guys. All the usual elements that you'd expect from a real-time strategy game on your desktop system are here: building, combat, multiple unit types, and more. (See Figure 11-17.) The most recent version offers supercharged performance on Palm OS 5 CLIÉ models and includes a Windows mission editor so that you can create your own add-on missions. Numerous missions are available for download as well.

Figure 11-17:
Send your virtual soldiers and sci-fi tanks into real-time battle in Warfare Incorporated.

ChessGenius

www.chessgenius.com

If you want to lose a game of chess, ChessGenius is the game for you. Optimized for the newest CLIÉs and packing startlingly good artificial intelligence, this handheld chess game — shown in Figure 11-18 — gives everyone this side of Garry Kasparov a real challenge. The good news is that the game features 40 playing levels, so you can adjust it to offer you a real challenge without always getting decimated. Hints and a tutor mode make ChessGenius an excellent choice for the new player.

Figure 11-18:
You won't feel rooked if you buy Chess-Genius.

Kingdom

www.grogsoft.com

Kingdom, shown in Figure 11-19, is very similar to the original version of the classic computer game Civilization. You start with a single city and build colonists and recruit soldiers as you expand your empire. You can go all Genghis Khan on your neighbors and try to wipe them out, or you can try to win a science victory by outpacing them technologically. As you play, you manage each city to make sure that it's properly exploiting the resources around it. Make wise choices on which units to build. Kingdom has good artificial intelligence and has the depth of play of the original Civilization. It's a must-have for war- and colonization-game fans.

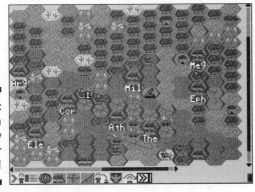

Figure 11-19:
A game, a game, my Kingdom for a game!

Adventures and RPGs

Adventure and role-playing games (RPGs) are like interactive books where you're the main character. Adventures typically involve interacting with other characters and solving puzzles to move on to the next chapter. RPGs also have storylines but often focus more on combat and building up your character's abilities as you solve heroic quests.

Legacy

```
www.redshift.hu
```

I first tried the newly released Legacy during the writing of this book, and it took a crowbar, a pound of butter, and a deranged squirrel to tear me away from Legacy long enough to finish writing. This stellar role-playing game looks like it belongs on a desktop computer, not a handheld. It includes all the requisite features, including dungeons to crawl through, monsters to slay, and recruiting parties of adventurers to join you in the fun, as shown in Figure 11-20. The graphics are stunning, and the overall game is reminiscent of computer classics like The Bard's Tale and Might and Magic. I highly recommend Legacy for role-playing-game fans.

Figure 11-20: Sleep? Who needs sleep? Legacy is so much better than sleep.

Kronos

```
www.codejedi.com
```

Kronos isn't actually a game. It's an *interpreter,* a program that lets you load and play classic Infocom text adventure games such as Zork and The Hitchhiker's Guide to the Galaxy. If you don't have these great old classics around, you can pick up one of the old Infocom CD collections on eBay for a song. Text adventures are interactive stories where you issue commands like "go west," "kill grue with sword," or "grab the stupid babel fish" to interact with the story. Text adventures are also perfect for handheld play because you look like you're working intently as you play them. (Figure 11-21 introduces you to a CLIÉ version of The Hitchhiker's Guide to the Galaxy.)

Figure 11-21: Kronos can help make having fun look like diligent work.

CLIÉ for Kids

Have your kids reached the age where you can feel confident handing them a device that cost you hundreds of dollars and whose most fragile component is a screen made out of the "you betcha I'll shatter if you drop me on a hard surface" variety of glass? If so, the CLIÉ makes an excellent time-killer for the kids — and a parental sanity-saver for you when they resort to the time-honored, parent-torture techniques of repetitive blasts of "Are we there yet?" and "I'm bored."

Even your everyday CLIÉ can entertain kids. They can draw with CLIÉ Memo or Photo Editor or go nuts shooting pictures with the built-in camera. Or you can take advantage of kids' affinity for multimedia by buying a second Memory Stick and filling it with their favorite songs from The Wiggles or a recording of their favorite episode of *Jay Jay the Jet Plane*.

Although the amount of educational software available for the CLIÉ pales in comparison to entertainment and productivity programs, some standout programs are designed just for kids. At palmgear.com alone, you can find about 400 programs targeted at educating grades K through 12.

If you are handing off the PDA to the kids, and they're not in a controlled, soft environment like a car or plane, invest in a good case. A hard case helps prevent scratches, but a soft, padded case offers better drop protection. Choose the type that best fits your needs — and the destructive tendencies of your children.

PDA Playground

www.dataviz.com

Designed for kids ages 3 through 7, PDA Playground offers a selection of six games aimed squarely at the little-kid market:

- **Paint:** Color in predrawn pictures.

- **Draw:** Draw uses the same interface as Paint but lets kids draw images from scratch.

- **Match:** This memory game has kids find matching tile pairs. Think of the game Concentration.

- **ScratchOff:** This is the weakest of the bunch. Kids can use the stylus to scratch a pattern off a drawing and try to guess what the image is before revealing it. It's boring alone but fun with two or more kids to see who can be the first to guess.

- **FollowMe:** Use the stylus to repeat patterns of images and sounds that flash on the screen. Remember the classic Simon electronic game? (Figure 11-22 gives you a peek at FollowMe.)

- **PuzzlePath:** Rearrange on-screen tiles to make a path so that a little girl can safely collect fruit while avoiding turtles.

Figure 11-22:
PDA
Playground
is fun for
younger
children.

The games are cute, but overall, they're more entertaining than educational. The coolest feature, though, is that it can keep the kids from deleting your important contacts or otherwise doing scary things to your data. To prevent such disasters, simply set it to require a password before it allows you to exit the program.

Even better, PDA Playground can launch not only the six included games, but also any other programs that you add to the Program Launcher. So you could, say, also let the kids use the CLIÉ Camera and play Bejeweled and Vexed, but lock them out of all the other applications.

Kids Pack

www.jsmart.com

For a slightly older crowd, check out Kids Pack, shown in Figure 11-23. Rated for ages 8 and up, this four-game pack includes the following:

- ✔ **Word Search:** Find the hidden words in the grid of letters.

- ✔ **Labyrinth:** For those sweet, innocent minds that haven't yet figured out that life itself is merely navigating a complicated maze of decisions, this graphical maze game is just the ticket.

Figure 11-23:
Kids Pack offers enjoyable brain teasers.

✔ **Peg Jump:** Did you ever stop at the Cracker Barrel restaurant and play that fun little wooden peg game where you try to jump the golf tees and remove all but one from the board? With Peg Jump, your kids can play the game without the need for a Cracker Barrel, and you'll need to find a new excuse to talk the spouse into stopping for a tasty plate of chicken-fried steak.

✔ **Simon Says:** Repeat the sequence of flashing lights, just like the old Simon game.

Note that this is merely a bargain bundle of four separate games, without the kid-safe Program Launcher included with PDA Playground. But it's also half the price.

Math123 Kids Math and Count

www.palmgear.com

Looking for something a little more educational? Math123 Kids Math and Count offers four levels of difficulty aimed at kids from preschool to elementary. At the easiest level, kids merely count the objects on the screen and tap the on-screen number, as shown in Figure 11-24. The program works all the way up to addition and subtraction with two more digits.

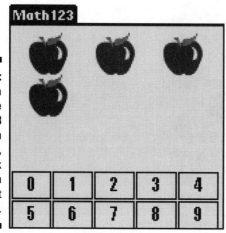

Figure 11-24: With a name like Math123 Kids Math and Count, you'd think this program taught spelling.

To be really attractive to kids, this program could be a little more game and a little less drill. Still, it's a great way for kids to practice their math skills, and it's very inexpensive.

Beret Study Buddy: Vocabulary

www.beret.com

Are your kids finding it frustrating to study for their vocabulary and spelling tests? The Beret Study Buddy: Vocabulary application lets kids or parents enter vocabulary words and definitions and then practice with them. Tech-savvy kids can even beam their vocabulary lists to each other.

The quiz mode is configurable, but in the fun department, kids also enjoy WordFind, Guess? (which is like Hangman), and Tic Tac Toe games for more entertaining practice, as shown in Figure 11-25. The AnswerTrack feature lets kids and parents see which problem words need extra drilling.

At the Beret Web site, you can also find a variety of math, reading, and civics programs, all hosted by the friendly Herbert the Caterpillar.

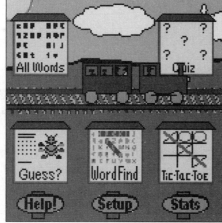

Figure 11-25: Beret Study Buddy: Vocabulary offers good gaming and quizzing options.

Kid Zone

www.beiks.com

Kid Zone is a replacement for the CLIÉ Program Launcher that lets you designate which programs your kids can launch, as shown in Figure 11-26, and then lets them launch *only* those. It locks out the hard buttons and the standard Program Launcher.

Set up all the kids' games and education programs in Kid Zone, and then launch the program before you hand the CLIÉ to the kids. They can swap back and forth between programs to their hearts' content. When you retrieve the CLIÉ, you can enter a password to access the normal Program Launcher and use all your usual applications.

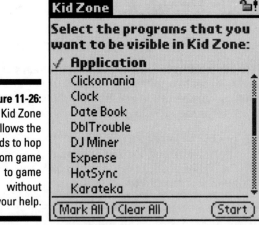

Figure 11-26:
Kid Zone
allows the
kids to hop
from game
to game
without
your help.

Missile Math

www.palmgear.com

Missile Math, shown in Figure 11-27, is a math drill program that uses arcade action to keep the kids playing. If you ever played the classic arcade game Missile Command, the screen will look awfully familiar. The difference is that you have to tap the number that answers the math problem presented at the bottom of the screen to stop the missile.

Nothing like the threat of nuclear annihilation to drill home the need for strong math skills, eh? Um, maybe that's not an appropriate thought to share with the kids.

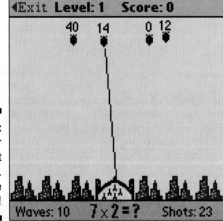

Figure 11-27:
It's better
than rocket
science.
It's Missile
Math!

MakeFaces

www.wagware.com

This one is a hoot. You start with a basic head shape and add eyes, ears, nose, mouth, hair, and so on to create a new face, as shown in Figure 11-28. It's simple enough for even the littlest kids to use, yet it's oddly entertaining. You'll probably find yourself "testing" it for a few minutes before you can bring yourself to hand the CLIÉ to the kids.

Figure 11-28: Don't worry. When you use MakeFaces to make a funny face, your CLIÉ won't stick that way.

eBooks for the kids

I cover eBooks in the section "Curl Up with a Good eBook," but I want to make sure that you know this is a great resource for kids who like to read. Although relatively few commercial eBook titles are aimed at kids, a ton of classic literature is available in the public domain and can be downloaded in Palm OS format.

The best place to look for classics for the kids is www.memoware.com. There you can find kid-friendly classics such as Mark Twain's *The Adventures of Huckleberry Finn* and *A Connecticut Yankee in King Arthur's Court*. You can also find everything from Jane Austen's *Pride and Prejudice* to Victor Appleton's *Tom Swift and His Sky Racer,* all at no charge.

Good, old-fashioned games

Hey, you don't make them do homework 24/7, so you don't have to limit the kids' CLIÉ time to math and word drills. Many of the games that adults enjoy also appeal to the kids. Astraware's ChromaGames features checkers, for instance, which is a perennial kids' favorite. Puzzle games like Bejeweled and Vexed teach basic matching skills and prioritization, and you can't find more entertaining spelling and vocabulary drills than Bookworm and Link Letters. You're not going to find anything as egregiously inappropriate as Grand Theft Auto on the CLIÉ, and you have to look pretty hard to find games that even have blood in them. So don't feel bad about letting your kids partake in a little handheld gaming.

Curl Up with a Good eBook

eRead a good book lately? Whether you enjoy curling up with bestsellers, science fiction, romance, or the classics, the CLIÉ is ready to deliver the eGoods. eBooks have come a long way since the early days when people struggled to read *public domain* electronic books on blocky, low-resolution screens. (Works that are in the public domain aren't protected by copyright law and can be reproduced and used at will.)

My, what a difference a few years makes! Today you can purchase the latest bestsellers, electronic versions of fiction magazines, and even short stories. And of course, the free classics are still available as well.

Reading eBooks on the CLIÉ is a pleasant experience. Its bright, backlit screen with a paper-white background and crisp, high-resolution text is easy on the eyes. It's the next best thing to paper. And eBook readers include features that take advantage of the electronic format by offering keyword searches, multiple bookmarks, and digital annotation.

I admit that I'd never give up my paper library for electronic books. There's something comforting about the feel of a paper classic in my hands. But I still keep an eBook or two on my CLIÉ because I never know when I'm going to find some downtime to sneak in a few pages. Not to mention the fact that it would be considered rude and unprofessional to pop out a book in a meeting when a coworker is on a ten-minute ramble about something that's only peripherally related to work. However, reading an eBook on a CLIÉ looks an awful lot like you're doing something productive and work-related. . . .

Where to find eBooks

An Internet account is your library card for a vast selection of electronic books, both commercial and free. All you need to get started is a CLIÉ, possibly a credit card, and an eBook reader. (I fill you in on readers in the later section "eBook readers.") Knowing which kinds of books you'll be reading comes in handy when choosing a reader, so it pays to check out the virtual bookshelves first.

Palm Digital Media

www.palmdigitalmedia.com

The premiere shopping destination for eBooks, Palm Digital Media offers thousands of fiction and nonfiction books by authors ranging from Stephen King to Moon Unit Zappa.

Prices are much more reasonable now than they were in the early days of the store, when new books cost as much as they did at a bookstore. Today you can find the hottest new novels at prices that are typically about 25 percent less than their hardcover counterparts. Paperbacks tend to run from $3 to $9, with most coming in at just under $6. If you don't mind an occasional commercial e-mail, subscribing to the Palm Digital Media e-mail newsletter will net you a weekly code that's good for 10 percent off every eBook that you purchase.

Those prices are reasonable when you consider that you're getting the exact same content you'd get in a printed book but in an extremely portable format. The biggest disadvantage is that you can easily pick up and read an old printed book 20 years from now, but who knows what kind of eBook readers will be around by then?

The Palm Digital Media eBooks are copy-protected and require an unlock code that's based on the credit card number that you used to purchase the book. (Don't worry, nobody else can read the number). This means the book is tied to you but not specifically to your CLIÉ. Thus, you can copy the book to a desktop or notebook system for some big-screen reading. But if you want to share the book with a friend or family member, it has to be someone you'd trust with your credit card number. Because of this copy protection, you must use the company's Palm Reader program to read its eBooks.

Palm Digital Media even lets you browse before you buy: You can read excerpts from most of their eBooks on your desktop system before you make a purchasing decision.

Fictionwise

www.fictionwise.com

Fictionwise started a few years ago as an online store selling primarily science-fiction short stories. The company has since then significantly expanded its selection, moving into mystery, romance, nonfiction, and other genres and adding full-length novels to the mix. The company has over 18,000 titles available.

Like Palm Digital Media, Fictionwise offers eBooks in secure Palm Reader format. However, the company also offers a number of titles in the standard, unencrypted Doc file format, which gives you more choices in eBook reader software.

Fictionwise's collection of short stories might be the best choice for you if you tend to do your CLIÉ reading when you find a few minutes of free time rather than curling up on the couch with a good PDA.

Fictionwise almost always offers a few short stories or classic texts for free download, which is a great way to sample the eBook experience.

MemoWare

```
www.memoware.com
```

If your favorite word is *free,* or your tastes tend to run towards the classics, check out MemoWare. MemoWare specializes in public-domain texts. You can find many books and short stories old enough that their copyrights have expired — think Mark Twain, Jane Austen, H.G. Wells, and the complete works of Shakespeare. MemoWare also offers government-sponsored works, reader-written texts such as *The Little Book of First Aid,* dictionaries, foreign-language translators, and a ton of computer and handheld reference works.

If you're not sure what you're looking for, MemoWare offers an excellent search engine that lets you look for books by keyword, author, format, reader rating, and more.

MemoWare also offers an excellent eBook primer section with detailed information on eBook formats, reader programs, and how to create your own eBook texts. If you're new to eBooks, www.memoware.com makes a good first stop to help you get started.

Other eBook resources

The Internet hosts numerous other spots for finding eBooks. They include:

- **Baen Books:** This publisher of science-fiction and fantasy novels not only offers many books in electronic format (including Mobipocket reader format for the CLIÉ), but also actually offers many titles online *before* they're available in bookstores. For a monthly fee, you get access to four brand new novels. Check them out at www.baen.com.

- **Mobipocket:** This is another good source for commercial eBooks. Your CLIÉ might have Mobipocket Reader included, either built in or on the CD that accompanied the unit. I've got one caveat: A search for *Star Trek* titles also brought up a racy erotica title in the "based on what others bought, you might also like this" segment of the results. So you might want to do any eBook shopping for the kids yourself on this site. And *Star Trek* book fans might want to get out of the house a little more. For a test run, point your Internet browser to www.mobipocket.com.

- **eBooks.com:** Offering books in Palm Reader format, eBooks.com has an extensive selection of mainstream fiction and nonfiction titles. But what makes this site stick out is the ability to do a full-text search, fantastically helpful if you're looking for texts that reference subjects such as

Alexander the Great or the Holy Grail. eBooks.com makes its home on the Web at (surprisingly enough) www.ebooks.com.

✔ **PerfectBound:** HarperCollins Publishers is offering is own titles online from authors such as Michael Crichton and Neal Gaiman. Most of the titles here can also be found at other sites, but the same titles at PerfectBound were almost always cheaper than at Palm Digital Media. Give them a try at www.perfectbound.com.

✔ **Contentlink:** This site offers books published by Random House Publishing and features authors such as Laurell K. Hamilton, Dan Brown, and Anne Rice. As with PerfectBound, many of these are available elsewhere, but the prices are sometimes better. See for yourself at www.contentlinkinc.com.

eBook readers

Okay, you've downloaded some eBooks. Now all you need is a reader to view them on.

Freeware and unencrypted commercial eBooks are stored in a format called Doc files. Despite the name, these have no relation to the DOC files saved by Microsoft Word. Rather, they're compressed eBooks designed for viewing on Palm OS and Pocket PC handhelds. All Palm OS eBook readers can read Doc files.

Encrypted commercial eBooks are specially designed to prevent copying, and they require a reader that supports their special format. Thus, if you're reading a book from Palm Digital Media, you have no choice but to use Palm Reader because it's the only reader that supports that store's format.

The next few sections fill you in on the most popular readers.

Mobipocket Reader

www.mobipocket.com

Mobipocket Reader, shown in Figure 11-29, isn't as universally supported as Palm Reader. Still, I mention it first because it's actually included with — or even built into — many CLIÉs. You can use it to read commercial eBooks from the Mobipocket Web site, as well as from Baen books and a few other publishers. The version bundled with the CLIÉ is full-featured with bookmarks; a built-in dictionary; and easy-to-read, smooth-edged fonts. Mobipocket's most unique feature is its ability to download news from a choice of more than 500 online channels and download it to your CLIÉ when you HotSync. Mobipocket also sells Mobipocket Reader Pro, which adds better searching, more screen orientations for reading text, highlighting, and several other features. The free version comes bundled with many CLIÉs and can also be downloaded from the Web site.

The Road to Oz 1 ▾   A ← 16▾

State of Kansas, was an experience that fairly bewildered
her.

"Will your folks worry?" asked the shaggy man, his eyes
twinkling in a pleasant way.

"I s'pose so," answered Dorothy with a sigh. "Uncle Henry
says there's ALWAYS something happening to me; but I've
always come home safe at the last. So perhaps he'll take
comfort and think I'll come home safe this time."

"I'm sure you will," said the shaggy man, smilingly nodding
at her. "Good little girls never come to any harm, you know.
For my part, I'm good, too; so nothing ever hurts me."

Dorothy looked at him curiously. His clothes were shaggy, his
boots were shaggy and full of holes, and his hair and
whiskers were shaggy. But his smile was sweet and his eyes
were kind.

"Why didn't you want to go to Butterfield?" she asked.

"Because a man lives there who owes me fifteen cents, and if
I went to Butterfield and he saw me he'd want to pay me the
money. I don't want money, my dear."

"Why not?" she inquired.

"Money," declared the shaggy man, "makes people proud and
haughty. I don't want to be proud and haughty. All I want is
to have people love me; and as long as I own the Love
Magnet, everyone I meet is sure to love me dearly."

"The Love Magnet! Why, what's that?"

"I'll show you, if you won't tell any one," he answered, in a
low, mysterious voice.

Figure 11-29:
Mobipocket
Reader
supports a
variety of
font sizes.

Palm Reader

www.palmdigitalmedia.com

By virtue of the vast majority of commercial eBooks for handhelds being
released in Palm Reader format, Palm Reader is a must-have for anyone who
plans to buy eBooks online. The good news is that it's an excellent program
overall, and because it supports Doc files, it's a good choice for reading free
eBooks as well. The program features multiple screen orientations, so you can
read in landscape mode, as shown in Figure 11-30, or even flip the text upside-
down if that makes the scroll buttons easier for you to hit while reading. Palm
Reader supports multiple bookmarks, and you can make annotations in the
text. Palm Reader is free, but Palm Digital Media also offers a commercial version that adds extra fonts, customizable colors, and a built-in dictionary.

Other readers

www.palmgear.com

Quite a few other readers that support uncompressed Doc files are available
for the Palm OS. Here are a few of the standouts, all of which are available
from Palm Gear:

- **CSpotRun:** This classic reader is easy to use, available in a variety of languages, and it's free. Its autoscroll feature lets you just sit back and read with no button-pressing or screen-tapping necessary.

- **iSilo:** The Doc format supports only plain-text files. If you want to create your own eBooks featuring text with colors, styles, multiple sizes, and more, iSilo is just the ticket. iSilo files are smaller than Doc files, and you'll find several files available online in iSilo format. iSilo reads standard Doc files, as well.

- **TealDoc:** This enhanced reader supports standard Doc files, PC-format text files stored on Memory Sticks, and enhanced TealDoc files. The TealDoc-format files can include graphics, links, multiple colors, and other enhancements that aren't available in regular Doc files. It includes TealDocMaker for the PC, a program for creating your own document files.

- **WordSmith:** This is actually a full-featured commercial word processor, but the author lets you use it as a Doc-format eBook reader for free. It's notable for its font support. It includes easy-to-read, smoothed fonts, and you can convert any TrueType font on your desktop system to Palm OS format for use in WordSmith on your CLIÉ.

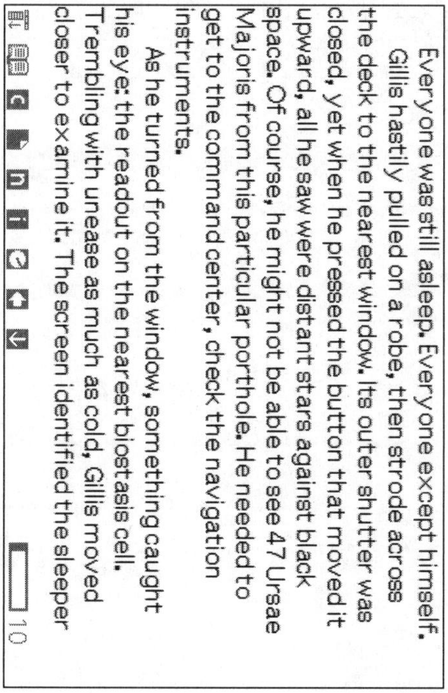

Figure 11-30:
Palm Reader
supports
landscape
mode for
widescreen
reading.

Everyone was still asleep. Everyone except himself. Gillis hastily pulled on a robe, then strode across the deck to the nearest window. Its outer shutter was closed, yet when he pressed the button that moved it upward, all he saw were distant stars against black space. Of course, he might not be able to see 47 Ursae Majoris from this particular porthole. He needed to get to the command center, check the navigation instruments.

As he turned from the window, something caught his eye: the readout on the nearest biostasis cell. Trembling with unease as much as cold, Gillis moved closer to examine it. The screen identified the sleeper

Listened to a Good Book Lately?

Audible is to audiobooks what iTunes is to digital music. Imagine an online store with an audiobook selection that's 100 times what you can find at even the largest local book superstore. That's Audible, found at www.audible.com, a Web site with spoken-word bestsellers ranging from *Cold Mountain* to *The Da Vinci Code.*

Audible doesn't stop with audiobooks. The service also offers a variety of radio programs, including such National Public Radio standouts as *Car Talk, Fresh Air,* and my personal favorite, *This American Life.* You can purchase individual episodes or buy subscriptions that let you download new episodes each week.

To download the player software for your CLIÉ, visit the Web site and sign up for an account. (The account is free, so you won't be charged until you buy something.) Then log in with your new user ID and click the Get Audible Software link to download AudibleManager, shown in Figure 11-31, for your desktop system . (If you're using a Mac, you can access Audible content simply by using iTunes.) After you install the software, load AudibleManager on your desktop system and choose Devices⇨Add New Devices. The Mobile Devices Update window appears. Select the AudiblePlayer for Sony CLIÉ check box in this window and click Okay. AudibleManager exits, automatically installs the necessary software, and then restarts itself.

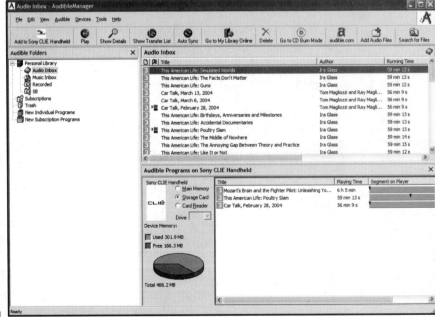

Figure 11-31: You can use Audible-Manager to download audiobooks and transfer them to your CLIÉ.

The program should prompt you to install the Palm OS AudiblePlayer on your CLIÉ. If not, you can find the Palm application on the Audible Web site. Just click the Get Audible Software link again, choose Palm OS from the list of available versions on the Web page, and then choose Sony CLIÉ on the page that follows. Download and run the program to install it.

When you have all the software installed, and you've purchased a book or radio program, you're ready to listen. To transfer a program, use the following steps:

1. **Launch AudibleManager on your desktop system and start Audible-Player on your CLIÉ by tapping its icon in the Program Launcher.**

    The screen shown in Figure 11-32 appears on your CLIÉ.

    Be sure that your CLIÉ is connected to your desktop system via cradle or cable when you do this.

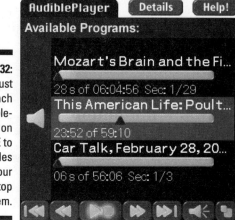

Figure 11-32:
You must launch Audible-Player on your CLIÉ to transfer files from your desktop system.

2. **Choose the Audible program that you want to download by dragging and dropping the program to the CLIÉ window at the bottom of the AudibleManager window, or by clicking the file once with the mouse and clicking the Add to Sony CLIÉ Handheld button at the top-left corner of the screen.**

    You're given the option to save files in main memory, to save the files on a Memory Stick, or to copy the files to a Memory Stick that's inserted into a reader on your desktop system.

    After you choose where to copy the file, the transfer starts automatically. You don't have to HotSync to move the file over.

    Status meters appear on both the CLIÉ and desktop system screens, showing you the progress of the file download.

Note that AudiblePlayer bookmarks the current position in an audiobook, so you can easily pick up where you left off when you stop listening. If you tap the Menu soft button in the program and choose Options➪Preferences from the menu that appears, you can enable background play, allowing you to switch to another program while listening to your Audible program. If you want to extend your battery life while you listen, use the Hold slider to turn off the screen.

Cars are among the most popular places to listen to audiobooks, but wearing headphones while you're driving isn't safe. If your car has a cassette player, you can buy a tape adapter at any local stereo or electronics store and plug that into your CLIÉ. Otherwise, take a look at an FM transmitter, which plugs into your CLIÉ's headphone jack and transmits its audio output on an unused FM radio frequency. I use the SF121 model from Arkon Resources, which works very well and is relatively inexpensive. You can find information on it at www.arkon.com.

Part IV
An Office in Your Pocket

The 5th Wave   By Rich Tennant

"Oh wait – this says, 'Lunch Ed from Marketing', not 'Lynch', 'Lunch'."

In this part . . .

This is the part where I put you to work. Today's CLIÉs let you bring files from all the major office applications along and even create or download new documents on the road. In this part, I show you how to use Documents to Go to view, edit, and create Word, Excel, and PowerPoint files. You also find out about Picsel Viewer, which lets you view desktop documents with all their formatting and graphics intact, and powerOne Personal, which lets you pass on the old calculator to the kids.

Also, you discover the best third-party productivity programs and two applications that any Microsoft Outlook users will want to check out.

Chapter 12

Office on the Go

In This Chapter

▶ Using Documents To Go to create and edit Microsoft Office files

▶ Putting the powerful Picsel Viewer to work

▶ Calculating with the powerOne Personal calculator

"*A*h," you think, "my CLIÉ is great, but I still need to bring my laptop along to get any real work done. I have a report to finish, numbers to crunch, a presentation to go over . . . None of *that* is going to fit in my pocket."

As Ed McMahon said to Karnak the Magnificent, "You're wrong, oh enlightened one!" The Documents To Go program lets you view, edit, and even create Microsoft Office–compatible files directly on your CLIÉ. And even better, chances are good that your CLIÉ already includes a copy of this powerful program.

Another weapon in the CLIÉ's office arsenal is Picsel Viewer, an amazingly fast program that lets you view (but not edit) Office files and PDF documents with all their graphics and formatting intact.

Finally, for those quick calculations where a spreadsheet is overkill, try the powerOne Personal calculator, a powerful little number-cruncher that's included on the CD that comes with every CLIÉ.

In this chapter, you get a chance to find out about these applications in detail. Be sure to check out Chapter 13 for some third-party alternatives as well, particularly if you're a heavy Outlook user.

The Lowdown on Documents To Go

Think of Documents To Go as a very small clone of Microsoft Office. The Professional Edition of the program includes handheld word processing, spreadsheet, and presentation programs, as well as charting, image display, and e-mail utilities. At the time this book was written, Sony was shipping the

Professional Edition of the program with all its CLIÉ models except the PEG-UX50 line, but in the past, it bundled the less expensive Standard Edition (which includes only the word processing and spreadsheet modules) with its CLIÉs.

If you didn't receive Documents To Go with your CLIÉ, or you got the Standard Edition and want to upgrade to the full Professional Edition, you can find upgrade and purchase information at www.dataviz.com.

Documents To Go Professional includes the following modules:

- ✔ **Word To Go:** This full-blown word processor can natively read Microsoft Word DOC files and covert files from WordPerfect, Word Pro, AppleWorks, and several other word processing formats by using the included desktop synchronization applications.

- ✔ **Sheet To Go:** This powerful spreadsheet can natively read Microsoft Excel files, and convert files from Quattro Pro, Lotus 1-2-3, and other spreadsheets by using the desktop synchronization program.

- ✔ **Slideshow To Go:** This presentation program can display files created with PowerPoint. Note that it can't read PowerPoint files directly; you first have to convert them during HotSync by using the desktop synchronization program.

The Documents To Go program also includes a desktop program designed to manage file synchronization. This program is available for both Windows and Macintosh. I focus on the Windows version here, but the Mac version operates in essentially the same manner.

The desktop application

What makes Documents To Go 6.0 special is its support for native Word and Excel files. For the first time, you can use your handheld to open documents and spreadsheets that are saved in their original format on a Memory Stick or received by e-mail with no translation step necessary.

However, you can likely still find use for the desktop application of Documents To Go. This handy utility controls how files are transferred to and from your desktop computer to your CLIÉ.

After installing Documents To Go on your desktop system, you can open the desktop application by choosing Start➪Programs➪Documents To Go➪ Documents To Go. The program's interface, shown in Figure 12-1, is very easy to use.

Figure 12-1:
The
Documents
To Go
desktop
application
manages
file transfers
between
CLIÉ and
desktop
system.

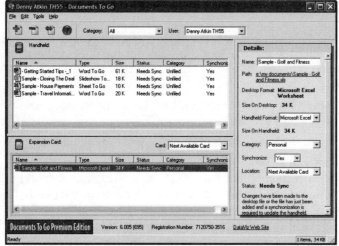

Storing and synchronizing files

When you open the Documents To Go desktop application, you see two areas, one labeled Handheld and the other labeled Expansion Card. If you're lucky enough to have a Memory Stick, you're better off using the Expansion Card area to hold your files, rather than the Handheld area, simply because doing so gives you added flexibility for transferring files in native formats by e-mail or memory card readers.

Selecting a file to synchronize with your CLIÉ is as simple as dragging and dropping the file icon on either the Handheld or Expansion Card area. You can also click the Add icon — the green plus sign (+) in the top-left corner of the program window — to open a file selection window. These files are copied to your handheld during the next HotSync, and then Documents To Go keeps them in sync by automatically updating the CLIÉ version of the file with any changes made to the desktop version, and vice versa.

When you drag a file into the desktop application, by default it's set to transfer in the *To Go format* — that is, a special format used by Documents To Go. Files in this format are smaller and are faster to load on your CLIÉ, but they can be loaded only by Documents To Go. Store files in native Word or Excel format instead if you plan to e-mail them, view them with Picsel Viewer, or access them by using other CLIÉ programs. You determine how files are stored by changing the settings in the Details pane, as shown on the right side of the window in Figure 12-1.

Options in the Details pane

From the top, the following options are available in the Details pane (refer to Figure 12-1):

✔ **Name:** The name that will be used for the file on the CLIÉ appears in this text box.

✔ **Path:** This shows where the file is stored on your desktop system. You can click the path to open a window for the directory containing the file, which is handy for quick access to a document's directory when you want to drag more files over to your CLIÉ.

✔ **Desktop Format:** This shows the original file format before translation during HotSync.

✔ **Size on Desktop:** This shows the size of the original file.

✔ **Handheld Format:** Here's where you choose which format to save the files in. Note that files stored on expansion cards offer additional options. If you want the smallest file, choose the native To Go format. If you want greatest compatibility with other programs, choose the native file format.

✔ **Category:** You can categorize files to help locate them quickly.

✔ **Synchronize:** Set this to Yes if you want changes made on the version of the file stored on your desktop system to be sent to the handheld, and vice versa. If you set it to No, no changes to the file are transferred.

Normally, you want to set Synchronize to Yes. If a file is changed on either the desktop or handheld, the other version is updated during HotSync. If you modify the file in both places, two copies are created during HotSync, one of which reflects the changes made in each location.

✔ **Location:** Here you choose whether to copy the file to main memory or Memory Stick. If you have multiple Memory Sticks, you see their names listed here, and you can choose which one you want to copy the file to. The file is transferred the next time that the correct Memory Stick is present during a HotSync. If this option is set to Next Available Card, the file is transferred during the next HotSync as long as any Memory Stick is present. (Note that you can manually copy Word or Excel files to a Memory Stick by using a card reader, but the Documents To Go desktop application doesn't support this transfer method.)

✔ **Status:** This tells you whether changes have been made to the file that haven't yet been transferred to your handheld. If this option is set to Current, the file is up to date, but if it's set to Needs Sync, the file is updated during the next HotSync.

Setting preferences

Note that you can change the default formats for files that you add to Documents To Go, as well as change the default directory where files are saved. Choose Tools⇨Preferences to get to the window shown in Figure 12-2.

Documents To Go Preferences

General | Exchange | HotSync Action | Graphics | Communications

For each destination window (Handheld or Expansion Card), you can set the format that will be applied to files added to Documents To Go on the desktop.

Handheld Destination Window

Choose the format for files added to the Handheld destination window.

Word Processing:	Word To Go
Spreadsheet:	Sheet To Go
Presentation:	Slideshow To Go

Expansion Card Destination Window

Choose the format for files added to the Expansion Card destination window.

Word Processing:	Microsoft Word
Spreadsheet:	Microsoft Excel
Presentation:	Slideshow To Go

Category

Choose the category to be applied to files added to Documents To Go.

Category:	Unfiled

☑ Always confirm removal of items

OK | Cancel | Apply | Help

Figure 12-2: Setting the default formats for files that you transfer to your CLIÉ.

The settings shown in Figure 12-2 are good defaults, spelling out that you want to store files on Memory Sticks in their native format and that files stored on the handheld are to be in the more compact Documents To Go format. Note that the current version of the program doesn't support presentation files in native PowerPoint format, so Slideshow To Go is your only option.

Even if you create all your files on the handheld, you still want to configure the Documents To Go desktop application because you use it to control how files are transferred from your handheld to your desktop system. Click the Exchange tab in the Documents To Go Preferences dialog box, and you find an option to change the directory where files created on the handheld are stored; the default is your My Documents folder.

When your preferences are set, click OK to return to the main program. Now you're ready to HotSync.

Documents To Go on your CLIÉ

To start the Documents To Go program, just tap the Documents icon in the CLIÉ Program Launcher. The File Selection screen, shown in Figure 12-3, appears.

Documents To Go		▼ All		
ℹ Name		Size	🔄	▣
📄 – Getting Started Ti...		61K	🔄	
📄 Annual Report		16K	🔄	▢
📄 billrog		76K	🔄	▢
📊 Sample – Closing Th...		18K	🔄	
📊 Sample – Golf and Fi...		34K	🔄	▢
📊 Sample – House Pay...		11K	🔄	
📄 Sample – Travel Info...		77K	🔄	▢
📄 simcity		4K	🔄	▢
📄 Test doc		20K	🔄	▢
New ▼	Show: ▼ All Formats			

Figure 12-3:
The main
Documents
To Go
screen.

Assuming that you've HotSynced some files to the CLIÉ already, you see them listed here. The icon in the first column shows the file type — word processing, spreadsheet, and so on. If you tap the icon, you access a pop-up menu that contains options for displaying the file's details, deleting the file, beaming it to another PDA, sending it by e-mail, or moving it between a Memory Stick and the handheld's main memory.

The second column displays the filename; just tap this to load the file. The third column shows the file size, and the fourth column shows HotSync status. If the column has the red-and-blue HotSync icon in it, the file will be synchronized with your desktop computer; if it has a dash, it won't be transferred during HotSync. You can change the sync status for any file by tapping in this column.

The final column shows whether a file is stored in handheld memory (no icon) or on a Memory Stick (a small card icon). You can tap the card icon to see what directory the file is stored in, which is handy if you plan to access it directly from a desktop computer.

You can tap any of the column headers to change the sorting order to sort by file type, name, size, sync status, or location. Tap the drop-down menu arrow next to the Show option at the bottom of the screen to display only files of a certain type.

To create a new document, tap the New button in the lower-left corner of the screen and select the file type. For more on the kinds of file types available, check out the next few sections.

Word To Go

Selecting either Word To Go or Microsoft Word from the New button launches the Word To Go module. The program offers a fairly decent suite of word processing features, although some advanced Word capabilities (such as inserting new graphics) are absent. What makes the current version of Documents To Go extremely useful is its ability to maintain formatting that it doesn't directly support. Any graphics, advanced formatting, and so on in a file transferred from the desktop system is maintained in the final document, even if those features can't be added or edited on the CLIÉ.

The functions of the Word to Go button controls, shown in Figure 12-4, should be obvious to anyone who's used Word on the desktop.

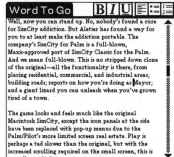

Figure 12-4:
Word To Go
in action.

Across the top are buttons for bold, italic, and underlined text, followed by paragraph alignment, bullet item, and numbered item buttons. Across the bottom, to the right of the Done button, you find font selection, paragraph format, search/replace, and bookmark buttons. The bookmark function is handy when you use Word To Go to read eBooks (Word To Go supports the Palm Doc format) or for quickly jumping back and forth between sections when working on a long document.

You find additional functions on the pull-down menus, which appear when you tap the Menu soft button. The File menu offers a word count function as well as a spell checker. The Insert button lets you add tables, hyperlinks, and more, and the Format menu gives you control over indentation.

Although you can create a word processing document with Graffiti 2 or your CLIÉ's keyboard, consider plugging in a larger folding keyboard when creating lengthy documents. See Chapter 17 for more details on add-on keyboards.

After you finish creating or editing a document, tap the Done button. You're given the opportunity to save the document in its original file, save as a new file, or discard your changes. If you're saving a file for the first time or saving it as a new file, you're given a chance to name the file, choose its format (Word To Go, generic Palm Doc, or Microsoft Word), and whether to save it on a Memory Stick or in main memory.

You can save a file in Palm Doc format if you want to share it with other hand-held owners who don't have Documents To Go or if you want to create your own eBooks. Be aware, though, that Palm Doc files contain no formatting, so you lose all bold, italics, images, tables, and so on.

Sheet To Go

Sheet To Go looks familiar to any Windows spreadsheet user. You can have multiple columns of text and numeric data, process ranges of data with sophisticated formulas, and so on. The biggest limitation is that Sheet To Go doesn't support macros or scripting. Also, if a spreadsheet uses a formula that's not supported by Documents To Go, it's loaded in a locked, read-only mode. That way you can still reference it, but you won't find yourself in the unenviable position of making changes to a spreadsheet only to discover that your results were incorrect due to an unsupported formula.

As shown in Figure 12-5, Sheet To Go can fit a lot of data on a single screen — thanks to the teeny fonts used.

Sheet To Go offers three Zoom levels, which control font size. To adjust the zoom, tap the Menu soft button and choose File⇨Zoom from the menu that appears. The new display shows three options. The Small option fits a ton of data on the screen at once but uses tiny fonts that require excellent vision to read. The Medium option is probably the best setting for most users. The Large option provides big, easy-to-read fonts but fits a mere three rows and nine columns on-screen at once. Select the check box next to the size of your choice and tap the OK button to return to your spreadsheet.

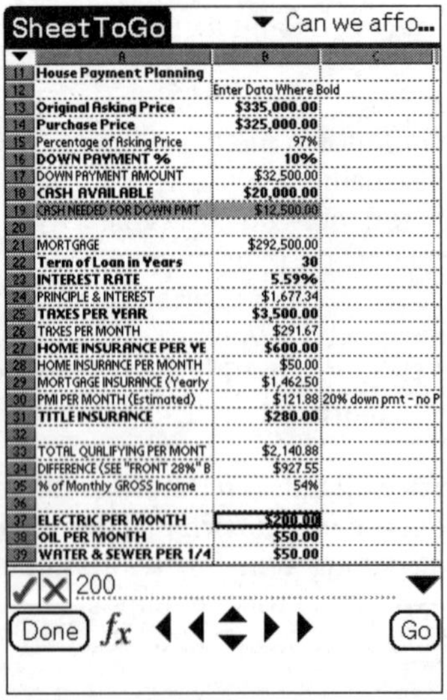

Figure 12-5:
If you have
good eyes,
use the
Sheet To Go
support for
small text to
get lots of
data on the
screen.

Below the sheet is a field where you can enter or edit the value contained in a spreadsheet cell. Tapping the *fx* button brings up a list of basic numeric operators. Tap the *fx* button in that list to bring up a list of supported mathematical and data functions to select.

When you finish entering a value or formula, tap the green check mark to confirm it. The spreadsheet automatically recalculates.

Use the arrows at the bottom center of the Sheet To Go screen to navigate around the spreadsheet. Also note that you can tap any row or column heading to automatically adjust its size, free a column, sort data, and so on.

Although you wouldn't want to manage Boeing's corporate finances on the Sheet To Go program — it starts to slow down with large, complex spreadsheets — it does offer a surprising amount of spreadsheet functionality for a PDA application.

Slideshow To Go

Slideshow To Go is the weakest of the major applications because you can't create or edit native PowerPoint format files with it, and files that you do create are very basic.

Although the program does support graphics, multiple colors, and other fancy formatting features, you can bring these into the program only by converting a PowerPoint presentation by using the Documents To Go desktop program. Files created from scratch are far more basic.

You can cheat and create files with some basic generic graphics and formatting by creating a *template file* (a file that contains the background graphics and formatting of a document without the actual data or content) with graphics on your desktop system and then syncing the template file to the CLIÉ. You can then modify the template file on your CLIÉ and save it under a new name.

The Slideshow To Go interface is extremely simple. You see three icons across the top of the main screen, as shown in Figure 12-6. You can use these icons to switch between Edit, Preview, and Presentation Notes modes.

✔ **Edit mode:** This mode shows your presentation as an outline. To add items to the current slide, tap the Menu soft button and choose Insert⇨ New Bullet Item from the menu that appears. To create a new slide, choose Insert⇨New Slide to start with a blank slide, or Insert⇨Duplicate Slide to create a copy of the current slide, which you can then edit.

Tap the middle icon at the top of the main Slideshow To Go screen to switch to Preview mode, as shown in Figure 12-7.

Edit Mode icon

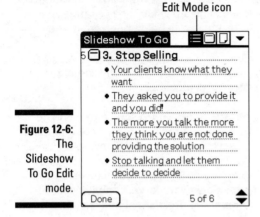

Figure 12-6:
The
Slideshow
To Go Edit
mode.

✔ **Preview mode:** This mode lets you look at your slides in their final form to preview and proofread them. The plus sign (+) button at the bottom of the screen lets you zoom in to a magnified view.

✔ **Notes mode:** Tapping the third icon at the top of the screen lets you create or view presentation notes for the current slide. The drop-down menu arrow in the top-right corner lets you quickly jump to any slide by tapping its title.

Notes Mode icon

Preview Mode icon

Figure 12-7:
The
Slideshow
To Go
Preview
mode.

To view your final presentation, tap the Menu soft button and choose Slide Show⇨View Show from the menu that appears. Tap the Start Timer button — shown at the bottom of the screen in Figure 12-8 — to start an on-screen stopwatch, which is handy if you're rehearsing a timed presentation.

You can move between slides by tapping the slide, by using the Up and Down hard buttons, or by tapping the pop-up slide menu in the lower-right corner of the screen.

You can actually use your CLIÉ to give a presentation on a projection screen or large monitor. You need MARGI's Presenter-to-Go Memory Stick, which adds a VGA output to the CLIÉ. Documents To Go can convert PowerPoint presentations directly to Presenter-to-Go format during HotSync.

Figure12-8:
The actual
slideshow
offers a
timer
function,
which is
useful for
timing
practice
run-
throughs.

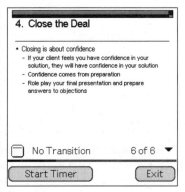

Getting a Quick Look with Picsel Viewer

Most CLIÉs now include a built-in copy of Picsel Viewer. This innovative program displays Word, Excel, PowerPoint, text, JPEG, and HTML files at blazing speed. And unlike Documents To Go, Picsel Viewer shows *Portable Document Format* (PDF, a common format for manuals and other electronic documents) with all graphics and formatting intact. As you scroll around a page with your stylus, whipping the virtual paper left and right, you'll marvel at how fast your CLIÉ can update the screen.

When you first load Picsel Viewer, you see the introductory document, as shown in Figure 12-9.

Place your stylus on the page and drag it around. Notice that the page not only moves with blazing speed, but it even has inertia — it keeps moving after you release, gradually slowing to a stop. This is mostly a gimmick, but it does help when scrolling around very large pages.

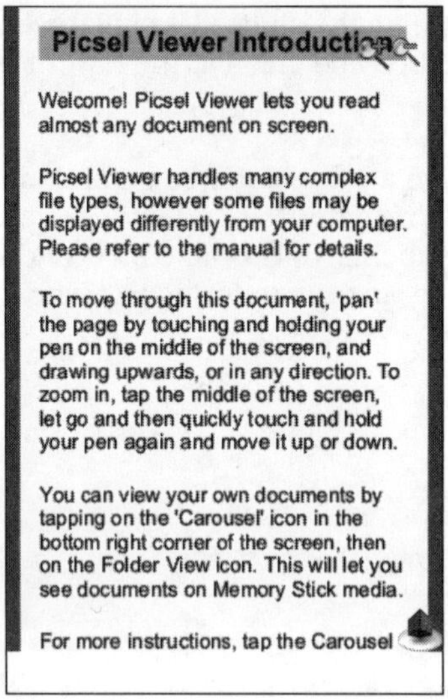

Picsel Viewer Introduction

Welcome! Picsel Viewer lets you read almost any document on screen.

Picsel Viewer handles many complex file types, however some files may be displayed differently from your computer. Please refer to the manual for details.

To move through this document, 'pan' the page by touching and holding your pen on the middle of the screen, and drawing upwards, or in any direction. To zoom in, tap the middle of the screen, let go and then quickly touch and hold your pen again and move it up or down.

You can view your own documents by tapping on the 'Carousel' icon in the bottom right corner of the screen, then on the Folder View icon. This will let you see documents on Memory Stick media.

For more instructions, tap the Carousel

Figure 12-9:
Picsel
Viewer has
a clean,
simple
interface.

The screen has just three controls: two icons in the upper-right corner that are for zooming in and out on the page, and the Carousel icon in the lower-right corner. Tap the Carousel icon in the lower-right corner to bring up the Picsel Viewer interface, an innovative if highly nonstandard group of icons. You can see what each icon does in Figure 12-10.

You can also pop up a short description of each icon by holding the stylus down on it for a couple seconds. For more detailed help, tap the question mark in the upper-right corner.

To open a new file in Picsel Viewer, tap the Folder View icon. The interface will be replaced by a Memory Stick icon. (Note: Picsel Viewer can display only files that are stored on a Memory Stick.) Tap the Memory Stick icon to get a list of folders on your card. Your screen should look something like Figure 12-11.

To view the contents of any folder, just tap it. A couple likely candidates for files to view are the DCIM folder, where your digital images are stored, and the Documents folder, where Documents To Go stores its native-format Word and Excel files. When you find a file to view, tap its icon to display it.

A couple of methods for quickly navigating to often-used files are available. You can set a bookmark for a file by tapping the Carousel icon to bring up the Picsel Viewer interface and tapping the Add Bookmark icon while viewing the file. Then you can quickly access it from a list of bookmarks by tapping the Bookmark View icon. Also, tapping the History View icon brings up a list of recently accessed files.

Document View

Rotate Screen   Bookmark View

Add Bookmark   Folder View

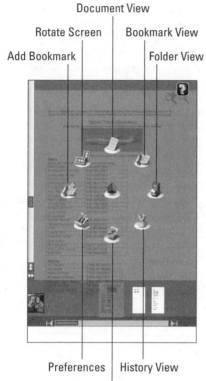

Figure 12-10:
Picsel
Viewer
has an
interesting
and
innovative
interface.

Preferences | History View

Refresh Current Document

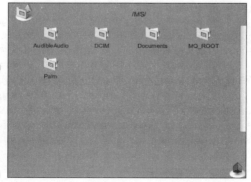

Figure 12-11:
The Picsel
Viewer
folder
navigation
screen.

Crunching Numbers with powerOne Personal

Like all Palm OS handhelds, your CLIÉ has a built-in calculator that's handy for basic number-crunching. However, Sony includes a far more powerful calculator on your CLIÉ's Installation CD: powerOne Personal. This super calculator is located on your CD under Additional Software/Personal Productivity. Tap the Install button and follow the instructions on the screen to install the calculator.

 Note that a demo version of the even heavier-duty powerOne Finance calculator, which includes loan and investment functions, is located under Additional Software/Business Utilities on the Installation CD. This is a trial version, however, and you can use it only for a limited time.

As shown in Figure 12-12, the powerOne Personal basic interface looks just like that of a high-end traditional calculator. But the program doesn't stop at division and multiplication. It includes everyday business functions, such as calculating markup and profit margins, as well as the ability to calculate ranges between dates. You can access these by tapping the Business and Calendar buttons at the top of the screen.

Figure 12-12: powerOne Personal is more powerful than meets the eye.

The calculator offers Normal, Scientific, and Engineering display modes, which you can alter by tapping the Menu soft button and choosing Preferences from the menu that appears. Although the interface seems basic, it has more functions than meet the eye. Pressing the Func key gives you access to about 20 functions spread across math, trig, and num lists. These range from logarithmic and trig functions to powers, roots, and percentages. A few functions are illustrated in Figure 12-13.

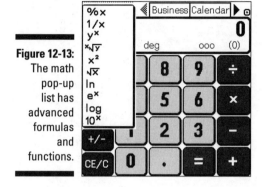

Figure 12-13:
The math
pop-up
list has
advanced
formulas
and
functions.

Making powerOne Personal the default calculator

After you try powerOne Personal, you won't want to go back to the stock Palm OS calculator. So why not set it as the default calculator that appears when you tap the Calculator soft button next to the Graffiti area?

To set powerOne Personal as the default, tap the Prefs icon in Program Launcher, and then tap the drop-down menu arrow in the upper-right corner of the screen and select Buttons.

Just tap the drop-down menu arrow to the right of the calculator icon and select powerOne Personal from the list, as shown in the following figure. Now when you tap the calculator button, you have instant access to the most powerful calculator on your CLIÉ.

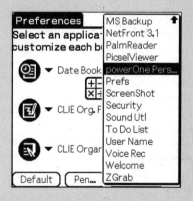

Chapter 13

Other Office Applications

*1*t's the kind of twist you might expect from Hitchcock: At the end of the film, the CLIÉ turns out to be a much better handheld for the Microsoft Office user than PDAs based on Microsoft's own Pocket PC operating system. (And the butler was done in by the vicar's daughter.) Why? Because he rejected her. Oh, you mean the CLIE. It's because all Pocket PCs ship with very basic versions of Word and Excel, so programmers have little incentive to try to reinvent the wheel.

The CLIÉ and other Palm OS PDAs, on the other hand, don't include Word and Excel support as part of the operating system. So that sets talented program-mers loose to try to create better handheld office applications — competition is a wonderful thing. Although these office applications aren't free, they're much more full-featured than the freebies that are included with Pocket PCs, so you're not likely to mind spending a few bucks.

Best of all, you can take each of these programs for a spin before you buy them. Just download the demo version from the Web site and try it on your CLIÉ. If you like it, simply return to the site, pay for the program, and you're given an unlock code that allows the program to continue functioning after the evaluation period ends.

In this chapter, I take a look at some of the best productivity applications available for the CLIÉ. If you're skipping around the book, reading it back-ward, or reading this one first because it's "Lucky Chapter 13," be sure to check out Documents To Go in Chapter 12. Documents To Go is included with many CLIÉs and is as worthy of consideration as any of these programs, even if you didn't get it for free.

Quickoffice Premier

www.quickoffice.com

Quickoffice Premier is a full-featured Office suite that includes word processing (Quickword), spreadsheet (Quicksheet), charting (Quickchart), and presentation support (Quickpoint). Though its feature set is similar to the Documents To Go set, it has some differences that might make it a better alternative for some users.

Like Documents To Go, Quickoffice supports reading Word and Excel files stored on Memory Sticks. However, it can also read PowerPoint files in their original format, which is something that Document To Go can't do. This could be really handy if you're on the road and someone needs to send you an updated presentation file by e-mail.

As you can see in Figure 13-1, the Quicksheet spreadsheet has an interface similar to Excel's with the addition of some handy features, such as a pop-up list of math operators. Quicksheet is acknowledged as the most powerful spreadsheet currently available for the CLIÉ. It offers over 80 functions, support for spreadsheets containing up to 996 rows and 254 columns, and the ability to link to shared Excel files on a network.

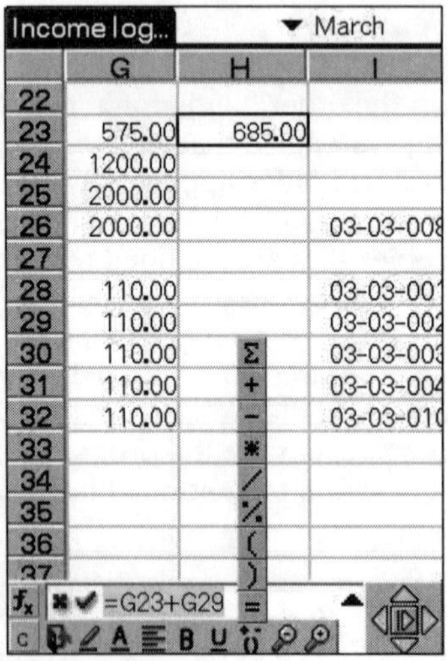

Figure 13-1: Quicksheet offers over 80 mathematical functions and can read Excel files directly.

Quickoffice includes a bundled copy of the PrintBoy printer utility. Most CLIÉ programs can't print — you have to transfer the files back to your desktop system to print them out. But what if you're on the road with just your CLIÉ? PrintBoy lets you print directly from your CLIÉ by using infrared, Bluetooth, Wi-Fi, or a modem connection.

Quickoffice is an excellent but not unusual application. However, the folks behind Quickoffice sell a very interesting version that offers a truly unique way for mobile workers to get their jobs done. Quickoffice Conference is a multi-user office suite that lets multiple handheld users collaborate on the same documents wirelessly.

This means that a group of wireless-equipped CLIÉ and Palm users in different offices or even different countries can collaborate on spreadsheets or other documents. "So, Bob, what happens if we allocate the widget budget to research on framistats instead?" Change numbers, and everyone else sees the same change reflected in their spreadsheets.

A free Quickoffice Conference viewer application is also available. It can be used to let people watch the documents being altered, but the watchers can't make changes.

A truly innovative and new way to work, Quickoffice Conference supports infrared, Bluetooth, and Wi-Fi connections.

You can find information on Quickoffice Conference at the following URL:

```
www.mobl.com/software/solutions/es_conference.html
```

Mobile Office 2004 Professional

```
www.mobi-systems.com
```

Because Mobile Office 2004 Professional doesn't include a spreadsheet, it's worth looking into only if you're primarily interested in other office functions besides number-crunching. Here's a look at what you do get:

- **Mobile Word 2004:** This is the most *what you see is what you get* word processor on the Palm. It has a full suite of text-formatting tools, and it displays fonts, styles, images, tables, and other advanced formatting features with aplomb. The only downside to the program is that you have to convert Word files back and forth during HotSync — it doesn't have native file support on the handheld. It includes the QuickSpell spell-checker program, which runs in the background and can work with other applications, such as your e-mail program. Mobile Word also bundles QuickWrite, a utility designed to allow you to enter words much faster with the stylus by popping up the words that it thinks you've started to enter.

- **Mobile Agenda 2004:** This program integrates the functions of the CLIÉ's personal information manager programs in one program, giving you a single place to look to see your To Dos, appointments, contacts, and memos.

- **Mobile Access 2004:** Although the name implies that this database program interfaces with the Microsoft Access desktop database, it's actually designed to synchronize with Microsoft Excel. This is a good thing for anyone who finds it easier to keep databases in Excel than in the more complex Microsoft Access. This powerful handheld database includes a forms designer (shown in Figure 13-2), sophisticated queries, and the ability to filter results.

- **Mobile Paint 2004:** A full-featured graphics editor and paint program, Mobile Paint includes over 25 painting tools, the ability to place text on images, unlimited Undo functions, and more. It's far more sophisticated than the Photo Editor application that's included with some CLIÉ models. You can use it to touch up digital images or just create fun doodles like the one in Figure 13-3.

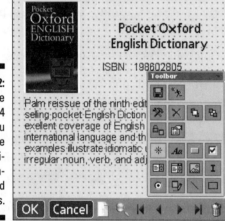

Figure 13-2:
Mobile
Access 2004
lets you
create
sophisti-
cated, form-
based
databases.

Figure 13-3:
A snowy
scene
created in
Mobile Paint
2004.

✔ **Mobile Money 2004:** A budgeting and money-management program, Mobile Money lets you track your finances directly on your handheld. Money managers on your desktop system are great, but having the ability to enter transactions when you're out of the house means that you're less likely to forget to do it. The program can synchronize date with Quicken, Microsoft Money, and Excel.

If you're not a spreadsheet user, Mobile Office 2004 Professional is a heck of a deal for its relatively low price.

WordSmith

www.bluenomad.com

If the only handheld office application that you really use is a word processor, WordSmith is the program for you. Portions of this book were created with this miniature word processor, in fact.

Like Mobile Word 2004, WordSmith relies on the HotSync process to translate Word files to handheld format — it can't read Microsoft Word files directly. Although it doesn't create or import graphics or tables, it does support the typical formatting that you use in everyday writing — bold, italics, centered text, bullet lists, and so on. Note, however, that some features get lost in translation. For instance, if you have graphics in your document, they're stripped out during the transfer process.

So given that other programs don't have these limitations, why am I even covering WordSmith? Well, if you're just looking for a tool to *write,* rather than create fancy documents, WordSmith is hard to beat. It's extremely fast and very easy to use. It supports a text display option called FineType that removes the jaggy edges from the fonts that it displays, which can make long writing sessions on the small screen much easier on your eyes. (See Figure 13-4 for an example of FineType at work.) You can convert any TrueType font on your Windows PC to a FineType font for use on your CLIÉ.

WordSmith also has a few nice bonus features. It replaces the built-in Memo Pad application so that you can use its more sophisticated editing tools when creating standard Palm OS memos. With its support for the Palm Doc format and its smooth font rendering, it makes a great reader for non-copy-protected eBooks.

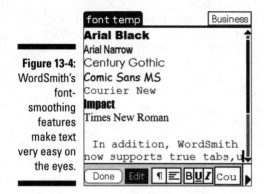

Figure 13-4: WordSmith's font-smoothing features make text very easy on the eyes.

Outlook Alternatives: Beyond Contacts and KeySuite

www.dataviz.com
www.chapura.com

If you're a serious user of Microsoft Outlook, you might find the CLIÉ's built-in information management applications limited because they support only a subset of the fields that are available in Microsoft Outlook. Luckily, two superb alternatives are available for Outlook users, and they bring all your important data to the CLIÉ.

Both DataViz's Beyond Contacts and Chapura's KeySuite replicate all the major functionality of Outlook right on your CLIÉ. They replace the built-in personal information manager programs with new versions that support all 19 phone number fields and all 3 address listings supported by Outlook, as well as Outlook-style categories and the various other fields in Outlook that aren't present in the CLIÉ's Address Book, Date Book, and so on.

The biggest difference between Beyond Contacts and KeySuite is the interface. As shown in Figure 13-5, Beyond Contacts offers an Outlook-style Today screen that gives you a quick look at pending appointments, To Dos, and unread e-mails.

KeySuite, on the other hand, offers four independent applications, each of which replaces one of the built-in information manager programs. Figure 13-6 shows the Contacts module. Although these programs don't share a common front end, as do the modules in Beyond Contacts, you can still link data between the various functions, such as associating contacts with a scheduled meeting.

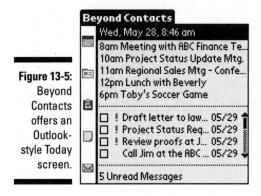

Figure 13-5:
Beyond
Contacts
offers an
Outlook-
style Today
screen.

Note that both programs take over the HotSync process between your desktop and the handheld, so the information in the built-in Address Book, Date Book, To Do List, and Memo Pad is no longer updated; you need to use Beyond Contacts and KeySuite instead.

Figure 13-6:
KeySuite's
Contacts
module
supports all
the Outlook
address
fields.

Which one should you choose? Beyond Contacts feels more like Outlook on your desktop, and KeySuite has more of the feel of a traditional Palm OS program. Trial versions of both are available online. You can find Beyond Contacts at `www.dataviz.com` and KeySuite at `www.chapura.com`.

Part V

Reaching Outside the CLIÉ Box

In this part . . .

This part shows you how to extend your CLIÉ's capabilities and reach far beyond what came in the box. You find out about Memory Sticks and how they not only give your CLIÉ more storage, but added functionality, as well. You discover the various wireless options for your CLIÉ and how to get connected to the Web, e-mail, and your favorite instant messaging service. And finally, I show you the accessories that can turn your CLIÉ into a completely equipped travel computer.

Chapter 14

All about Memory

. . . .

In This Chapter

▶ Discovering memory basics

▶ Understanding file management

▶ Making your Memory Stick think it's a disk drive

. . . .

"**Y**ou can't have everything," says comedian Steven Wright. "Where would you put it?" Why, put it on Memory Sticks, of course! Every CLIÉ includes a Memory Stick slot, which lets you add up to a whopping gigabyte of memory. Although the built-in memory offers enough space for contacts, appointments, and quite a few add-on applications, you still have plenty of reasons to consider buying a Memory Stick for your CLIÉ:

✔ **Music:** MP3 music files can be stored only on Memory Sticks.

✔ **Video:** You can carry around full-screen videos — home movies of the kids or your favorite TV shows. The files are huge, and they need the space afforded by Memory Sticks.

✔ **Room to grow:** Although the CLIÉ's built-in memory can hold a lot of data, if you start adding third-party programs, shooting pictures with the built-in camera, and making voice recordings, you can fill the memory before you know it. Even an inexpensive 128MB Memory Stick should eliminate any chances of running out of room for a *long* time.

✔ **Interchangeability:** If you have a camera, camcorder, or MP3 player that uses Memory Sticks, you can pop the stick out of that device and into your CLIÉ to access its files, view pictures, play MPEG-4 videos, or play MP3 music.

✔ **Security:** If your battery dies or your CLIÉ has a severe crash, you can lose the contents of your main memory. As with the Backup and Internal Media memory found in the UX series, Memory Stick data survives dead batteries and the worst crashes.

Whether or not you equip your CLIÉ with a Memory Stick, you still want to take advantage of some basic memory-management tricks, such as how to delete a freeware game that you downloaded and haven't played since last December.

Memory 101

You might encounter the following kinds of memory when using the CLIÉ, depending on the model that you own:

- ✔ **Handheld memory:** This is built-in memory in your CLIÉ. It's the area where programs actually run and where your personal information manager records are stored, and it's the fastest memory for launching applications and accessing data. However, it relies on your CLIÉ's battery to maintain its data, and its contents can be lost in the rare event of a severe crash.

- ✔ **Memory Sticks:** Sony's design for a memory card, these cards are slightly smaller than a pack of chewing gum and come in several varieties. Memory Sticks are available not only from Sony, but from other companies as well, such as the SanDisk card shown in Figure 14-1.

- ✔ **Internal Media memory:** So far, this has appeared only on the CLIÉ PEG-UX40 and PEG-UX50 models, which have 30.2MB of Internal Media storage. This memory is built in, but it acts like a Memory Stick. Programs treat it like it's a memory card, and it can survive power failures and hard resets.

Figure 14-1:
Memory Sticks are available from a variety of manufacturers, including SanDisk.

✔ **Backup memory:** This is so far found only on the PEG-UX40 and PEG-UX50 models. It provides 16MB of memory that's used to back up the contents of the units' Handheld memory. For more on the UX Backup memory, see Chapter 19.

✔ **CompactFlash memory:** The PEG-NX73V and PEG-NX80V both feature a CompactFlash expansion slot that's designed primarily for using the CLIÉ Wi-Fi card. However, you can also use the slot with a CompactFlash memory card, such as the huge 4GB card shown in Figure 14-2. Note that many of the built-in CLIÉ applications don't support this memory, so you're better off using a Memory Stick. The PEG-NX60V and PEG-NX70V also boast CompactFlash slots, but you must purchase third-party software to use memory cards in the slot. On these models, the slot was officially supported only by Sony for Wi-Fi use.

I focus on Handheld memory and Memory Sticks in this chapter because every CLIÉ sports those. If your CLIÉ has Internal Media or CompactFlash Memory, it essentially works the same way as Memory Sticks, though not all programs will recognize it.

When buying memory, keep in mind that all Memory Sticks are not created equal. Various Memory Sticks are available. The good news is that all work with your CLIÉ. Still, I recommend being familiar with all the types out there so that you don't spend more money than necessary.

Figure 14-2: CompactFlash cards are generally less expensive than Memory Sticks of the same capacity.

The following list is a rundown of Memory Stick models, present and future. Some of these designs are being phased out in favor of newer models, but you can find the most current models at major electronics and office supply stores.

✔ **Memory Stick:** The standard Memory Stick is purplish in color. These are available in sizes up to 128MB and are good for basic storage. It's the least expensive Memory Stick model and is fine for CLIÉ use, but it's not the fastest type.

✔ **MagicGate Memory Stick:** These white Memory Sticks are similar to basic Memory Sticks but with the addition of the ability to copy-protect data that's stored on the stick — which protects music publishers but just makes for more potential hassles for you. They're generally more expensive than the purple sticks, and they offer no real advantages. The only reason to buy a white MagicGate Memory Stick is if, for some reason, you want to listen to songs in Sony's ATRAC3 music format.

✔ **Memory Stick Pro:** The original Memory Sticks were limited to 128MB. Memory Stick Pro cards eliminate this restriction and are available at sizes up to 2GB. They're also much faster than the original Memory Sticks, reducing the time to copy or load files. They include MagicGate support for copy protection without adding a price premium. Note the MagicGate logo in Figure 14-3. All Palm OS 5-based CLIÉs can use Memory Stick Pro cards, but some older models require a software upgrade from Sony's support site.

✔ **Memory Stick Select:** Designed for older CLIÉs, cameras, and other Sony products that can't be updated to support Memory Stick Pro cards, the Memory Stick Select cards offer 256MB of storage by essentially cramming two 128MB cards into one Memory Stick. You have to flip a physical switch to swap between the two 128MB memory banks, which is awfully inconvenient. If your CLIÉ supports Memory Stick Pro cards, they're a much better option.

✔ **Memory Stick Duo:** These smaller cards — about the size of the Secure Digital cards used by PalmOne-brand PDAs and many cameras — are designed for very compact devices. They include an adapter, as shown in Figure 14-4, which lets you use them in standard Memory Stick slots. Buy one of these only if you own another device that requires them.

✔ **Updated Memory Stick:** You can tell these from the original Memory Sticks because they're dark blue and now feature the MagicGate logo, signifying that Sony's digital rights management copy protection is supported on the cards. These are replacing the old purple sticks on the market. Along with the inclusion of MagicGate support, the new sticks are somewhat faster.

Figure 14-3:
Memory
Stick Pro
cards are
the best
choice for
today's CLIÉ
models.

Phew! That's a lot of Memory Sticks! However, unless you're worried about sharing the stick between two devices, or you're using an older Palm OS 4 CLIÉ, you really don't even have to make a choice. If you're looking for a card supporting 32 to 128MB, buy one of the new dark blue updated Memory Sticks. Otherwise, buy a Memory Stick Pro card.

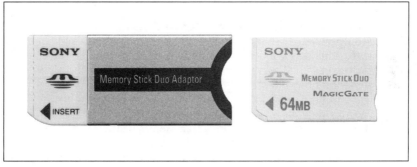

Figure 14-4:
Memory
Stick Duo
cards are
designed for
devices that
need tiny
expansion
cards.

What about capacity? Here are a few general numbers that you can use when calculating how large a card you need:

- ✔ **Music:** A minute of MP3 music recorded at 128 Kbps (the most common quality) takes about 1MB. You can fit about two hours of music on a 128MB Memory Stick if nothing else is on there.

- ✔ **Video:** A minute of video at the CLIÉ's standard motion video quality fills about 2MB, and high-quality video fills about 3.75MB per minute. If you want to watch an entire movie stored on Memory Stick, you want to spring for at least a 256MB card. Get a 512MB card if you plan to use high quality.

✔ **Photos:** Images shot with the VGA-resolution camera included on current CLIÉ models are typically less than 150K in size, so even the smallest 32MB Memory Stick holds hundreds of shots. If you also plan to use the card in a dedicated digital camera, keep in mind that the size of the images varies depending on the resolution of the camera. A 4-megapixel camera generates shots that typically run about 1.5 to 2MB in size, but an uncompressed 8-megapixel image on Sony's high-end DSC-F828 camera can fill a whopping 16MB.

✔ **Programs:** Palm OS programs are pleasantly compact. If you're just looking for extra program storage and room to back up your CLIÉ and you don't plan to, say, download every game known to man, a 64MB card should suffice.

Now that the basics are out of the way, I look at how to manage memory.

File Management

Okay, the previous section establishes what kind of memory your CLIÉ has and demystifies the various flavors of Memory Sticks. Now I show you how to put that memory to good use!

When you install a Palm OS program or its related data file, you're given a choice whether to put it in Handheld memory or on a Memory Stick. Put the programs that you use most often in Handheld memory because they load faster and are always available even if you remove the Memory Stick. For more on how to install files, see Chapter 3.

So you know how to get files into your CLIÉ. But what if you want to move them from Handheld memory to a Memory Stick? Or even delete them completely? No problem. You can perform basic file management from the Program Launcher, and Sony includes the CLIÉ Files utility for more sophisticated file-management tasks.

Deleting, copying, and moving files

At times, you might need to move files around or trash a stale old program that's outlived its usefulness. Doing so makes room for fresh, new programs.

The easiest and safest way to do this is by using the menu commands in the Program Launcher. Although the menus are different in CLIÉ Launcher compared to the standard Program Launcher, as illustrated in Figure 14-5, the actual file manipulation commands are identical.

First, look at the Delete command. Tap the Menu soft button and then choose App⇨Delete. You see the window in Figure 14-6.

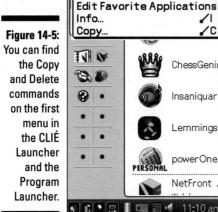

Figure 14-5:
You can find
the Copy
and Delete
commands
on the first
menu in
the CLIÉ
Launcher
and the
Program
Launcher.

At the top of the screen are options that display the currently selected memory area and how much space is currently being used. By default, the window allows you to delete files from Handheld memory. If you want to delete from a Memory Stick or Internal Media, just tap the drop-down menu arrow next to the Delete From option and select the memory area that you want to work with. (Note that Memory Sticks are identified by their card names.)

Deleting a file couldn't be simpler. Just scroll through the list until you find the program or data file that you want to delete, tap it to highlight it, and finally tap the Delete button. The program asks you to confirm that you really want to delete the file. Tap Yes.

When deleting programs, note that they might have associated data files as well. For instance, in Figure 14-6, you see WordToGo and WordToGoFonts listed. The second file is related to the first one, so you'd want to delete both if you were deleting the WordToGo program.

Before deleting any file, make a backup with a backup program like MSBackup or by HotSyncing your CLIÉ. That way, if you make a mistake, you have another copy that you can restore. If you accidentally delete a file, you can find it your Palm Desktop user directory, typically `C:\Program Files\Palm\`*yourusername*`\Backup`. Locate the file that you accidentally deleted and double-click it to add it to the Install queue. Note that you must do this before you HotSync again; the file will be removed from your Backup directory during the next sync.

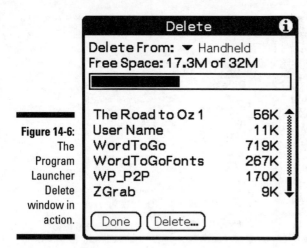

Figure 14-6:
The
Program
Launcher
Delete
window in
action.

You can also use the Program Launcher to move files between Handheld memory and a Memory Stick. This is useful if you need to free up more Handheld memory by moving files to a card or if you want to move files to Handheld memory before removing the card.

For some reason, the CLIÉ doesn't include an actual Move command. Rather, you have to copy the file and then delete it manually. It's rather annoying, since you're far more likely to want to move a file from one place to another than to need it in two places. Still, moving a file is a fairly easy process: Copy it to its new location, and then use the Delete command to zap the original.

To copy a file, tap the Menu soft button and choose App⇨Copy from the menu that appears. At the top of the Copy window, illustrated in Figure 14-7, is a pair of drop-down menu arrows for specifying the source and destination for the copy. Note that the Copy To option is the destination directory, where you want the file to end up. The From option is the source directory. This order seems reversed because most programs put the source directory at the top, but the labels make the procedure obvious.

On typical CLIÉs with only Handheld and Memory Stick storage, you just need to select the source to change the destination to the only possible location. If you have a UX series unit with Internal Media memory or an NX unit with a CompactFlash memory card, you need to make sure that you select the proper destination location because more than one possibility exists.

After you set your source and destination directories, just tap the file that you want to copy and tap the Copy button at the bottom of the screen. The CLIÉ has the smarts to put the files in the right place on the Memory Stick. Programs typically go in the /Palm/Launcher directory, and data files usually end up in the /Programs/programname directory, where programname is the program that actually uses that data file.

Figure 14-7:
The
Program
Launcher
Copy
window.

Note that on the Copy window some files have a padlock icon next to them. These files are system files or copy-protected commercial programs, and they can't be copied or moved to another directory.

After the copy is complete, you're returned to the Copy window so that you can copy additional files. When you finish copying files, tap Done. At this point, you might want to return to the Delete screen and delete the originals.

This is easy enough, but what if you want to copy or delete multiple files at once? That's where CLIÉ Files comes in.

Advanced file management: CLIÉ Files

CLIÉ Files is a full-fledged file manager (similar to Windows Explorer on your desktop system) that gives you full control over copying, moving, and deleting files.

Be aware that with this control come more opportunities to mess up. When you delete a program by using Program Launcher, for instance, the system is smart enough to delete related data files, as well. CLIÉ Files gives you individual control over what you delete and where you move files. This means that you could unintentionally delete a program and leave stray data files lying around taking up memory. You could also accidentally move a program file to a spot on the Memory Stick where it can't be launched. So until you're absolutely certain which files you want to manipulate, stick with the Program Launcher file-management commands.

Figure 14-8 gives you an overview of the various CLIÉ Files functions. At the very top of the screen is a status line that shows you how much memory is free. To the right of that is a drop-down menu arrow that lets you choose which memory area to work with.

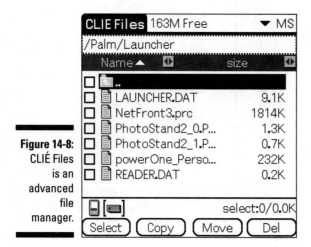

Figure 14-8:
CLIÉ Files
is an
advanced
file
manager.

The file information line below the status line shows the current directory (if you're working with a Memory Stick) or the types of files being shown (if you're working with Handheld memory). Below this line is the File List area.

At the very bottom of the screen are icons that let you select which area of memory to work with (the icons duplicate the functionality of the drop-down menu arrow at top-right corner) and the File Command buttons.

To copy, move, or delete a group of files, simply tap the check boxes next to the files to select them, and then tap the appropriate command. If you're copying from Handheld memory to a Memory Stick, the Directory List screen appears.

If you're copying a program, it should typically go in the Palm/Launcher directory, shown in Figure 14-9. Data files normally go in subdirectories of the Programs directory, but under normal circumstances, those should be copied or moved by using the program that they were created in.

When working with files in Handheld memory, you can tap the file information line of the main CLIÉ Files screen to filter which files are displayed. It defaults to All Databases, which shows a rather cluttered list of all files in the handheld. If you tap the line and select Application, the display changes to show only programs. If you're trying to clean up all files related to a particular program, the

Creator Group option is just the ticket. In the All Databases view, select the program that you plan to delete or one of its data files. Then select Creator Group from the filter list. Now only files related to that program are shown in the File List area. (See Figure 14-10.) You can now select them for deletion or archiving to a Memory Stick.

Figure 14-9:
Selecting a
destination
directory.

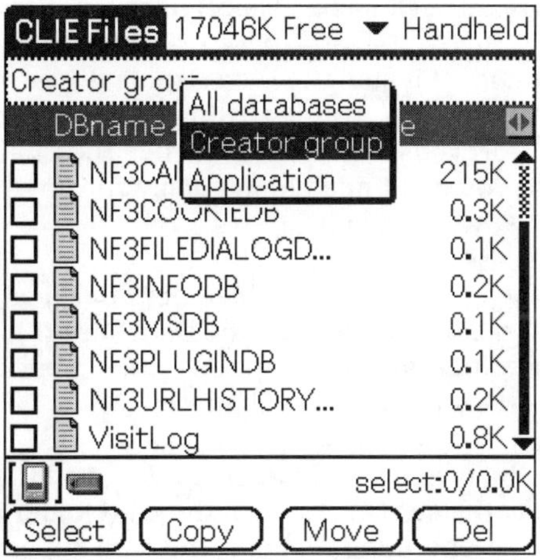

Figure 14-10:
The Creator
Group
option lets
you see all
files related
to a
particular
program.

Using Your Memory Stick as a Disk Drive

When it comes to transferring Palm OS programs and their data to your CLIÉ, HotSync rules the roost. It's easy to use, and you can just tap the button and walk away.

When it comes to large files, though, HotSync doesn't hold up as well. Transferring an hour's worth of MP3 songs or a large animation file can take *forever*. Well, okay, by *forever*, I mean more than a few minutes. But in today's instant-gratification world, who can stand a process that might take (gasp) five or ten minutes?

These large files are always stored on Memory Sticks, so the solution is easy: just copy the file directly to the Memory Stick by mounting it on your desktop system as a disk drive, leaving HotSync out of the process completely. In fact, even some of Sony's own programs do this. Image Converter, for instance, requires you to specify a drive letter for your Memory Stick before you can install files.

You can go about this in two ways. The first is to insert your Memory Stick directly into a reader connected to your computer. Some desktop systems (particularly Sony VIAO computers) and printers have Memory Stick slots built in. If yours doesn't, you can purchase an inexpensive USB Memory Stick drive such as the SanDisk ImageMate. With either of these solutions, the Memory Stick works just like a giant floppy disk drive — plug it in, and it appears in My Computer as a disk that you can work with just like a floppy or hard disk.

You don't have to use an add-on card reader, though. Your CLIÉ can do double duty as a card reader by using the Data Import program, which lets you mount the CLIÉ's Memory Stick slot as a disk drive on your computer.

Before using Data Import, you must install the Data Export driver on your desktop system. It's located in the CLIÉ Utilities listing on the CD that came with your handheld. Data Export runs automatically when the CLIÉ is connected, so after you install it, you don't need to manually run anything on your desktop system to take advantage of it.

When you're ready to copy files to or from your Memory Stick, just connect the CLIÉ's HotSync cable or cradle, and then tap the Data Import icon in Program Launcher. When the program starts, tap the Connect button at the bottom of the Data Import screen, as shown in Figure 14-11.

If you're running Windows XP, a window pops up and offers you the chance to copy photos, play music on the card, or to open the card folder to view and copy files. On XP and other operating systems, the card appears as an additional drive in My Computer.

Table 14-1 lists some of the common directories where you can find various CLIÉ files.

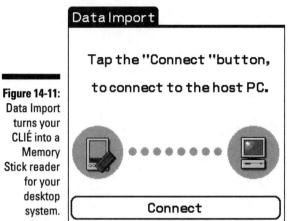

Figure 14-11:
Data Import
turns your
CLIÉ into a
Memory
Stick reader
for your
desktop
system.

Table 14-1	Mapping Your Memory Stick
Directory	*File Types*
DCIM	Digital Camera images are stored here.
Documents	This is where Documents To Go stores files saved in native Word and Excel formats.
MQ_ROOT	Here you can store QuickTime movies.
Palm\Launcher	This is where programs and data files are stored on the Memory Stick.
Palm\Programs	Individual programs store their data files in sub-directories here.
Palm\Programs\MSAUDIO	This is the audio folder, where you copy MP3 files for playback in Audio Player or AeroPlayer.
Palm\Programs\MSSOUND	Voice Recorder files are stored here in WAV format.
Palm\Programs\MSBackup	MS Backup files are stored here.

Chapter 15

The CLIÉ Goes Wireless

Chances are that you don't live in a solitary shack in the hills of South Dakota, cut off from everyone around you. (If you do, where on earth did you find this book? Did you pick it up off a geek wandering in the wilderness?) People thrive from connections to the outside world — and so does your CLIÉ. Just as the Internet turned personal computers from solitary workstations into amazing tools that can be used for e-mail, chatting, and important research such as tracking the color of Christina Aguilera's hair, wireless networking transforms the CLIÉ into an amazing tool for sharing data and on-the-spot communications.

Even if your CLIÉ doesn't include a wireless radio, you don't want to skip this chapter. Every CLIÉ includes an infrared port that's designed to allow wireless beaming of data. At business conferences and even social events, beaming contact information is the chic replacement for swapping business cards.

Beam Me Data, Scotty!

Sorry, but it's a rule that every technology book has to include at least one *Star Trek* reference. But your CLIÉ in many ways has already surpassed the Tricorder technology used by Captain Kirk and company. The CLIÉ is smaller, and even the *Star Trek* writers didn't foresee a technology as useful as beaming data from one device to another. Your CLIÉ includes an infrared transmitter port that can both send and receive data — using invisible light! Talk about *Star Trek*!

The great thing about beaming is that if you have a use for beaming data in a certain application, that application most likely supports it. In Address Book, you can beam a single record or an entire category. Date Book lets you beam individual appointments. CLIÉ Camera and CLIÉ Viewer both support sending photos. The only requirement is that the receiving handheld have a program that can read the data being sent. That's not an issue with the built-in information manager applications but might be with some of the multimedia applications like CLIÉ Camera because some Palm OS PDAs might not have photo viewers.

Many add-on applications also support beaming. You can even beam many kinds of data to PDAs based on Microsoft's Pocket PC operating system. Not only was I able to successfully send a picture that I'd taken with my CLIÉ's camera to an iPAQ, but I was also able to beam a saved game from the superb game Legacy (see Chapter 11) and then use that saved file in the Pocket PC version of the game.

In most programs, you find the Beam command on the first drop-down menu. Generally, you select the record that you want to beam, and then hit the Menu soft button and choose Beam from the first menu that appears. (Some programs offer menu choices for beaming individual items or entire categories.) A window pops up on-screen and lets you know that the CLIÉ is searching for the receiving unit, as shown in Figure 15-1. Aim your CLIÉ's infrared emitter at the receiving PDA.

Figure 15-1:
Preparing
to beam a
To Do item.

Resist the temptation to put the devices as close together as possible. Beaming actually seems to work best when the two devices are about six inches apart.

If you're on the receiving end of a beam, the CLIÉ asks you to confirm whether you want to accept the data and, when appropriate, what category you want to place it in, as illustrated in Figure 15-2.

Figure 15-2: Accepting a To Do item before it's beamed.

You can see the filename or the first few characters of the item. This confirmation step keeps someone from beaming wacky joke To Dos (such as, oh, an author running around an airport beaming a file that says "Buy *Sony CLIÉ For Dummies*" to every PDA owner in sight) or unwanted programs. ("No, honey, I don't know how Strip Poker Deluxe got on my CLIÉ, I swear!")

If you designate a business card in Address Book, you can beam that by holding down the Address Book hard button. For the full scoop on beaming business cards, see Chapter 4.

You can use the infrared port for more than just beaming data. If you're on the road with a laptop, and you've forgotten your HotSync cable, for instance, you can actually HotSync by using an infrared connection. It's slow, but it works just fine.

Turn your CLIÉ into a super remote

Okay, what's the one thing in your house with an infrared port on it that you just can't live without? If you said your CLIÉ, I'll give you brownie points for trying to butter me up, but an even better answer is your TV remote. Anyone born before 1980 now regales younger acquaintances with tales of the bad old days when a person actually had to *get up* to change the channel on the TV — sometimes with a pair of pliers because something called a dial had broken off. Today, the remote is such an indispensable household tool that you probably have a coffee table full of them. So wouldn't it be nice to hear that your CLIÉ can take the place of a $300 universal remote control? Sure, you probably don't want to leave your PDA lying around the coffee table all day long, but it's mighty handy to have it double as a remote control when your toddler has hidden the TiVo remote, and the season finale of *Law and Order: Special Parking Violations Unit* is about to come on. With one of these programs, a CLIÉ can duplicate the functionality of a dedicated programmable remote.

A number of Sony models, including the NX series and the PEG-TG50, actually include built-in remote control software. CLIÉ Remote Commander, shown in the following figure below, is a basic but useful product that can control up to four home-theater components.

More sophisticated third-party remote control programs are available. They offer support for more devices, better programmability, and even interactive program guides. Perhaps the best-looking is NoviiRemote, as you can see in the following figure. It has a colorful, customizable interface that's very intuitive. NoviiRemote also allows you to program your CLIÉ's hard buttons so that you can access your most-used functions quickly, without having to tap the correct spot on the liquid crystal display (LCD). Best of all, NoviiRemote includes over 100 preprogrammed settings, so chances are that you can start using it immediately, without having to train it with your standalone remotes. For more information on NoviiRemote, including a list of CLIÉ models that the program is compatible with, check out www.novii.tv.

Another remote control program worth checking out is ConnectedTV. This slick application lets you forget about channel numbers and choose your programs by name. Every couple weeks, you download the latest listings from the ConnectedTV servers, complete with descriptions for almost every program, as shown in this sidebar's last figure. The interface is very similar to the excellent TiVo program guide — down to an option for setting up a page with your favorite programs so that you can find out when they'll be on next. When this book was written, it was compatible only with some CLIÉ models, but you can find a full list on which PDAs work with the latest version at `www.connected.tv`.

Keep in mind that various CLIÉ models have different infrared ranges. Some work up to about 15 feet or farther from your home-entertainment equipment with no problems, but a few are limited to a piddly 6 feet or so. Your best bet is to download a trial version of the program and test it with your equipment to see what kind of range your CLIÉ has before making a purchase.

Who knows. You might be so enamored of the versatility of these programs that you decide to buy an older, used CLIÉ just to use as a remote.

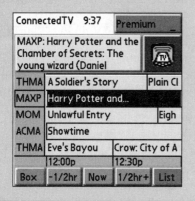

To set your system up to HotSync by infrared, do the following:

1. **Click the blue-and-red circular HotSync icon in the lower-right corner of your laptop's Windows Task bar.**

   Assuming that your laptop has a working and enabled infrared emitter, you see Infrared as a choice below Network on the HotSync menu that pops up.

2. **Choose Infrared.**

   Note that you can have both Infrared and USB selected, and the laptop works with whichever HotSync method you're using at the moment.

3. **Tap the HotSync icon in the CLIÉ Program Launcher to start the HotSync program.**

   The HotSync main screen appears.

4. **Tap the drop-down menu arrow below the HotSync button on the screen and change the setting from the Cradle/Cable option to the IR to a PC/Handheld option.**

5. **Point the CLIÉ's infrared port at the laptop's infrared port and tap the HotSync button on the CLIÉ's screen.**

   You should hear the usual HotSync beep and see the HotSync window open on the laptop. From there, the HotSync proceeds normally, but at about a quarter the usual speed.

Tune In to Wi-Fi

Wi-Fi is all the rage. Sony is building this wireless networking technology into most of its CLIÉ models today. Wi-Fi is a short-range networking standard that's designed for use in offices, homes, and public spots like airports and coffee shops. To use Wi-Fi, you must be within roughly 300 feet of a an *access point* — a base station that transmits the wireless signal and connects you to the Internet — so it's not going to help you on the road or in the country.

But with Wi-Fi popularity growing by leaps and bounds, finding access points is getting easier and easier. Many hotels, coffee shops, and bookstores offer Wi-Fi access as an enticement to draw in customers. These Wi-Fi zones, sometimes free but often available at a small charge, have come to be known as *hotspots.* Conferences and trade shows often offer free Wi-Fi coverage. In major cities, you can just roam the streets and find open Wi-Fi networks to leech onto, where individuals and businesses have left their networks unsecured. (It's not very polite, though, unless the access points were left open intentionally.) Adding Wi-Fi capabilities to your own home network costs well under $75.

What is Wi-Fi?

Wi-Fi works just like a traditional wired network card. Its primary function is to give wireless access to a network's Internet connection. *Wi-Fi* is short for *wireless fidelity,* a term that doesn't make a whole heck of a lot of sense. (It's a play on the well-known audio term *Hi-Fi.*) You can also see Wi-Fi referred to by the extremely unfriendly designation 802.11, which was the official designation given to the wireless standard by the Institute of Electrical and Electronics Engineers (IEEE). The flavor of Wi-Fi that you find on CLIÉs is the original standard, 802.11b, which supports transmission rates of up to 11 Mbps. Now, most of the home-networking equipment that you find at your local electronics superstore uses the new 802.11g standard, which supports 54 Mbps transmissions. The good news is that these 802.11g base stations are compatible with 802.11b devices, so your CLIÉ can talk to them without problems.

Note that Wi-Fi has certain security issues. Without security features enabled, anyone within radio range can access a Wi-Fi network. For people living in apartment buildings, an unsecured Wi-Fi network could provide free Internet access for all your neighbors. Worse, in an office, it could allow outsiders to snoop your company's files. The ubiquitous Wired Equivalent Privacy (WEP) security standard requires you to input a special code on all devices that access a particular Wi-Fi network. The problem is, WEP networks can be fairly easily cracked in just a few hours by using readily available programs. The new Wireless Protected Access (WPA) protocol that's found on newer equipment is more secure but hasn't yet found its way onto the CLIÉ. The good news is that WEP security is adequate to keep casual snoopers and free-loaders off your network. The even better news is that the way the CLIÉ's Wi-Fi access is designed, even someone who's broken into the network can't snoop around in the data stored in the unit. The worst they could do would be to intercept e-mail and Web data you're sending across the Internet.

Configuring your Wi-Fi connection

Okay, you have a Wi-Fi network set up at home, or you located one at work or the local coffee shop. Now you need to get connected.

Connection is more trouble-free if you can find out the wireless network's Service Set Identifier (SSID). The SSID is the name given to the network during setup. You don't absolutely have to have the SSID, but it can save some headaches if you're having problems connecting. You also need to find out whether the access point is using WEP encryption; if so, you need the password, called a *WEP key.*

If you're using an NX series CLIÉ, you need to install the drivers for your CompactFlash Wi-Fi card before proceeding. They came on a disc with your card, but I suggest downloading the latest drivers for the WL100/WL110 Wi-Fi cards from Sony's CLIÉ Support Web site at `www.sony.com/clie/support`. If you're using a TJ-, TH-, or UX-series CLIÉ with built-in Wi-Fi, no drivers are necessary.

Wi-Fi setup on the CLIÉ

Wi-Fi setup is handled in the Preferences application, as is manually connecting to the network. Tap the Prefs icon in the Program Launcher, and then tap the drop-down menu arrow in the top-left corner of the screen and choose Network. You see the screen in Figure 15-3.

Figure 15-3:
The
Network
Preferences
screen
gives
simplicity a
whole new
meaning.

Tap the Service drop-down menu arrow and choose Wireless LAN (local area network). Now you need to tell the CLIÉ about the network that you want to connect to.

Tap the Details button to bring up the Wireless LAN Setup screen. If you have an NX-series CLIÉ with a CompactFlash Wi-Fi card, you see the basic setup screen shown in Figure 15-4. If you have a UX, TJ, TH, or newer CLIÉ, you see the more full-featured interface in Figure 15-5.

Figure 15-4: The Wireless LAN Setup screen on NX-series CLIÉ models is plain but functional.

Figure 15-5: The Wireless LAN Setup screen on newer CLIÉs can scan for access points.

The main difference between the old interface and the new one is that the interface for CLIÉs with CompactFlash Wi-Fi cards requires you to manually enter an SSID for the network that you want to connect to, but the newer version can scan for any wireless networks in range.

I show you in the following sections how to configure your CLIÉ to connect automatically to the nearest available access point.

CLIÉs with built-in Wi-Fi

Tap the Prefs icon in the Program Launcher, tap the drop-down menu arrow in the upper-right corner of the Preferences screen, and then choose Network. Tap the Service drop-down menu arrow and choose Wireless LAN. Now tap the Details button at the bottom of the Preferences screen to open the Wireless LAN Setup screen, shown previously in Figure 15-5.

If you select Auto Connect on this screen, the Wi-Fi radio attempts to connect to the unencrypted access point that's the strongest and closest. This setting should work in most situations. However, in cases where you're within range of more than one access point, you might want to specifically choose which network you're going to connect to. You also need to do some manual configuration if the access point that you're using has WEP encryption active.

In this case, just tap the Scan button at the bottom of the screen. The Scan Result screen opens and gives you a list of access points in range, as shown in Figure 15-6.

Figure 15-6: A list of available wireless access points.

The WEP column tells you whether an access point is using WEP encryption. (If you see an X in that column, you need the WEP key to access this network.) The Mode column reads Infra (short for *infrastructure mode,* the mode that's used by access points; the alternative is Adhoc, which lets you connect to only one computer). The Signal column tells you how strong the signal is, ranging from 0 to 100.

On the ScanResult screen, tap the access point that you want to configure for use. When you're not using your own network, you generally want to select the strongest unencrypted signal reading. Then tap the Select button. The Wireless LAN Setup window appears, as shown in Figure 15-7.

For access points that aren't using WEP encryption and that can automatically register devices on their network, all you need to do is tap OK, and you're ready to connect to the new network.

Figure 15-7: Setting the configuration details.

If your network is using WEP, you need to get the WEP key from the system administrator — or whoever set up your wireless router, as the case may be. When you tap the WEP drop-down menu arrow, you're given four choices for entering encryption keys: 40-bit characters , 40-bit Hex, 128-bit characters, or 128-bit Hex. Select the type that's used by your access point, and then enter the encryption key. If your network doesn't automatically assign *IP addresses* (which stands for *Internet Protocol,* unique numeric identifiers that every computer connected to the Internet must possess) using a DHCP (Dynamic Host Configuration Protocol) server, you need to manually configure the IP address. You can get info on the access point and how to configure the IP address from your network administrator. Tap the Advanced Setup button to get to the screen shown in Figure 15-8. Deselect the Auto check box next to IP Address and enter the appropriate data for your network.

Figure 15-8: Manually entering IP address data for a wireless network.

Now tap OK to return to the main Wireless LAN Setup screen. (Refer to Figure 15-7.) Tap OK again to return to the Network Preferences screen. Finally, tap the Connect button. If all goes well, a Connecting status window pops up, and the Connect button changes to read Disconnect. You're now on the network, ready to browse the Web, process e-mail, and more.

CLIÉs with CompactFlash Wi-Fi cards

If you're using an NX series CLIÉ with a CompactFlash Wi-Fi card, the WL100/110 CF card drivers don't have the ability to list available Wi-Fi access points. However, a special trick lets you connect to unencrypted access points even if you don't know the network's SSID.

On the Wireless LAN Setup screen (refer to Figure 15-5), tap the Create button to create a new profile. Now enter the information so that it matches Figure 15-9. This takes advantage of a poorly documented trick with these cards: If you set the value of the SSID to Any, WEP to None, and leave all other settings set to their defaults, the card then attempts to connect to any unencrypted access point in range.

Figure 15-9:
Setting up
a Wi-Fi
Compact-
Flash card
to connect
automat-
ically to the
strongest
available
network.

If you use WEP encryption on your home or work network, you can configure an additional profile for that access point with the proper SSID and WEP code, and select the Any Access Point profile when you're roaming outside of the home or office environment.

Wi-Fi setup with the Mobile Connection Wizard

Sony has released a Windows program called the Mobile Connection Wizard designed to run on your desktop computer and simplify Wi-Fi and Bluetooth configuration. The program is included on the Installation CD with the newest CLIÉs, but I recommend that you skip that copy and download the latest version, even if it came with your unit, because Sony constantly updates it to support new profiles. You can download the latest version from Sony's CLIÉ Support Web site at www.sony.com/clie/support.

After you first launch Mobile Connection Wizard on your desktop system, HotSync your CLIÉ so that the program can gather information about it. (For more on how to HotSync, see Chapter 3.) Then click the Select User Account button on the Connection Wizard screen and choose your CLIÉ's HotSync ID. Finally, click New to create a new connection profile.

On the next screen, click the drop-down list, and you see just one Wi-Fi profile, which is for using your wireless LAN with the T-Mobile HotSpot commercial Wi-Fi service. If you do plan to use your CLIÉ with T-Mobile's service, you can select this option, click Next, and follow the on-screen prompts to configure your CLIÉ to work with it. However, I'm going to assume that you might use your CLIÉ with other networks, as well. Select the Show Advanced check box to see the more advanced drop-down list shown in Figure 15-10.

Figure 15-10: The Connection Wizard's Advanced Options menu lets you configure a Wi-Fi connection.

Select the *Your CLIÉ model* Internal Wireless LAN option and click Next to continue. The screen shown in Figure 15-11 appears and prompts you to enter your network's SSID. Note that some wireless networks are configured with a blank SSID; if this is the case with yours, simply leave the Network ID (SSID) field blank. Click the Next button when you're done.

The next Connection Wizard screen prompts you to enter the WEP encryption for the network that you entered. If no WEP encryption is active, select None from the drop-down list. Otherwise, choose the type of encryption (40/64 or 104/128 bit) and the method for entering the code (text characters or hex), as shown in Figure 15-12. You can get this information from your system administrator or from the person who configured your wireless router.

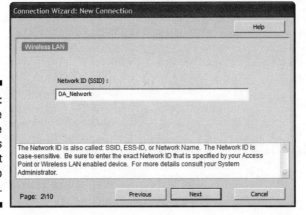

Figure 15-11:
Enter the
SSID of the
wireless
network that
you want to
connect to.

Figure 15-12:
Choosing
the type of
encryption
in use.

Click Next to move on to yet another Connection Wizard screen. If you chose a WEP encryption type, you need to enter it in the Enter WEP Key field. Unfortunately, Sony chose to obscure the entry with asterisks, as shown in Figure 15-13. This can make code entry difficult, particularly when entering a 128-bit encryption key in hex format — that's 26 characters!

If you'd like to verify the code rather than typing it blind, enter it in another program, such as Word or Notepad, and check to make sure that the characters are correct. When you're ready, highlight it, choose Edit➪Copy, and then click in the Enter WEP Key field in the Connection Wizard and press Ctrl+V, which is the Paste command. Your verified WEP key is pasted into the field. Click the Next button.

Figure 15-13:
Blindly
entering
26 charac-
ters is a
challenge.
Check out
the cut-and-
paste tip
to avoid
headaches.

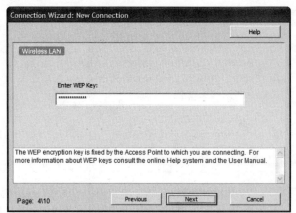

The screen that appears asks you to tap a button to select the network type, and your choices are Infrastructure or Adhoc. You use Infrastructure to connect to network access points, and choosing Adhoc connects your CLIÉ to a wireless network card on a single computer. I assume that you're using an access point here because Adhoc use is very specialized and limited in potential usage. Select Infrastructure and click the Next button.

The next screen, shown in Figure 15-14, prompts you to enter your IP address, which is your computer's address on the local area network. Home network and public access networks are typically set up to use a technology called DHCP, which assigns an IP address automatically to a computer when it tries to connect to the network. So chances are that you can just select the DHCP check box and click Next to move on to the following screen. If you're on an office network that requires each device to have its own IP address, you need to deselect the DHCP check box; get the information for the Address, Mask, and DNS values from your network administrator; and enter that information here. For reasons that defy logical explanation, for some CLIÉ models the wizard puts IP and DNS address information on a single screen, but on others, the wizard breaks them into two separate screens.

Next, you're given the chance to choose whether to activate Power Save Mode. I suggest selecting the Power Save check box to enable the feature — at least to start with. If you find that your connection is weak or intermittent, you can edit the connection settings and disable power savings. Click Next after you make your choice.

Next is Auto Connect. With this active, the CLIÉ attempts to connect to the access point on the network you're configuring if it's in range, even if you've selected Auto Connect rather than this specific network in the Wireless LAN Setup screen. Unless you're using an Adhoc network, enable Auto Connect. Click Next after you make the selection.

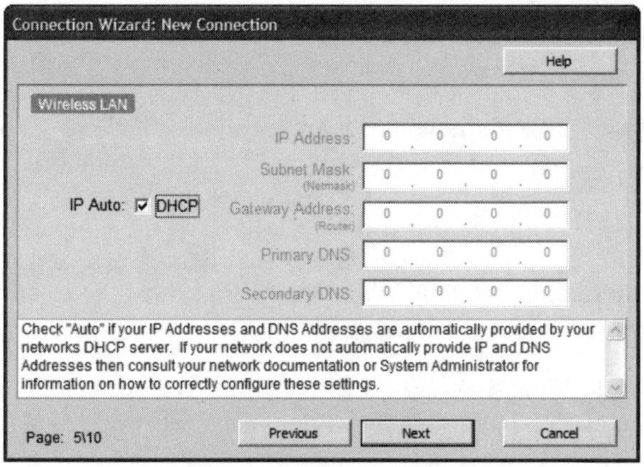

Figure 15-14:
If your
network
requires you
to manually
assign an IP
address,
choose
it here.

The next wizard screen prompts you to enter a name for the connection, as shown in Figure 15-15. This is simply an identifier for your own reference, so that you can use anything you'd like: Work LAN, Home Wi-Fi, Starbucks Setup, and so on. Click Next after entering the name. The final wizard screen gives you the opportunity to enter an optional comment describing the name.

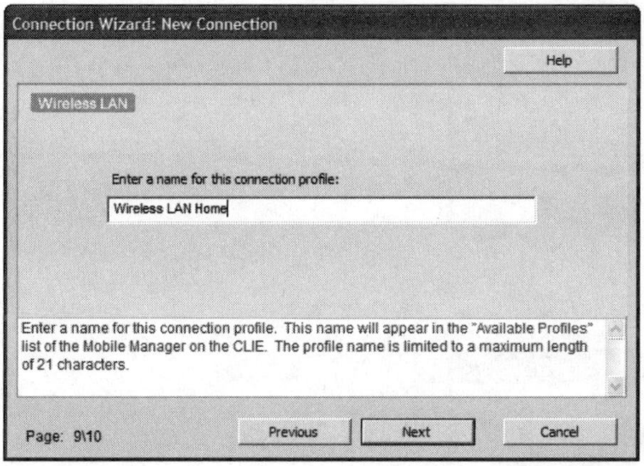

Figure 15-15:
Finally, time
to name the
network!

You're configured! You also probably have a better idea why they give pretty, frameable certificates of accomplishment to people when they find out how to set up computer networks.

Putting Wi-Fi to use

The previous section sets up your Wi-Fi connection. The good news is that actually using Wi-Fi after it's been configured requires little or no interaction from you. If you're using a CLIÉ with built-in Wi-Fi, after you configure the access points that you'll be using you can just set the Wireless LAN Setup to Auto Connect, as shown in Figure 15-16. As long as you've manually set up any networks that require a WEP key or a preset IP address, and they're set to be able to connect automatically, the CLIÉ should be able to find and connect to your network without further intervention.

If you're using a CLIÉ that's equipped with CompactFlash Wi-Fi, you need to select the profile manually when using a network that requires WEP or a preset IP address. For normal use on unencrypted access points, leave the configuration set to Any, as shown in Figure 15-17, and just choose the proper profile manually when using a protected network.

Figure 15-16: Typically, you want to leave CLIÉs with built-in Wi-Fi set to Auto Connect.

Figure 15-17: On CLIÉs with a Compact-Flash Wi-Fi card, you must select the proper profile when using a protected network.

Where to find Wi-Fi

If you have a Wi-Fi CLIÉ, you might want to set up Wi-Fi in your home. Just imagine streaming MP3s tunes off the Internet onto your CLIÉ as you work out in the basement, or picture yourself sending e-mail from the comfort of your couch.

To install Wi-Fi at home, you need to connect a wireless router to your home network. These are relatively inexpensive (from $40 to $299), and most also include a firewall feature to protect your home network from Internet hacking. Just connect at least one computer to the router, and then connect your cable or DSL modem to the router's wide area network (WAN) port. (If you're using a dial-up modem, you also need to use the Internet Connection Sharing software built into Windows. See the Windows Help feature for details.) Almost any router works fine with a CLIÉ Wi-Fi setup. Just be sure that the router supports either the 802.11b or 802.11g standard.

To liberate yourself from wired networking at the office, talk to your network administrator to find out the network SSID, the WEP encryption code, and whether you need a fixed IP address. Plug the info into your Network Preferences as outlined in this chapter, and then you're good to go.

The real versatility of a wireless CLIÉ, though, comes from public access points. Some are free, but others charge a small fee. Numerous companies now offer Wi-Fi access services — great for people who travel often and can take advantage of them.

Some commercial Wi-Fi services allow you to log on to your account by using a standard Web browser. Any Wi-Fi CLIÉ can access these Wi-Fi services. Other services require special software to be installed on your compute or handheld to log on to the company's Wi-Fi networks, so be sure that the correct software is available for the CLIÉ before you sign up.

Boingo's service (www.boingo.com), for instance, is available for Pocket PCs but not CLIÉs. The Earthlink Wi-Fi software requires Windows, so handheld users are completely out of luck. Complain to Earthlink at www.earthlink.net.

Happily, most of the major players do support handhelds. T-Mobile HotSpot (www.t-mobile.com/hotspot/) offers hourly, daily, and monthly rate plans and lets you log on with a standard Web browser, so it works fine with the CLIÉ. The service is available at over 3,100 locations in 34 states, including many Starbucks coffeehouses and Borders stores.

The other big player is Wayport (www.wayport.com), which also works on the CLIÉ. It primarily serves hotels (over 600 of them), but it also has access points in 12 airports, including Oakland, San Jose, and Seattle-Tacoma. And West Coast fast-food fans can rejoice: Wayport is running trials in Bay Area McDonalds restaurants. ("Would you like fries with your McWi-Fi?") Wayport offers daily and monthly plans.

Keep in mind that plenty of legitimate, free Wi-Fi access points also exist. Many public libraries, for instance, offer Wi-Fi access for their patrons, as do a number of mom-and-pop coffee shops. Panera Bread Company has 602 locations nationwide and offers free Wi-Fi access at all its stores. Even a few Laundromats have hopped on the free Wi-Fi bandwagon. If that's not enough, some towns now offer free Wi-Fi access in their business districts. Boulder, Colorado, for instance, offers free outdoor Wi-Fi access in its Pearl Street Mall shopping district. Even downtown Mount Airy, North Carolina — population 8,500 and the real-life model for Andy Griffith's Mayberry — has kicked off its own free Wi-Fi service. An excellent resource for finding out whether a free Wi-Fi hotspot is available in your area is www.wififreespot.com.

To manually connect to a network, tap Prefs in the Program Launcher, tap the drop-down menu arrow in the upper-right corner and select Network, make sure that Wireless LAN is selected (refer to Figure 15-3), and tap the Connect button. If you leave the network preferences set to Wireless LAN, however, you don't need to connect manually. When you attempt to go online with a Web browser, chat program, or e-mail application, the system asks you whether you want to connect. Tap OK, and your CLIÉ connects automatically.

You can also use the Mobile Manager to swap between profiles if they were initially created by using the Mobile Connection Wizard on your desktop system. Just load the Mobile Manager by tapping its icon in the Program Launcher, tap the profile that you want to use, and tap Activate.

Bluetooth: Weird Name, Great Technology

Wi-Fi has caught on like wildfire, yet its little brother, Bluetooth, is having problems even igniting a spark. Part of this is because the technologies are often compared, whereas in fact, they're typically used for completely different purposes.

Wi-Fi is designed specifically to connect your PDA wirelessly to a network or the Internet. Bluetooth is designed to connect a PDA to anything that would typically require a cable to make a connection (for example, cell phones, printers, GPS receivers, and HotSync cradles).

By far the best use for Bluetooth is connecting to a Bluetooth-capable cell phone, which lets the CLIÉ utilize the phone as a wireless modem. This isn't as fast as a Wi-Fi connection — it's just a little faster than a traditional dial-up modem — but you can use this technology anywhere that your cell phone works. You don't even have to hunt for access points.

My second favorite use is to connect to a Bluetooth GPS (Global Positioning System) receiver. These wonderful mouse-size gadgets track a constellation of orbiting GPS satellites and can locate your exact position within just a few feet. They're a life-saver when driving in strange cities. Particularly Munich.

Instead of having to deal with a Rube Goldberg combination of a CLIÉ, a cable to an external GPS receiver, and chargers for both strewn around your dashboard, you can connect the CLIÉ to a compatible GPS (such as the Navman 4460) through a wireless connection. This lets you place a tiny, pager-sized

GPS on your dashboard and hand the map-equipped PDA to your passenger or mount it in a convenient spot on your dash. If you're running on batteries, no cables are involved at all.

Sony has released a few CLIÉs with built-in Bluetooth, including the PEG-TG50 and the PEG-UX50. Oddly, the PEG-TH55 ships with both Bluetooth and Wi-Fi in its European edition, but the American version includes only Wi-Fi. Bluetooth-savvy CLIÉ fans have been known to pay an extra $100 to get an imported Bluetooth-equipped model.

When you first use two Bluetooth devices together, they must be *paired,* which means that you tell them it's okay to talk to each other. (This helps keep wily Bluetooth bandits from wirelessly snooping around your PDA or laptop in public places.) The good news is that after you complete the initial configuration and pairing, Bluetooth devices can connect to each other automatically.

Sony's Mobile Connection Wizard makes connecting the CLIÉ to a phone via Bluetooth super easy. If your phone and your cell phone company are both supported, the process is point-and-click and requires none of the technical knowledge that sometimes comes up when dealing with Wi-Fi.

Setting up a Bluetooth phone: Part 1

Setting up a supported Bluetooth phone is a snap when using the Mobile Connection Wizard. After you first launch the Mobile Connection Wizard on your desktop system, HotSync your CLIÉ so that the program can gather information about it. (For more on how to HotSync, see Chapter 3.) Then click the Select User Account button on the Connection Wizard screen and choose your CLIÉ's HotSync ID. Finally, click New to create a new connection profile.

On the Setup screen, shown in Figure 15-18, you get Bluetooth setup choices for Cingular, AT&T Wireless, and T-Mobile Wireless, the three major carriers currently offering Bluetooth phones in the USA. Choose your cell phone provider and click Next. (If you're using another carrier, you need to get specialized setup instructions from the carrier.)

Next, you choose your cell phone model, as shown in Figure 15-19. If your phone isn't listed, try the Generic GSM Phone setting.

Figure 15-18:
To get
started,
select your
cell phone
carrier in
the Mobile
Connection
Wizard.

> Connection Wizard: New Connection
>
> Help
>
> Bluetooth
>
> Please select a connection type: ☐ Show Advanced
>
> Quick Setup for T-Mobile Wireless Internet using a Bluetooth Phone   ▼
>
> Connect your PEG-UX50/U to the T-Mobile high-speed GPRS network using your
> Bluetooth (BT) enabled phone. This simple setup uses the most common settings. If
> your configuration needs require more control try one of the Advanced Setups. NOTE:
> Quick setups cannot be edited on the Mobile Manager
>
> Page: 1\4   Previous   Next   Cancel

Figure 15-19:
Select your
cell phone
model.

> Connection Wizard: New Connection
>
> Help
>
> Bluetooth
>
> Please select your phone model:
>
> Sony-Ericsson T68i   ▼
>
> Select your phone from the list of provider supported phone models. If your phone model
> does not appear in the list, select the generic model.
>
> Page: 2\4   Previous   Next   Cancel

If your phone isn't directly supported, and the Generic GSM setting doesn't work, try another phone of the same brand. Typically, the Bluetooth commands are similar enough that the phones will be compatible. Also, download the latest version of the Mobile Connection Wizard from the Sony CLIÉ Support Web site at www.sony.com/clie/support. Your phone might have been added to the latest version. If all else fails, contact your cell phone carrier or use Google (www.google.com) to search for a Web site devoted to your phone. For instance, you can find lots of information on configuring the relatively rare Sony-Ericsson T608 Bluetooth phone to work with the CLIÉ at www.sprintpcsinfo.com.

Next, enter a name for this connection, as illustrated in Figure 15-20; click Next; and enter an optional comment describing the connection.

Figure 15-20:
Enter a name for your wireless connection.

You now have a the Bluetooth profile for your phone. Simply HotSync the CLIÉ to transfer the profile over to the PDA.(For more on how to HotSync, see Chapter 3.)

Setting up a Bluetooth phone: Part 2

All that's left is to select the new profile and pair your phone to the CLIÉ. First, make sure that your CLIÉ's Bluetooth radio is turned on by tapping Prefs in the Program Launcher, and then selecting Bluetooth from the drop-down menu arrow in the top-right corner of the screen. Set Bluetooth to Enabled, as shown in Figure 15-21.

Figure 15-21:
Use the Preferences application to turn on your CLIÉ's Bluetooth radio.

Tap the Mobile Manager icon in the CLIÉ Program Launcher. (This program was installed when you did a HotSync after you installed the Mobile Connection Wizard on your desktop system.) You see a screen similar to the one in Figure 15-22. Tap the name of the profile that you created in the previous section and tap the Activate button.

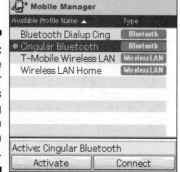

Figure 15-22: The Mobile Manager simplifies switching between connection profiles.

Next, the Mobile Manager program brings up a screen asking you to Select Trusted Device. Before proceeding, you need to set your Bluetooth phone up so that it's *discoverable,* which means that the CLIÉ can detect it. Check your phone's manual for specific instructions on how to do this; the menu procedures vary between phone models.

When the phone is in Discoverable mode, tap the Discover button at the bottom of the Mobile Manager. The CLIÉ searches for Bluetooth devices and then presents a list of the devices that it located, as shown in Figure 15-23. Tap the one that represents your phone and then tap OK. The Mobile Manager program asks whether you want to add the device to your Trusted Device list. Tap Yes so that you don't have to pair the device every time you use it.

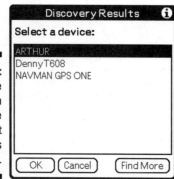

Figure 15-23: Tap the Bluetooth device name that represents your phone.

Next, you're asked to enter the passkey for your Bluetooth device, as shown in Figure 15-24. This is a secret password that each device has. The default password should be listed in the documentation for your phone, or your phone might have prompted you to set your own password when you were activating its Bluetooth features. Enter the password and tap OK. Check your phone's screen because it might ask you to verify that you want to pair the devices.

You can now see your phone's name listed on the Trusted Device window. Make sure that it's highlighted and tap Done.

Your Bluetooth phone profile is now active. As long as you don't switch profiles, all you have to do to connect to the Internet is make sure that your phone is on, its Bluetooth feature is active, and your CLIÉ's Bluetooth radio is turned on. Simply going online with a Web browser, e-mail program, or chat application causes your CLIÉ to connect with your phone wirelessly and dial the Internet.

Figure 15-24:
A passkey prevents strangers from pairing with your Bluetooth devices.

Connecting a non-Bluetooth phone

If you have a cellular phone that doesn't support Bluetooth, you might still be able to use it to connect to the Internet by attaching it to your CLIÉ with a cable. Your phone must use the GSM or CDMA digital networks. (TMDA networks, which are in the process of being phased out, don't support cellular data.)

You can find cables at a variety of sources, but the chances of your locating them locally are pretty slim. The best source is SupplyNet at www.thesupplynet.com. The company not only has cables for just about every CLIÉ model (the UX series is the exception) to connect to a wide variety of cell phones, but it also includes step-by-step instructions for configuring your CLIÉ and phone to work with all the major cellular carriers.

Setting up other Bluetooth devices

When it comes to setting up other Bluetooth devices, such as GPS receivers or printers, the procedure varies by device. The basic process is to put the device that you want to connect in Discoverable mode, and then go to the Bluetooth section of the Preferences application, as shown previously in Figure 15-21, and tap Trusted Devices to pair the two devices. This works the same way as selecting Trusted Devices does in the previous sections.

From there, it's up to the program that you're running to connect to the Bluetooth device. If your application supports Bluetooth, it should include detailed instructions on how to proceed.

Chapter 16

Internet on the Go

· ·

In This Chapter

▶ Discovering CLIÉ Mail

▶ Browsing the Web with NetFront

▶ Using instant messaging and other applications

· ·

Sure, playing games or watching a video on your CLIÉ is fun when you have a little downtime, but if you're really busy, you might need to kill the e-mail backlog instead of zapping aliens from Planet 13.

All current CLIÉ models are set up to handle e-mail whether or not they have built-in wireless capabilities. (The nonwireless varieties use the HotSync process to transfer e-mail.) Wireless CLIÉs include the added benefit of Web browsing. Any CLIÉ can accept add-on programs that enhance e-mailing and browsing capabilities, and some add-ons offer other online tricks, such as instant messaging.

The Versatile CLIÉ Mail

CLIÉ Mail is a powerful e-mail program that's included with all current CLIÉ units, even the units without wireless capabilities. CLIÉs that lack wireless features can still take advantage of the program by transferring e-mails when you HotSync your CLIÉ. However, with a Wi-Fi card or Bluetooth wireless connection, you can process your e-mails on the go. On many CLIÉs, CLIÉ Mail is built in and available from the moment that you first turn on the unit. On some CLIÉs, you must first install the handheld version of CLIÉ Mail from the CD that came with your CLIÉ; you can find it in the CLIÉ Utilities section.

Transferring CLIÉ Mail using your desktop system

Transferring e-mail by using your desktop system is a relatively painless process. First, you have to install a HotSync conduit on your desktop system. Insert the Installation CD that came with your CLIÉ and look for CLIÉ Mail Conduit, which can typically be found by clicking the CLIÉ Utilities tab on the installation menu. Click Install, and the installation proceeds automatically.

Now you must activate the conduit. Here's how:

1. **Click the red-and-blue HotSync icon in the lower-right corner of your Windows screen.**

   The menu shown in Figure 16-1 appears.

Figure 16-1:
Click the
HotSync
icon on your
Windows
screen and
choose
Custom.

2. **Choose Custom on the menu.**

   The Custom window appears.

3. **Select CLIÉ Mail from the list of conduits in the Custom window, and then click the Change button.**

   The CLIÉ Mail conduit settings window appears, as shown in Figure 16-2. (You use this window to configure the conduit you just activated.)

4. **In the CLIÉ Mail conduit settings window, click to choose the synchronization option that you want.**

   You typically want to select the Synchronize the Files option. It downloads all new e-mails to your CLIÉ and uploads any e-mails that you've written on the CLIÉ. With the e-mails uploaded to your desktop system, you can send them by using your desktop e-mail program. If you select the Overwrites Handheld option, new e-mails that you created on the CLIÉ aren't transferred, and any existing e-mail on the CLIÉ is replaced by the e-mail currently on your desktop system. Selecting the Do Nothing option results in nothing being transferred.

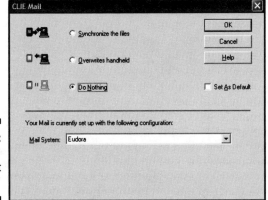

Figure 16-2:
Conduits!
Get your hot
conduits!

5. **Select the Set As Default check box.**

6. **Using the Mail System drop-down list, select the e-mail program that you're currently using.**

   CLIÉ Mail supports Microsoft Outlook, Outlook Express, and Eudora.

7. **Click OK to close the CLIÉ Mail window, and then click Done in the Custom window.**

   The Custom window closes, and you're about set to go.

You also need to ensure that the Messaging Application Program Interface (MAPI) feature is enabled in your desktop e-mail application. The MAPI feature lets your e-mail program communicate with other applications. It's enabled by default in Outlook Express 5.0 or later and in Outlook. To enable it in Eudora, open Eudora, choose Tools⇔Options, and then click the MAPI icon in the Options window. Select Always Available from the MAPI options that appear.

You're almost ready to start using HotSync mail. All that's left to do is to choose your e-mail retrieval options on the CLIÉ. Launch the program by tapping the CLIÉ Mail icon in the Program Launcher. Tap the Menu soft button and choose Options⇔HotSync Options from the menu that appears. You see the screen illustrated in Figure 16-3.

If you leave it set to All, the default option, all messages are synchronized between the desktop system and your CLIÉ. All new messages are downloaded to the CLIÉ, and any messages that you write on the CLIÉ are uploaded to the desktop system and put in your e-mail program's outbox. Note that you can limit how many days' worth of messages to transfer. You definitely want to do this the first time you sync, and you might also want to set a low number if you haven't HotSynced in a while. Otherwise, I leave the number set at 999 to ensure that I get all my new e-mail.

HotSync Options

All | Send only | Filter | Unread

All messages will be syn-
chronized between the
handheld computer and the
e-mail application.

Only transfer messages from
the past ......3 days

OK | Cancel

Figure 16-3:
The CLIÉ
Mail
HotSync
Options
screen.

If you select Send Only, the CLIÉ sends any e-mail that you write on your CLIÉ
but doesn't download any e-mail from your desktop system. This is useful if
you want to be able to compose quick e-mails when you find a free moment,
but you don't want to read and respond to e-mails on your CLIÉ.

The next setting, Filter, lets you choose to download only messages containing a certain word in their headers or to ignore all messages with a particular
header word. You might use this, say, to grab all new messages from a particular sender or to ignore all messages for an e-mail list that you belong to —
choose Ignore and put the list's address in the From line.

Finally, the Unread option uploads any e-mails that you've written on your
CLIÉ to your desktop system but downloads only e-mails that you haven't yet
read on your desktop system.

Note that any e-mails you delete on your CLIÉ are also deleted on your desktop system. If you don't want to do this, use the Custom settings on your
desktop system's HotSync conduit, which I describe at the beginning of this
section, to set the conduit to the Overwrites Handheld option for the next
sync. The new e-mail is downloaded to the CLIÉ, but any deletions or new
messages that you've created are deleted instead of being sent to your desktop system.

Sending and receiving e-mail directly

If you want to grab e-mail directly without having to HotSync on your computer, CLIÉ Mail is up to the task. Just be sure that you have a wireless connection set up, either by Wi-Fi or a cell phone. (Chapter 15 takes you through
the wireless setup process.)

You need to set up your personal e-mail account first. Here's how it's done:

1. **Tap the CLIÉ Mail icon in the Program Launcher.**

   The CLIÉ Mail application opens on-screen.

2. **Tap the Menu soft button and choose Options⊅Accounts from the menu that appears.**

   The Accounts screen appears.

3. **Tap the New button on the Accounts screen.**

   You need the username, password, and server information for your Internet e-mail account to proceed.

   Note that CLIÉ Mail can't send or receive AOL e-mail. For details on AOL's software for the CLIÉ, see the "Instant Messaging and Other Applications" section at the end of this chapter.

4. **Enter your name on the Account Setup screen that appears, and then tap Next.**

   Recipients will see this name in the From field, and because it's for display purposes and not part of the actual address, it can be anything you'd like. Of course, your actual name is the logical thing to put there.

5. **Enter your actual e-mail address in the new screen that appears, and then tap Next.**

   If the address is incorrect here, replies to your e-mails won't get through.

6. **Enter the server addresses of the incoming mail server (called POP3) and the outgoing mail server (called SMTP) in the new screen that appears (see Figure 16-4), and then tap Next.**

   This information should be available in the signup information that you received from your Internet service provider (ISP). If not, call your ISP or visit its support Web site to find the proper values.

   Because of the spammer abuse, most e-mail providers let you use only their SMTP servers when you're actually connected to their network. So if you enter, say, your cable modem ISP's SMTP address, you're able to send mail from home but not when you're using someone else's network. In this case, you might need to contact the network administrator, find out that network's SMTP address, and change the value temporarily to that address. Incoming POP3 e-mail servers don't have this limitation, so you can receive e-mail no matter what network you're on.

Figure 16-4:
You can get
the real
addresses
from your
ISP and
enter them
here.

If you find that you can't send e-mail by using CLIÉ Mail on a strange network due to the SMTP problem, check and see whether your e-mail
provider offers a Web mail interface. Most do, and you can use Web mail
on any network. In that case, you can use the NetFront Web browser,
which I cover in more detail later in this chapter, to access the Web mail
interface and compose your outgoing e-mail.

7. **Enter your logon information — account name and password — on
   the next screen that appears, and then tap Next.**

   Again, this information should be included with the setup information
   from your ISP — otherwise, look for it on the ISP's support site or call
   the ISP's technical support number. Typically, the account name is the
   first part of your e-mail address — everything preceding the @ sign —
   but some ISPs use the entire address.

8. **Tap the Finish button to close the final screen.**

   That's it! You're ready to send and receive e-mail over your network.

Note that you can repeat this process if you have more than one e-mail
account. When you have multiple accounts, you can choose which one you
want to use to send outgoing e-mail by using to the Accounts screen. To get
there, tap the Menu soft button and choose Options⇨Accounts from the
menu that appears. When the Accounts screen appears, select the account
that you want to use, and then tap the Set to Outgoing Server button, as
shown in Figure 16-5.

If you don't want to check all your e-mail accounts next time you log on, just
use the Accounts screen to deselect the accounts that you don't want to check.

Figure 16-5:
CLIÉ Mail
supports
multiple
e-mail
accounts.

Composing and reading e-mail

When you first start CLIÉ Mail, you see a screen like the one in Figure 16-6.
The most important controls are all located on the icon bar at the bottom.

Tap the first icon to compose a new e-mail. You see the screen in Figure 16-7.
You can enter a recipient's e-mail address manually or choose addresses from
your address book by tapping the word *To,* and then tapping the Lookup
button on the Address screen that appears. You can include multiple recipients separated by commas. The same procedure works for the CC (carbon
copy) and BCC (blind carbon copy) fields. Finally, enter a subject, and then
enter your e-mail in the text area below.

CLIÉ Mail supports attachments, but they're limited to media files: graphics,
movies, and voice recorder files. To attach a file, tap the Insert button on the
blank e-mail screen and select the file that you want to send. You can repeat
the process to attach multiple files. A paperclip appears in the top-right
corner of the screen to indicate that an attachment is present. You can tap
the paperclip to verify or delete the attachment.

After you finish composing your e-mail, tap the Send button. A menu pops up
with two choices: Send Now and Send Later. Send Later queues your e-mails
for later sending, which is handy if you're not currently able to connect to the
network, if you plan to send e-mails using the HotSync process, or if you want
to compose multiple e-mails before going online. Otherwise, select Send Now,
and the CLIÉ connects to the Internet and sends your e-mail. If you want to
come back to your e-mail and finish it later, tap the Draft button instead of
the Send button.

Sort by Sender, Subject, or Date

Read/Unread Status   Choose Category

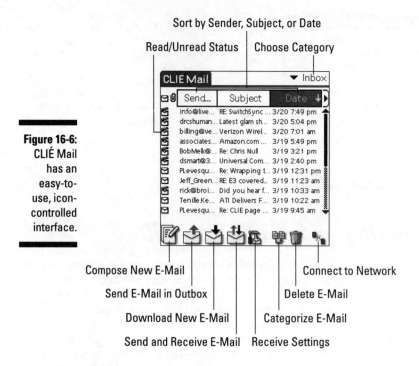

Figure 16-6:
CLIÉ Mail
has an
easy-to-
use, icon-
controlled
interface.

Compose New E-Mail   Connect to Network

Send E-Mail in Outbox   Delete E-Mail

Download New E-Mail   Categorize E-Mail

Send and Receive E-Mail   Receive Settings

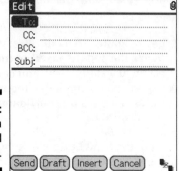

Figure 16-7:
Creating a
new e-mail
message.

Reading an e-mail is as easy as tapping it in the E-Mail list. Sometimes, however, you might see gibberish, such as in Figure 16-8. This is because the
sender created an e-mail by using *Hypertext Markup Language* — HTML, the
fancy formatting used on Web pages — which CLIÉ Mail doesn't understand.
This is a common problem with people who use Microsoft Outlook for e-mail.
Alas, the only solution is to ask senders to use standard, plain-text e-mail
when writing you, or to bug Sony's feedback line with requests that they add
HTML support to CLIÉ Mail.

Figure 16-8:
HTML
e-mails
have
gobbledy-
gook
formatting
characters
added. The
actual text
is hidden in
the mess.

If you get a lot of e-mail in HTML format, I recommend looking at an add-on e-mail solution, such as SnapperMail, which I cover in the "Instant Messaging and Other Applications" section later in this chapter.

By default, CLIÉ Mail doesn't show e-mail headers. If you're reading an e-mail, and you really need to see the e-mail's sender, subject, or date line, just tap the square icon in the top-right corner of the screen to display the headers. When you're done reading an e-mail, use the arrows at the top of the screen to move forward or backward through your E-Mail list. Tap OK to exit the screen and return to your E-Mail list, tap Reply to compose a reply to the sender, tap Move to place the e-mail in another category, or tap Delete to delete the mail.

Categories are extremely useful if you like to keep e-mails around for reference or if you want to separate e-mails as they come in based on certain criteria. To manually move letters to another category, tap the Categorize E-Mail icon on the main screen. (Refer to Figure 16-6.) The screen in Figure 16-9 appears.

Figure 16-9:
Selecting
e-mails to
move to
another
category.

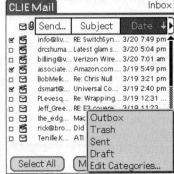

You can also create filters that will automatically categorize e-mails as they're received. Filters can automatically separate e-mails that are received by different accounts into their own folder or place all e-mails relating to a particular topic in their own folder, for instance. You can even choose not to download e-mails from a particular sender or with a particular subject line.

To set up filters, just do the following:

1. **Tap the Menu soft button and choose Options⇨Filters from the menu that appears.**

   The Filters screen appears. Initially, the screen is empty.

2. **Tap New to create a filter.**

   You see the screen in Figure 16-10.

3. **Enter a name for the new filter in the Filter Name field.**

4. **Using the first drop-down menu arrow, select which field you want to search for the trigger string of characters.**

   Your selections here are To, From, Subject, and CC.

5 **Use the next drop-down menu arrow to apply the filter either to every message that contains the specified text string you enter or to every message that doesn't have that string.**

6. **Use the Retrieve/Don't Retrieve drop-down menu arrow to toggle between receiving and not receiving the e-mails you are filtering for.**

7. **If you chose Retrieve in Step 6, use the Move To drop-down menu arrow to select a category.**

   Any e-mail that matches the filter goes into the category that you select.

   In the example in Figure 16-10, the filter looks for any message sent to my work e-mail address, retrieves that message, and then places it in the Work E-Mail category.

8. **When you finish creating the filter, tap OK.**

   You return to the Filters screen, where you must select the filter name to activate it. This ability to turn filters on and off is useful if, say, you want to use a filter that doesn't retrieve personal e-mail while you're at work.

To round off this discussion of CLIÉ Mail, I want to draw your attention to the Receive settings. These allow you to choose to receive only a portion of downloaded e-mails and to fetch only the most recent messages. The Receive settings are handy if you're on a slow connection, such as an older digital cell phone. You can access these settings by tapping the Receive Settings icon. (Refer to Figure 16-6.) The Receive Settings screen appears.

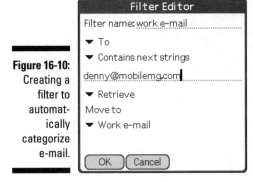

Figure 16-10:
Creating a
filter to
automat-
ically
categorize
e-mail.

The first setting, Retrieve Lines, defaults to All, which retrieves the entire message. If you change the setting to Headers+Bodies by tapping the Headers+
Bodies button, you can specify how many lines of a message to retrieve by
tapping the Retrieve Number button. Setting it at 20 to 40 speeds up retrieval
dramatically. A Retrieve on Next Connection check box is added to the end of
the message. Selecting the check box means that the CLIÉ downloads the rest
of the message next time you check your e-mail.

The second Receive setting, Retrieve Number, also defaults to All, but you
can set it to retrieve up to a set number of the most recent messages. If you
haven't checked your e-mail on your handheld for a while, but you have
checked on your desktop recently, you might want to limit the number of
messages retrieved to somewhere between 20 and 50 so that you don't get
deluged with old messages. Also, you can choose whether or not to use filters when customizing the Receive settings.

Browsing the Web with NetFront

NetFront is a full-featured, handheld Web browser that's optimized for the
CLIÉ's screen and wireless capabilities.

Sony includes the NetFront Web browser with its CLIÉ models that feature
built-in wireless capabilities, as well as with the NX series units, which can
accept add-on Wi-Fi cards. Unfortunately, the company doesn't make the program available to CLIÉ owners as a separate purchase, so if your CLIÉ doesn't
include it, you have to find a third-party solution.

You see the NetFront interface and function icons in Figure 16-11.

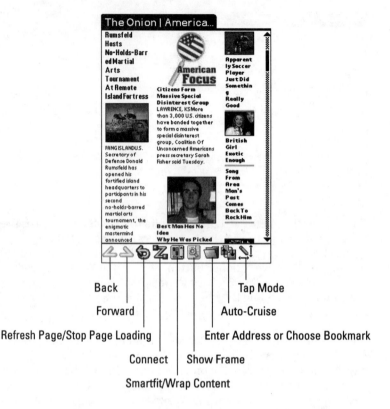

Figure 16-11:
The
NetFront
browser
control
icons reside
at the
bottom of
the screen.

Back

Forward

Refresh Page/Stop Page Loading

Connect

Smartfit/Wrap Content

Show Frame

Enter Address or Choose Bookmark

Auto-Cruise

Tap Mode

Most of the functions are similar to the functions on your desktop Web browser. Handheld-specific functions include the following:

- **Smartfit/Wrap Content:** Tapping this icon toggles the screen's word wrap between three modes that attempt to better fit the Web site to the CLIÉ's small screen in an effort to avoid the need to scroll sideways. This function is available only in NetFront 3.1, the newest version.

- **Show Frame:** On pages with multiple frames, you can use this to display a frame with the full screen.

- **Auto-Cruise:** Tap this icon to automatically download all the Web pages that are bookmarked in a particular category.

- **Tap Mode:** By default, tapping the screen highlights and selects text, but if you tap this button, you can use the stylus to drag the screen around to scroll it.

Although you can find hundreds of Web sites optimized for handheld browsing, NetFront lets you browse most desktop Web sites without difficulty. To get started, just tap the Enter Address icon and enter the address of a site that you want to visit. You might try tapping the Smartfit/Wrap Content icon a few times to check out the various screen-resizing options and find the one that fits your favorite sites.

Instant Messaging and Other Applications

CLIÉ Mail and NetFront are the only online applications that Sony bundled with the CLIÉ, but you don't have to stop there. Dozens of excellent add-on programs are capable of beefing up the CLIÉ's Internet suite.

The most egregious omission in the CLIÉ's online repertoire is an instant messaging (IM) client. But fear not: IM addicts can keep connected on their CLIÉs with a couple excellent applications:

- **AIM for Palm OS:** This is a handheld version of AOL Instant Messenger (AIM) for America Online. It's a basic but nice chat program, and it's one of the first programs for the Palm OS that actually runs in the background. You can start AIM, switch to another application to do some work, and then re-launch AIM to catch any IMs that you missed. Alas, although the program used to be free, AOL has started charging about $20 for it without improving it, which makes the more powerful VeriChat an attractive alternative. You can find the AIM software at `anywhere.aol.com/pda`.

- **VeriChat:** VeriChat is a unified IM client that supports not only AOL, but also MSN, ICQ, and Yahoo! chat networks. As with AIM, you can stay online while working in other applications and jump back into VeriChat to check your messages. It's $24.95 for the first year and $19.95 per year after that, but it's worth it if you depend on IM to stay in touch. This is the best handheld chat program that I've tried on any platform. For more information, check out `www.pdaapps.com`.

On the e-mail front, CLIÉ Mail is an excellent application, but its lack of support for HTML-formatted e-mails is becoming more and more troublesome as those become common in online correspondence. Here are two great alternatives to CLIÉ Mail:

- **Eudora Internet Suite:** The Eudora for Palm program included here is fairly basic — it doesn't support attachments or graphics. It does support multiple accounts and HTML e-mail, and it can synchronize with your desktop e-mail program just like CLIÉ Mail. Best of all, it's free at `www.eudora.com/internetsuite`.

- **SnapperMail:** The king of all Palm OS e-mail programs, SnapperMail supports both POP3 (common with personal accounts) and IMAP (often used by businesses) e-mail standards, encrypted e-mail using Secure

Sockets Layer (SSL) technology, and HTML-formatted messages. It also has full-blown attachment support, with the ability to attach or download any file that you can save on a Memory Stick, not just multimedia files like CLIÉ Mail. The program does lack the ability to transfer e-mail during a HotSync, but it's the perfect e-mail companion if you have a wireless connection. Check it out at www.snappermail.com.

Finally, alternative Web browsers are available. If your CLIÉ came with NetFront, you're set for most Web sites. Unfortunately, NetFront isn't offered separately, so if your CLIÉ didn't include the program, check out one of the following alternative browsers:

✔ **AvantGo:** This superb program is actually designed to let you download Web pages by using your desktop system so you can view them on the go without having to connect to the Internet. However, it also works when you're connected to the Internet, providing basic wireless Web browsing capabilities with full color and high-resolution support. Even if you have NetFront, check out AvantGo for its offline browsing capabilities. Visit www.avantgo.com for info.

✔ **WebToGo Mobile Internet:** This is actually a suite of Internet applications that also includes an e-mail client. It offers very fast downloads, and it reformats pages for the screen. However, pages pass through a proxy server in order to be reformatted, so corporate users concerned about security won't find it appropriate. For more information, see www.webtogo.de.

✔ **PocketLink:** This basic Web browser doesn't use proxies and offers encryption on Palm OS 5.2 CLIÉs, so it's more appropriate for accessing corporate information. It has full support for CLIÉ high-resolution screens and for using the jog dial to navigate pages. See www.mdevelop.com for more information.

Chapter 17

CLIÉ, the Ultimate Travel Companion

● ●

In This Chapter

▶ Add-on keyboards

▶ Modems and communications

▶ GPS modules

▶ Vital travel accessories

● ●

*W*hen you see the ultimate CLIÉ travel kit and what it can do, it's not hard to imagine this exchange taking place. . . .

"Ah, good, you're here, 007. I have your laptop replacement ready. The entire kit fits in a large coat pocket, yet it offers wireless Internet access, a folding keyboard, the ability to create and edit Office files, voice-prompted GPS navigation, a week of battery life, international recharging, and a stylus that fires tranquilizer darts."

Except for the tranquilizer-dart stylus, you don't need to be James Bond to put together a powerful, pocket-sized computing toolkit. In this chapter, you find the must-have add-ons for the savvy traveler. The products that I mention here will have you ready for all but the most intensive business and personal trips alike.

I've gotten into the habit of packing my CLIÉ and about a pound of accessories on most trips, and the laptop gets left at home. With a CLIÉ and an add-on keyboard, I can write articles, check data in spreadsheets, process my e-mail, get restaurant recommendations and directions, listen to MP3s or watch videos while traveling on a plane, navigate in strange cities, and play games when I have some down time. The only time that I feel the need to bring along the full-sized laptop is when I know I'll be doing a lot of Web browsing. The CLIÉ's small screen is fine for doing quick information lookups, but the cramped handheld views on Web pages aren't so good for extended research sessions or reading message boards.

Without further ado, take a look at the essentials for the well-equipped CLIÉ road warrior.

Folding Keyboards

The stylus and the little thumb keyboards that are built into some CLIÉs are fine for entering short bits of data: addresses, brief e-mails, notes from a meeting, and so on. But try to write a six-page report for your boss with either option, and chances are your hand will hate your brain for putting it through that.

Luckily, a few excellent keyboard solutions are available for the CLIÉ line. In addition to the models listed here, you can find some CLIÉ-compatible infrared keyboards from Targus, Belkin, and other companies. Don't be tempted by the low prices or easy availability of other models. I've tried them all, and the models not listed here all have various driver, ergonomic, or other problems, and they can't compare to the following three excellent choices:

- **CLIÉ PEGA-KB100:** Sony's official folding keyboard works with all CLIÉs released in the past few years except for the UX-series units, which lack the HotSync port that the keyboard plugs into, and the PEG-NZ90, which places its HotSync port halfway up the back of the unit. This sleek, silver unit, shown in Figure 17-1, has an excellent feel and a superb layout. It's a bit small, but with a little practice, you can touch-type at full speed. The only downside is the lack of OK, Cancel, and New function keys, which means that you still find yourself reaching for your stylus fairly often. It's available at `www.sonystyle.com/clie`.

- **Stowaway XT:** The Think Outside Stowaway XT folding keyboard, marketed by Fellowes, is the slimmest, most compact PDA keyboard around. It has a fantastic feel, amazing portability, and a center fold that locks solidly so that you can use it on your lap. The one downside is that it lacks a number-key row, so you must use a function-shift key to enter numerals. This slim keyboard, shown in Figure 17-2, works with all CLIÉs except for the NZ and UX series and is a superb choice if you don't type a ton of numbers. It's available at `www.thinkoutside.com`.

Figure 17-1:
Sony's
PEGA-
KB100
keyboard.

Figure 17-2:
The
Stowaway
XT is
compact
but lacks
a number-
key row.

✔ **Stowaway:** If you're going to be typing on a solid, flat surface, and you don't mind a slightly thicker package when the keyboard is folded, consider the original Stowaway. Although it doesn't lock open, it offers a larger typing area that's exactly the same size as a typical laptop keyboard, complete with a standard number-key row. When folded, it's not much larger than your CLIÉ. For sheer typing comfort and potential input speed, the original Stowaway, shown in Figure 17-3, is the best keyboard for the CLIÉ. It works with the same models as the Stowaway XT and is available from www.thinkoutside.com.

✔ **Stowaway Wireless:** I saved the best for last. This versatile keyboard, shown in Figure 17-4, looks just like the Stowaway XT — and has the same unfortunate lack of a dedicated number-key row — but instead of connecting to the HotSync connector, it uses an infrared (IR) transmitter to communicate with the CLIÉ through its IR port. This means that it works with all CLIÉ models — even the UX- and NZ-series units. Not only that, it also works with other Palm OS and Pocket PC units. This is great news for multi-PDA families, and it means that you can continue to use the keyboard should you someday (gasp) switch to a non-CLIÉ PDA. It's available from www.thinkoutside.com.

Figure 17-3: The original Stowaway folds into a compact package and unfolds to full laptop keyboard size.

Figure 17-4:
The
Stowaway
wireless
uses
infrared
technology
and thus
works with
virtually all
CLIÉs and
other PDAs.

Modems and Communications

If you have a CLIÉ with built-in Wi-Fi, or you have a digital cell phone that can connect by cable or Bluetooth to your PDA, you're all set to browse the Web to your heart's content. If you're not so lucky — and you find e-mail more addictive than caffeine or computer games — you probably want some way to connect online. Here are a couple devices that can connect wireless-challenged CLIÉs to the outside world:

✔ **Infrared modem:** If you often find yourself in hotels without wireless access, an old-fashioned dial-up modem can be a sanity saver. Sony no longer markets a clip-on modem for the CLIÉ line, but 3JTech has an excellent solution: a modem that connects to your CLIÉ by using the infrared port. You can use their Pegasus III modem, shown in Figure 17-5, with any PDA or laptop that has an infrared port. It can work off batteries or wall power and supports speeds up to 56 Kbps. An optional add-on Bluetooth module is available for it. You can find it at www. pocketirmodem.com.

Figure 17-5:
The
Pegasus III
modem
connects to
your CLIÉ by
using the
infrared
port.

✔ **Bluetooth modem:** Although similar to the 3JTech dial-up modem offering, the Socket's Cordless 56K Modem with Bluetooth Wireless Technology shown in Figure 17-6 uses, you guessed it, Bluetooth wireless technology instead of infrared to communicate with your CLIÉ. The advantages over IR are that you can use your CLIÉ with the modem while it's mounted on a portable keyboard (even an IR keyboard, which is impossible to use with the 3JTech model) and up to 30 feet away from the modem. It's available from www.socketcom.com.

✔ **Wi-Fi Memory Stick:** If you have a CLIÉ that lacks built-in Wi-Fi and doesn't have a slot for Sony's CompactFlash Wi-Fi card, you're not out of luck. Hagiwara Sys-Com has released a Wi-Fi card in the form of a Memory Stick card that works with all Palm OS 5 CLIÉ models. (See Figure 17-7.) It includes excellent driver software that lists available Wi-Fi access points. It's available from www.hsc-us.com.

Figure 17-6:
Socket's
Cordless
56K modem
uses
Bluetooth to
commu-
nicate with
the CLIÉ.

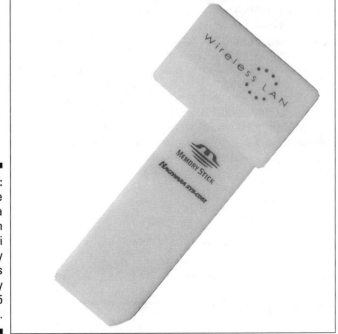

Figure 17-7:
The
Hagiwara
Sys-Com
Wi-Fi
Memory
Stick works
with any
Palm OS 5
CLIÉ.

GPS Modules

When traveling to a new city, a GPS navigator makes the best companion. These devices utilize the constellation of Global Positioning System (GPS) satellites that the U.S. Air Force is kind enough to share so that you can pinpoint your position within just feet on a map. If it weren't for a PDA GPS, I'm convinced that my wife and I would still be lost in Munich, Germany, three years after our trip there started.

A couple excellent GPS solutions exist for the CLIÉ. If your CLIÉ is equipped with Bluetooth, a Bluetooth GPS is an excellent solution because it does away with connecting cables and lets you place the GPS receiver on your dashboard while using the CLIÉ anywhere else in the car. Otherwise, a cabled solution is a little more cumbersome but still beats the heck out driving around the Mittlerer Ring in Munich 11 times.

Check out the following GPS options:

- **Mapopolis Navigator:** The first serious GPS navigation program for the Palm OS has been greatly enhanced for Palm OS 5. The new version issues spoken prompts for every turn and can automatically reroute you if you get off the planned route. Mapopolis offers GPS receivers that plug into your CLIÉ's HotSync port, as well as a Bluetooth model. See www.mapopolis.com for more info.

- **Navman GPS 4460:** The most advanced GPS solution available for the CLIÉ, the Navman 4460, shown in Figure 17-8, offers all the most advanced navigation features: on-the-fly rerouting, address-to-address map planning, the ability to program favorite routes and destinations, lists of attractions in the area, and voice-guided navigation. But what makes it really cool is the 3D map perspective. This isn't just a gimmick; it really does help you keep track of the direction that you're traveling when you can afford only a quick glance at the screen while stopped at a traffic light. The GPS connects to your CLIÉ by using Bluetooth wireless communication. Check out www.navman.com for more details.

Figure 17-8:
The Navman 4460 GPS module communicates with the CLIÉ by using Bluetooth wireless technology.

Other Essentials

Make sure to pack few other goodies in your travel kit:

- ✔ **Charging kit and/or backup batteries:** You don't want your CLIÉ to poop out because it ran out of power halfway through a trip. Be sure to bring along a charger. Wall chargers are good, but battery power chargers are an excellent option if you plan to use the CLIÉ while you're away from AC plugs. I take a look at power options in Chapter 20.

- ✔ **Plug adapters:** If you're heading to a foreign country, don't forget a plug adapter for your CLIÉ's charging brick. The good news is that the CLIÉ includes a universal power supply, so you don't need a voltage converter. A basic plug adapter that costs just a few bucks will do.

- ✔ **Memory Stick and Backup software:** Before you hit the road, make a backup of your CLIÉ's contents. (See Chapter 19 for details on how.) And keep making backups while you travel. The last thing that you want to do is lose all your data when you're 500 miles away from your HotSync cable.

✔ **Protection for your CLIÉ and accessories:** Pack a case to keep all your CLIÉ materials together and to protect it in your luggage. Of course, pack your CLIÉ in a briefcase or carry-on for easy access and for security reasons.

✔ **Your CLIÉ's Installation CD and a HotSync cable:** If you're going to be near a computer while you're on the road, you never know whether you might want to download and install a new program, use a full-sized computer to enter some data, or so on. Pack these, and your PDA can be friendly with strange computers.

✔ **Headphones:** If you're going to listen to music or watch videos, chances are that the guy in the seat next to you might not want to share the experience of your Weird Al Yankovic MP3s.

Part VI
Securing and Protecting Your CLIÉ

The 5th Wave   By Rich Tennant

"Well, here's what happened—I forgot to put it on my 'To Do' List."

In this part . . .

Some disasters you just can't protect against. Such catastrophes include earthquakes, flash floods, and toddlers who think it'd be fun to see what a CLIÉ looks like dipped in yogurt. However, you can do at least some preparation for more common calamities.

In this part, I show you the CLIÉ's security features and how to make backups to protect your data in case of damage or theft. You find out about solutions for keeping your CLIÉ powered on the road and for protecting it from bumps, scratches, and (hopefully) drops.

Chapter 18

Protect Your CLIÉ's Data

● ●

In This Chapter

▶ Setting a password

▶ Locking your CLIÉ

▶ Hiding private records

▶ Protecting desktop data

▶ Using industrial-strength security

● ●

*I*f you've taken advantage of the advice laid out in previous chapters of this book, your CLIÉ very likely contains everything from contact information to photos of the kids to your spending records.

This is wonderfully handy. But it also means that anyone who picks up your CLIÉ has access to all your business contacts, your financial transactions, and a series of pictures of you dressed as Captain Feathersword at your son's second birthday party . . . not to mention your To Do list, which includes the entry Rent *Gigli*. This is not information that you want falling into the wrong hands.

Luckily, the Palm OS includes security features that let you completely lock access to your CLIÉ — no password, no access. As an added layer of security, you can choose to hide or mask only specific records, thus keeping your important data (and your taste in films) safe and private.

Setting Your Password

To get started, tap the Security icon in the Program Launcher. The screen shown in Figure 18-1 appears.

Figure 18-1:
The Security
application
lets you set
your CLIÉ's
system
password.

The first thing that you need to do is select a password. The usual password caveats apply here. Don't choose something too obvious, like *password, 123,* or your own name. The best passwords are composed of a series of random characters, but because your password needs to be something that you can remember, *da5r340* might not be the way to go.

Keep in mind that you enter this password with the stylus (unless your CLIÉ has a built-in keyboard), so you probably want to keep it fairly short. Also, avoid difficult Graffiti characters: If you have problems drawing a *k* that your handheld can consistently recognize, *kooky1* isn't a good password.

When you decide on a password, use the following steps to set up your CLIÉ's security feature:

1. **Tap in the Password text box — where it says Unassigned.**

   The Password screen appears, as shown in Figure 18-2.

2. **Enter your password on the appropriate line.**

   Below the password-entry line is a Hint field. In this field, enter a clue that will jog your memory if you forget your password. For example, if you choose your first pet's name as your password, enter **first kitty** in the Hint field. Your CLIÉ displays this hint when anyone enters an incorrect password.

3. **Tap OK. The Password confirmation screen shows your hint and asks you to confirm the password.**

   Just re-enter your password. The CLIÉ is making sure that you didn't make a typo.

On the Password confirmation screen, note the warning that alerts you that any private records will be deleted if you select the Lost Password option later on. Though it sounds ominous, don't worry. You probably haven't yet marked any records as Private, and even if you do have to use the Lost Password option later, you can restore the deleted records by HotSyncing.

```
         ┌──────────────────────────────┐
         │          Password            │
         │ Enter a password:            │
         │ rosebud3                     │
         │ ────────────────────────     │
         │                              │
         │ Hint:                        │
         │ sled                         │
         │ ────────────────────────     │
         │ If you assign a password, you│
         │ must enter it to show private│
         │ records.                     │
         │                              │
         │  ( OK )   ( Cancel )         │
         └──────────────────────────────┘
```

Figure 18-2:
Including a
hint can
help remind
you of your
password.

4. **Tap OK again to return to the main Security screen. (Refer to Figure 18-1.)**

   Your password is now set, but until you select your privacy and lock settings, your data is still unprotected.

If you'd like to try entering your password now, tap the Lock & Turn Off button. After you tap the Off & Lock button on the System Lockout screen that follows, the CLIÉ powers off. The next time you turn it on, it requires the password before you can use the device.

Any time the CLIÉ prompts you for a password, you can tap the little a icon at the bottom of the writing area and use the on-screen keyboard to enter your password.

Locking Your CLIÉ

The best way to keep your personal information away from prying eyes is to set your PDA so that it's locked at power-up, which means that the only way to access its contents is to enter the password at startup. The only way that someone could access the device without the password is to perform a *hard reset* — which erases all its contents, keeping your data out of nefarious hands.

To activate the power-up password, first tap the Security icon in the Program Launcher to access the Security application. (Refer to Figure 18-1.) Be sure that you've set a password. (See the previous section.) Tap the Auto Lock Handheld text box — the default text there is Never. After entering your password, you're taken to the Lock Handheld screen (as shown in Figure 18-3), which offers you four options:

✔ **Never:** This is the default setting. It lets you turn on your handheld and start using it immediately without entering a password.

✔ **On Power Off:** Whenever you turn off your CLIÉ, or if it shuts down automatically after a period of inactivity, it locks. You need to enter your password every time you turn it back on.

✔ **At a Preset Time:** This setting is useful primarily if you keep your CLIÉ with you all day but leave it on a desk at the end of the workday. You can set the PDA to lock at a particular time of day so that, for instance, anyone turning the device on after 5 p.m. has to enter the password.

✔ **After a Preset Delay:** This is the best compromise between safety and convenience. You can set the handheld to lock after a set number of minutes or hours. You need to enter your password only if you haven't used the CLIÉ for a while. Set it for, say, 15 minutes, and you can turn the device on and off to look up information without hassling with the password, but it locks soon after you stop using it. With the time set at 15 minutes, you never have to enter the password more than three times in an hour.

Figure 18-3:
The CLIÉ offers several password lock options.

Note that locking the CLIÉ protects only the contents of the PDA itself, not the Memory Stick expansion card. A dastardly villain (or nosy co-worker) could easily remove the Memory Stick from your handheld, place it in another CLIÉ or a PC card reader, and view the contents. If you want to protect the data on your expansion card as well, be sure to check out one of the third-party encryption programs that I discuss at the end of this chapter in the section "Industrial-Strength Security."

Personalize your password screen

When the CLIÉ requests a password on power-up, it also displays the device's owner information, if it's present, as you can see in the following figure. Entering your name, e-mail address, and telephone number — and possibly an offer of a reward, as well — gives you a much better chance of recovering a lost CLIÉ. To set your owner information, tap the Prefs icon in the Program Launcher. Then choose Owner from the menu at the top-right of the screen. Enter your personal information on the Owner information screen that follows. Note that the System Lockout screen shows only the first three lines of owner information without scrolling, so put the important contact info there, where it's sure to be seen even by someone unfamiliar with operating a CLIÉ.

Hiding Private Records

Rather than locking access to your entire handheld, you can use the privacy settings to simply hide or mask the data that you don't want others to see. (You can lock your CLIÉ as well, doubling your protection.)

Private records are available in the standard organizer applications (Address Book, To Do, and so on), as well as in some third-party programs.

Private records aren't highly secure. Casual users can't access them, but knowledgeable hackers can get to them relatively easily. For information that truly, vitally needs to be kept from prying eyes, such as confidential business data, you should look into a third-party security application. I cover such applications at the end of this chapter in the section "Industrial-Strength Security."

To set the privacy level, tap the Security icon in your CLIÉ's Program Launcher to launch the Security application. (Refer to Figure 18-1.) Near the bottom of the screen, you see Current Privacy, with a pop-up selection menu. Choose one of these options:

✔ **Show Records:** The default option, which shows all your data.

✔ **Mask Records:** Obscures any private records with a gray bar and places a lock icon next to them, as shown in the top half of Figure 18-4. That way, you know that more data is there, but you need to enter your password to actually view the records.

✔ **Hide Records:** Hides private records completely. They aren't visible at all until you change your security settings to show private records.

Figure 18-4:
Masked records are covered by a gray bar and indicated by a lock icon.

Which option should you choose? Masking is a bit more convenient because it reminds you that some records are hidden, and you can simply tap a masked record to bring up the password prompt and reveal the obscured data. If you choose to hide the records completely, you could very well forget that they're there. To reveal hidden records, tap the Menu soft button to access the Options menu in your application, choose Security, and change the setting to Show Records.

If you hide a record, it doesn't show up when you use the Find command. If you're, say, looking for all your contacts who live in a certain ZIP code, you want to be sure to set security to Show Records before searching.

To flag an individual record as private in one of the built-in information manager applications, edit a record, tap the Details button, and select the Private check box in the Details settings, as shown in Figure 18-5. See Chapters 3 through 6 for more information on how to edit records in the information manager applications..

Figure 18-5:
You flag
records as
Private by
using the
Details
settings in
the CLIÉ
organizer
applications.

Defend Your Desktop Data

If you've chosen to hide or mask records on your handheld, they're also password-protected in the Sony Palm Desktop and CLIÉ Organizer applications on your desktop system. Note that you can change the display between Hide Records and Mask Records without the password — this doesn't give snoopers a look at your hidden data, but it lets them know that you're hiding something.

Just as you can lock access to your handheld, you can require a password to access your desktop organizer data as well, as shown in Figure 18-6. In the Sony Palm Desktop application on your desktop system, choose Tools⇨ Options from the menu bar, and then click the Security tab. Finally, select the Require Password to Access the Palm Desktop Data check box. This is a per-user setting, so if someone else also HotSyncs a Palm OS handheld with your desktop system, changing this setting doesn't affect the other CLIÉ's security. In CLIÉ Organizer, you can find the check box under the Tools⇨Options menu.

Note that desktop security works only if you're HotSyncing with the Sony Palm Desktop or CLIÉ Organizer applications. If you're HotSyncing Microsoft Outlook, all your private or masked records are visible on the desktop computer. In this case, you want to be sure to use the Windows security and password features to ensure that prying eyes can't access your Outlook data, because Outlook itself doesn't hide individual records.

Figure 18-6:
Private and
masked
records are
hidden
under Palm
Desktop,
but not if
you use
Microsoft
Outlook.

Industrial-Strength Security

The CLIÉ's built-in security is fine for casual use, but if you're keeping truly sensitive data, such as company financial information, a private client list, or the location of your weapons of mass destruction on your handheld, you want to consider using an add-on application that offers advanced security features and industrial-level data encryption. Here are a few of the top choices.

PDA Defense

Hearing a program's publisher brag that its product is used by all branches of the military, by the FBI, and in the White House should give you a feeling of security. PDA Defense offers 128-bit encryption of data files created by both built-in and add-on applications. It protects data on expansion cards and can even be set to make your data self-destruct if someone tries the wrong password too many times. My favorite feature is the ability to use a combination of button presses in place of standard password entry — still secure, but much faster. Figure 18-7 shows the Activation, Bomb, and Owner setting options. For more information, visit www.pdadefense.com.

Figure 18-7:
If PDA
Defense is
secure
enough for
the White
House, it's
likely secure
enough for
your needs.

PDADefense Options

Activation:
☑ Lock on power-off   ☑ Smart
☑ If off more than ▼ 2 min

Bomb:
☑ Attempts limit ▼ 5
☑ If not synced 30 days ▼ 2 hours

Owner:
☑ Show owner information
☐ Stealth mode

(OK) (Encryption...) (Buttons...)

TealLock

TealLock offers a feature set similar to that of PDA Defense, including the ability to encrypt expansion cards and to destroy data if too many attempts are made to guess a password. Among its unique features are the ability to put an image on the lock screen (handy as a password hint, or just another excuse to see your baby pictures) and the ability to set guest passwords that offer limited data access. Figure 18-8 shows the lock screen. If you're using your handheld in a medical environment, TealLock is compliant with United States Health Insurance Portability and Accountability Act (HIPAA) privacy regulations. For more information, visit www.tealpoint.com.

Fri Aug 22, 2003 4:46 pm

rosebud

(OK) Show Mask Hide

Figure 18-8:
TealLock
lets you use
a picture as
a password
hint.

Cloak

Rather than providing security for your entire CLIÉ, the Chapura Cloak software, shown in Figure 18-9, acts as an electronic safe where you can store critical but private information, such as credit card numbers, personal identification numbers (PINs), passwords, and other personal data. Cloak has preset forms for data such as credit card and bank accounts, and you can create your own custom fields as well. It also offers a Windows companion program that keeps your data private on your desktop system. Cloak offers top-notch security without adding any password hassles to your day-to-day PDA use. For more information, visit www.chapura.com.

Figure 18-9:
Cloak is a repository for your important private data.

Chapter 19

Backups: As Vital to Your Day as a Good Breakfast

*Y*our CLIÉ has become a trusty companion — the Andy Richter to your Conan O'Brien. And just as Sir Edmund Hillary wouldn't want to find himself climbing Mount Everest without the Sherpa mountaineer Tenzing Norgay, you don't want to find yourself far from home without the information that's stored in your CLIÉ.

But what if disaster strikes? A dead battery or severe system crash can wipe your CLIÉ's memory clean, leaving you in the lurch without any of the information that you depend on. More horrifying still is the thought of a lost, stolen, or broken CLIÉ. Even if you scrounge up a replacement unit on the road, without a backup you're left staring at an empty screen.

Memory Stick to the Rescue

In the early days of PDAs, a lost, stolen, or broken unit could be a real problem. But every CLIÉ ships with a Memory Stick expansion slot, so CLIÉ owners can hit the road with no worries. You can easily create regular backups of the information contained on your handheld on a Memory Stick — shown in Figure 19-1— secure in the knowledge that your backup can be easily restored to the unit if something goes awry. And thanks to falling Memory Stick prices, you could even bring along an extra Memory Stick with an emergency backup in case something irreparable happens to your CLIÉ or its Memory Stick.

Figure 19-1:
An extra
Memory
Stick just for
backups
can be a
life-saver if
your CLIÉ is
lost or
stolen.

As much as the technology writer in me cringes to even suggest such a stone-knives-and-bearskins approach, the best way to truly ensure that your vital information is available when you're on the road is to use the Print function in the Sony Palm Desktop software to print a copy of your schedule and your vital contacts. In all my years of PDA usage, I've had to fall back on this only once — when a battery inexplicably wouldn't recharge — but it was a life-saver.

Your CLIÉ's contents are backed up to your desktop system each time you HotSync. If your CLIÉ's memory is wiped clean after a crash or battery problem, you can simply HotSync the handheld again to restore all its contents. Of course, this doesn't help you when you're in Seattle and your home desktop system is in Baltimore, which is why we're looking at other backup options.

Choose Your Backup Weapon

Most CLIÉ models include a built-in backup program called MS Backup, which is shorthand for *Memory Stick Backup*. (The PEG-UX40 and PEG-UX50 models use a different backup method.) This simple program lets you back up the entire contents of your CLIÉ on a Memory Stick with just a few taps of the stylus. Restoring the contents of your CLIÉ is just as easy. And because MS Backup is built in, you don't have to reinstall it to restore your data after a crash.

Some newer CLIÉ models, such as the PEG-UX40 and PEG-UX50 (shown in Figure 19-2), actually contain dedicated backup memory designed to protect the contents of your PDA in case the power dies. The backup process is engaged automatically when power gets low; you don't have to run a program to create a backup of your data.

Figure 19-2:
The CLIÉ
PEG-UX50
includes an
additional
16MB of
memory for
emergency
backups.

The CLIÉ is also compatible with the wide variety of third-party backup programs designed for the Palm OS. Even though your CLIÉ probably has built-in backup software, these are still appealing because they offer advanced features such as the ability to restore individual files, to automatically back up your CLIÉ's contents at a specific time of day, and to encrypt backup data in case your Memory Stick falls into the wrong hands.

Working with MS Backup

To access the backup program, tap the Applications soft button to the left of the Graffiti area and then choose MS Backup from the Program Launcher.

The MS Backup screen appears, as shown in Figure 19-3, with a list of existing backups and available slots. The program can keep up to five backups on a single Memory Stick.

You might be asking, "Why create multiple backups?" When installing new programs, you might want to try a new add-on application while you're on the road. However, the add-on application might not play nicely with the other programs on your CLIÉ. If you create one backup before you install the new program and a second backup after installation, you can always revert your CLIÉ to its original configuration if the program that you just installed causes problems. Simply restore the first backup, and the problem program — and the headaches it was causing — will be history.

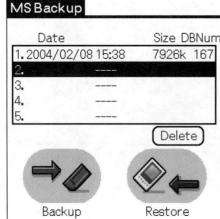

Figure 19-3: Five slots for backups means never having to say, "Oops."

Below the backup list, you find two large buttons, Backup and Restore, as well as a smaller Delete button that's used to eliminate older backups. MS Backup is a simple application; no additional options exist.

Creating a backup

Follow these steps to create a backup of your CLIÉ's contents:

1. Insert a Memory Stick into your CLIÉ's card slot.

You must insert your Memory Stick card before launching MS Backup. (Note that you can insert a Memory Stick with the CLIÉ turned on.) If you launch MS Backup with no card in the slot, the program complains that the card isn't present and sends you back to the Applications screen. Then you have to start up MS Backup all over again after you insert the card.

Remember that you need enough space on your Memory Stick to contain the entire contents of your CLIÉ. If you have 2MB free on a 16MB CLIÉ, you need approximately 14MB of free space on your Memory Stick. MS Backup displays an error message if the Memory Stick doesn't have enough room. To free up space, you can delete old backups or delete application and media files that you no longer need.

MS Backup doesn't support CompactFlash cards. On CLIÉs that also feature CompactFlash slots, such as the PEG-NX73 and PEG-NX80 models, you still must use the Memory Stick slot for backups that you create with MS Backup. If you prefer to use a CompactFlash card, you need to use a third-party backup application.

2. **Tap the Applications soft button to the left of the Graffiti area, and then choose MS Backup from the Program Launcher.**

   The MS Backup screen appears.

3. **In the MS Backup screen, tap to select a backup slot.**

   The MS Backup screen always displays a list of five backup slots at the top of the screen. Tap one of these slots to select it for the backup. A highlight indicates the backup slot that you selected.

   If you have an older backup that you no longer need, you can simply tap its slot and overwrite it by making a new backup. If you want to create an additional backup without deleting existing backups, select an empty slot if one is available.

4. **Tap the Backup button.**

   If you're using a slot that contains an existing backup, MS Backup asks you to confirm whether you want to overwrite it. Tap Yes unless you really *didn't* mean to overwrite an older backup.

5. **The program then displays a pop-up message, shown in Figure 19-4, giving you one last chance to change your mind. Tap OK to start the backup or Cancel to abort it.**

   A progress screen appears, showing you what percentage of the backup is complete. The backup shows up in the slot you chose. You can't name a backup, but the slot shows the date and time you performed the backup.

Figure 19-4:
Because
a backup
can take
a couple
minutes,
MS Backup
asks for
confirmation
before
starting.

Restoring a backup

Now, don't get panicky from all this backup talk. In many years of testing a wide variety of PDAs, I can count on one hand (well, and perhaps a couple of extra fingers) the number of times I've lost my data and had to restore a backup file. But far better to be prepared: You probably don't regularly drive into lamp posts, but you still buy a car with seatbelts and airbags. . . .

In a couple of special situations, you might need to restore a backup file. The obvious case is when you lose all your data due to a power failure or system crash. But on rare occasions, you might need to restore a backup even without losing your data. Perhaps you installed a poorly written add-on program that is causing your CLIÉ to become unstable, perhaps crashing randomly. Or maybe you accidentally deleted your only copy of the picture you took of a UFO landing on your back lawn.

Before restoring a backup to CLIÉ that already contains other data, do a hard reset. (If the term *hard reset* doesn't ring any bells, check out Chapter 2.) This ensures that you don't end up with a mixture of new and old information.

Remember, restoring a backup overwrites any existing files with the same names, possibly with older versions, so be sure that this is really what you want to do.

To restore a backup of your CLIÉ's contents, follow these steps:

1. **Insert the Memory Stick containing the backup files into your CLIÉ's card slot.**

   Remember, Memory Stick Backup launches only if it detects a Memory Stick installed in your CLIÉ.

2. **Tap the Applications soft button to the left of the Graffiti area, and then choose MS Backup from the Program Launcher.**

   The MS Backup screen appears.

3. **In the MS Backup screen, tap the backup file that you want to restore.**

   If you have multiple backups, note that the date is listed for each one. The bottom backup in the list might not be the most recent one, so be sure that you select the right backup. A highlight indicates the backup name that you selected.

4. **Tap the Restore button.**

   A pop-up message asks you to confirm whether you really want to restore all files from the backup.

5. Tap OK.

Because restoring a backup overwrites any changes that you've made since the last backup, MS Backup is cautious and asks you whether you *really, really* want to restore the backup with a Confirm Restore window, shown in Figure 19-5.

6. Tap OK again to indicate that you weren't under the influence of alien mind control and that you do indeed want to restore the backup.

After the restoration is complete, the CLIÉ resets, and you're sent back in time to the point of your last backup. Actually, only your data is sent back, but boy, wouldn't the time-travel thing be a handy feature for future CLIÉs?

Figure 19-5: MS Backup asks for confirmation.

 What if you just want to restore a file or two and not the entire contents of your CLIÉ? You can use CLIÉ Files (see Chapter 14) to copy a single file back to your CLIÉ's main memory. Just navigate with CLIÉ Files to the /Palm/Programs/MSBackup directory and select a backup folder. (They're numbered 0 through 4.) Tap the folder to see a list of files. Select the check boxes next to the files that you wish to restore, tap the Copy button at the bottom of the screen, and finally tap the Handheld button at the very top of the directory list. If another version of the file already exists, you're asked to confirm that you want to overwrite it. Tap the Yes to All button to confirm. To be safe, do a soft reset after restoring individual files. (Chapter 3 has more on soft resets.)

Using the Internal Backup Function

Sony's micro-laptop-style CLIÉ models, the UX40 and UX50, both include 16MB of specialized backup memory designed to protect your data in case your battery dies. That's a great feature, but unfortunately, the CLIÉ creates a backup only when the battery is about to go. If you're meticulous about keeping your battery charged, you might find that your backup dates back to the day you purchased your CLIÉ — that is, it's a backup of an empty device.

However, you can cheat and manually force the CLIÉ to perform an internal backup by using the Power Saving feature, which is actually designed to protect your data in case you put your CLIÉ in storage for a while.

The UX series CLIÉ models don't include the MS Backup application. If you want to create multiple backups or store a backup to Memory Stick, you need a third-party backup program. I suggest a few such programs later in this chapter, in the section "Backups with All the Bells and Whistles."

Performing a manual internal backup

To force your CLIÉ to perform an internal backup, follow this procedure:

1. **Tap the Applications soft button to the left of the Graffiti area and then tap on the Prefs icon in the Program Launcher.**

   The Preferences screen appears.

2. **Tap the menu button in the top-right corner of the screen and select Power Saving.**

   The Power Saving screen appears, as shown in Figure 19-6.

3. **Tap the Turn Off button on the Power Saving screen to shut down your CLIÉ.**

   A pop-up message asks you whether you really want to save a backup and turn off the system.

4. **Tap Yes to start the procedure.**

   The existing backup is overwritten with the current contents of your CLIÉs main memory.

You can now rest assured that your current information is safely protected in crash-proof memory.

Note that the 29MB Internal Media storage area built into the UX-series CLIÉ models is actually flash memory and isn't susceptible to loss from crashes or dead batteries. You don't need to worry about backing it up, but I suggest keeping critical files on Memory Sticks instead — you can still lose the contents of such flash memory if you misplace or damage your CLIÉ, and these files aren't saved to your desktop system during a HotSync.

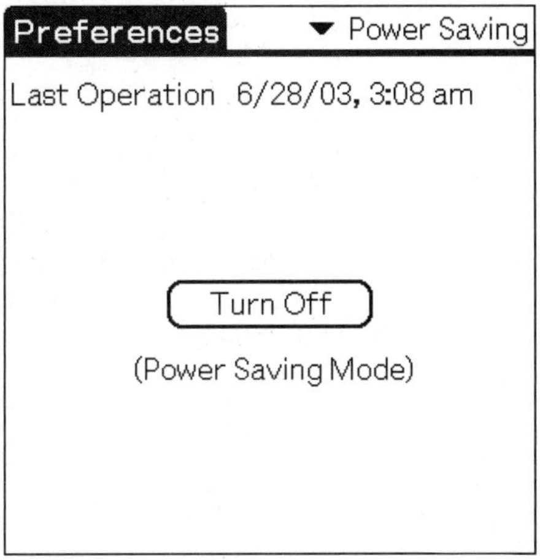

Figure 19-6:
The UX-series handhelds hide their backup command in the Preferences application.

```
┌─────────────────────────────────────────┐
│ Preferences      ▼ Power Saving          │
│ ─────────────────────────────────────── │
│ Last Operation  6/28/03, 3:08 am         │
│                                          │
│                                          │
│                                          │
│            ╭─────────────╮               │
│            │  Turn Off   │               │
│            ╰─────────────╯               │
│          (Power Saving Mode)             │
│                                          │
│                                          │
└─────────────────────────────────────────┘
```

Restoring an internal backup

When turning on your CLIÉ after using the Power Saving function or after performing a hard reset, the CLIÉ asks you whether you want to restore your backup data. The date and time of the backup are shown.

If you've done a HotSync of your CLIÉ more recently than the date of the internal backup, you should select No when it asks you if you want to restore your backup and restore your data by doing a HotSync instead, because your desktop system's backup contains the newest versions of your files. (See Chapter 2 for more on HotSyncing.)

If you tap Yes, a bar indicates the progress of the Restore process, and your CLIÉ resets when the procedure is complete. If you tap No, your CLIÉ becomes a clean slate with nothing stored in its main memory.

Backups with All the Bells and Whistles

A variety of add-on backup programs with additional features is available, such as automatic timed backups. These add-ons are worth checking out just to avoid that sinking feeling after a crash when you realize that you last remembered to back up your CLIÉ's data three months ago. . . .

BackupBuddyVFS

BackupBuddyVFS (shown in Figure 19-7) is the granddaddy of all Palm OS backup programs. It offers basic scheduled backup support, file encryption, and the ability to create a backup every time you turn off the CLIÉ. Perhaps its slickest feature is the program's ability to back up on your Memory Stick any files that you delete, so that you never have to worry about accidentally deleting a file again as long as you make regular backups. For more information, visit www.bluenomad.com.

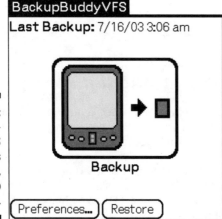

Figure 19-7: Backup-BuddyVFS offers simple, one-tap backups.

BackupMan

Bits 'n Bolts Software's BackupMan, shown in Figure 19-8, is as easy to use as MS Backup, but it boasts of many advanced features despite its low price. It allows you to schedule daily — or even hourly — backups and to trigger a backup each time you HotSync. It even supports restoring individual files. For more information, visit www.bitsnbolts.com.

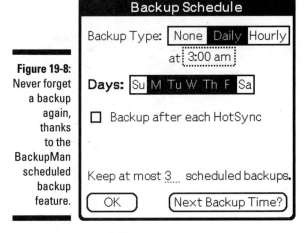

Figure 19-8:
Never forget
a backup
again,
thanks
to the
BackupMan
scheduled
backup
feature.

FlyBackUp

FlyBackUp, shown in Figure 19-9, can protect your backup data from prying eyes by password-encrypting it. FlyBackUp means no more worries about evil agents in black helicopters stealing your Memory Stick and restoring your data to their own CLIÉs to see what you've been up to. The program also compresses your information as it copies to the Memory Stick, which has the double benefit of speeding up your backup and taking up less space on the card. It also offers the usual frills, such as scheduled backups. The downside is that it doesn't let you restore individual files. For more information, visit www.fly-zip.com.

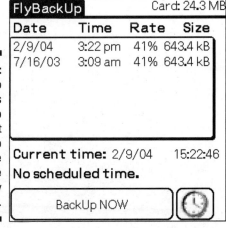

Figure 19-9:
FlyBackUp
compresses
your backup
files so that
they take up
less space
on the
Memory
Stick.

Chapter 20

Power Struggle: Getting the Most from Your CLIÉ's Battery

*W*hether your personal CLIÉ is a basic organizer or is loaded to the gills with options like MP3 players and built-in cameras, one particular component trumps all the others in importance: the battery. Without a battery charge, your CLIÉ is nothing more than a stylish Japanese paperweight that cost you hundreds of dollars.

Though I'm not so bold as to deny that a market for stylish $300 Japanese paperweights exists, I'm guessing that you probably value the CLIÉ's functionality above all else. And to keep it functional, you need to keep your battery charged. On CLIÉ models with virtual Graffiti screens, you can tap the battery icon on the command bar at the bottom of the screen to see how much juice remains. (See Figure 20-1.)

Figure 20-1:
This CLIÉ is
charged
and ready to
hit the road.

Battery Basics

Your first question is probably "What's the proper procedure for charging my battery?" Should you drop the handheld back in its cradle immediately after use or let the battery run down first? Battery technologies have evolved dramatically since the first PDAs were introduced, so some of the advice that you might have received a few years back for maximizing battery life is no longer valid.

The good news is that today you can recharge whenever it's convenient. With modern batteries, charge retention and battery longevity aren't affected by how often you recharge. The lithium-based batteries used in CLIÉs aren't affected by the *memory* issues found in older rechargeable batteries — older rechargeable batteries would lose the ability to hold a full charge if you didn't drain them completely before recharging. Your CLIÉ's batteries perform equally well whether they're charged after just a few minutes' use or after they're almost completely drained.

The lithium polymer batteries that Sony uses are designed for three to five years of overall use. For the most part, you can't alter your usage habits to extend that longevity, though extreme heat can reduce battery capacity over time. (In other words, don't leave your PDA on a car's dashboard or take it with you on your next vacation to the planet Venus.)

What happens if the battery does stop holding its charge after a few years? If your CLIÉ is a PEG-NZ90 (shown in Figure 20-2), you can just buy a new battery, but at the time that this book was written, that was the only CLIÉ with a user-removable battery. If you own any other model, you either need to send the CLIÉ back to Sony and pay to have a replacement battery installed or use battery death as a convenient excuse to upgrade to the latest and greatest new model.

If you're the adventurous techie type, you can replace the battery yourself. (Although the warranty should no longer be any use by the time the battery dies, keep in mind that CLIÉs aren't designed to be opened by the users, and a botched self-repair might give you an excuse to upgrade after all.) GetHighTech (www.gethightech.com), for instance, sells a variety of CLIÉ replacement parts, including batteries for a variety of models. The batteries cost around $40 to $50.

Figure 20-2:
The CLIÉ
PEG-NZ90
is the
only current
model
with a
replaceable
power
source.

Maximizing Battery Life

Although laptop computers typically offer general guidelines on how long their batteries last, such ratings aren't available for your CLIÉ. That's because battery consumption varies dramatically, depending on how you use your PDA. A CLIÉ might last seven or eight hours in light usage, such as looking up addresses or reading eBooks, but might support only three or four hours of playing games or listening to MP3 tunes.

On a day of normal usage, you probably drop the CLIÉ in its cradle after a few hours of use, and battery life typically isn't an issue. But if you're going to be away from your cradle for a while — say, on a long plane flight or an extended business trip — you might want to squeeze a little extra juice out of the battery. Here are a few tips for extending your battery life:

✔ Turn down the screen brightness. Reducing your CLIÉ's brightness level to about 30 percent almost halves the battery drain during basic operations. The screen remains very readable; you're not likely to even notice the difference after a few minutes.

Just tap the little star icon below the Menu soft button in the writing area to bring up the Adjust Brightness slider, shown in Figure 20-3. See Chapter 2 for full details on how to adjust screen settings.

Figure 20-3:
Turning the brightness level down to the lowest comfortable level can greatly improve battery life.

✔ Adjust the Auto-Off After setting, shown in Figure 20-4, from the standard two minutes down to one minute, or even 30 seconds. If you tend to turn on your CLIÉ several times during the day rather than use it for extended sessions, this can do wonders for extending battery life. (You access this setting by tapping the Applications soft button to the left of the Graffiti area, choosing the Prefs icon from the Program Launcher, tapping the menu button at the top-right corner of the screen, and then selecting General Settings.)

✔ Also in the Prefs⇨General settings are a few other adjustments that can give you a little more usage on a charge. Turning sound off when it's not needed helps a little. If you don't expect people to be beaming you business cards and other data via your CLIÉ's infrared (IR) port, turn off the Beam Receive setting. (Don't forget that you turned it off, though, because you might be in for a huge headache the next time someone tries to beam data to you and you can't figure out why your CLIÉ is just sitting there, twiddling its virtual thumbs.)

✔ On MP3-equipped CLIÉs, you can turn off the screen to reduce power when you're just listening to music. Find the Hold slider on the side of your CLIÉ and slide it toward the top of the unit. The screen turns off, but the music continues to play.

Figure 20-4:
Reduce
battery
usage by
setting the
Auto-Off
After option
to 30
seconds
and turning
off Beam
Receive and
sounds.

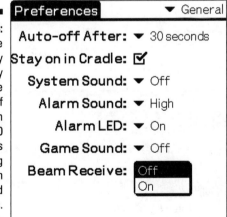

A few CLIÉ models, such as the PEG-UX40/50 and PEG-TH55, use a smart custom Sony processor chip that slows itself down during light usage in order to save power. If you're using an older CLIÉ with a Dragonball processor or a CLIÉ that uses an Intel ARM processor, you can use add-on programs to adjust the processor speed. These are typically designed to speed up your handheld, a process called *overclocking,* but they can also slow it down to increase battery life. If you have an older Dragonball processor-based CLIÉ that runs Palm OS 4, look for Afterburner 3.2. Newer ARM-based CLIÉs can use a program called PXA Clocker, shown in Figure 20-5. Both Afterburner and PXA Clocker can be found at `www.palmgear.com`. Note that adjusting your PDA's clock speed can cause crashes or even overheating, and these programs should be used by only the most tech-savvy users.

Figure 20-5: Techies only! Slowing your CLIÉ with an over-clocking utility can extend battery life, but such programs are very risky.

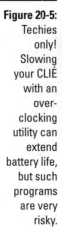
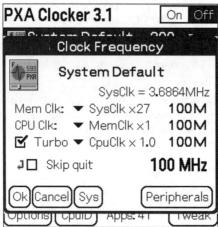

It's dead, Jim. Or is It?

If your CLIÉ appears to be dead and unresponsive, the Hold slider is the first thing you can check. An anonymous relative — who may or may not be known as *mom* — called me to tell me that her CLIÉ PEG-NR70V wouldn't power on even after a full charge. If she hit the power switch or dropped it in the cradle, the screen would flash for a second and then go black. Thinking the worst, our first thought was that we'd have to replace a failed battery. Then she just moved the Hold slider down to the inactive position, and her CLIÉ was as good as new!

If your battery is completely drained, I hope that you either made a backup (see Chapter 19) or HotSynced your CLIÉ recently, because a data drain means that any newly added data has likely been lost. Before you panic, though, drop your CLIÉ in its cradle for a few minutes and then turn it on. The CLIÉ is smart enough to reserve some power to keep the contents of its memory intact when the battery gets very low. When your battery is so drained that the PDA can't even turn on, you typically have a day or so to get it to a charger before data is irrevocably lost.

Charge Anywhere

What can you do when you're far from your cradle, and your charge is running low? Fear not — a wide variety of charging solutions can handle just about any situation. The most flexible is Sony's PEGA-BC10 battery adapter, shown in Figure 20-6. This little gadget holds four AA batteries, which can be used to recharge your CLIÉ literally anywhere. It plugs into the HotSync cradle port, which means it works with all models except for the UX series. If you exhaust your CLIÉ's battery, you can even run the device off the PEGA-BC10 while it recharges your handheld. This is a must-have gadget for the frequent traveler.

If you're on the road with your laptop — or you're visiting a location where you know that a computer is available — one of the least expensive and most portable charging solutions is a USB sync-and-charge cable. These cables use the voltage that's normally used to power USB peripherals (such as mouses and Webcams) to top off your CLIÉ's battery. Note that the USB cables included with some CLIÉ models are simply synchronization cables and don't charge the unit unless you have the power brick plugged in as well. A number of third-party companies offer dual-purpose cables. Incipio Technologies (www.incipiodirect.com), for instance, offers USB Sync-n-Charge cables for a wide variety of handheld models.

A couple of caveats apply to USB charging. First, some notebook computers have a particularly wimpy voltage level on their USB ports, making for extremely long charge times. This situation is getting better — it's not a problem with newer laptops — but you should be sure to try a charge before hitting the road. Even USB ports that supply optimal voltage don't charge your handheld as quickly as your cradle does.

Figure 20-6:
The PEGA-BC10 can charge your CLIÉ with a set of standard AA batteries.

USB charging cables can be made even more versatile with the addition of USB-to-AC or -DC adapters. Cables Unlimited (www.ziplinq.com), for example, sells adapters that let you plug a USB charging cable into an AC wall plug or a DC cigarette-lighter socket.

If you typically travel with a notebook computer, your CLIÉ, and a cell phone, iGo (www.igo.com) has the ultimate charging solution. A little device they call the Juice replaces your notebook's power brick and lets you plug in to wall sockets, as well as car and airplane charging ports. What makes the Juice power brick truly unique is its Peripheral Powering System (PPS) — a second port that allows you to simultaneously recharge two devices. (PPS cables are available for most major handhelds and phones for about $20 each.) Instead of hauling a laptop charger and a pair of power bricks for your CLIÉ and cell phone, simply bring along the Juice and the appropriate PPS cables in the handy included travel case.

Laptops for Less (www.pdainternalbattery.com) sells replacements for built-in handheld batteries, as well as innovative external solutions. The PDA External battery is a rechargeable external battery about the size and shape of a stick of butter. It's available for a variety of handhelds, but for the CLIÉ, you want the PR2-CLIÉ model. It offers 3500mAh of external battery power, which is more than triple the capacity of most built-in PDA batteries.

If you have patience (and you don't live in Seattle or a similarly gloomy place), you can even get a solar charger for your CLIÉ. The Aurora Solar (www.aurorasolar.com) POCKET-PAL Solar Charger ($49.95 for the charger plus $4 for PDA adapter) can recharge both PDAs and cell phones. Note that you need a sunny day and plenty of time — a typical handheld requires most of a day to fully recharge. For extended camping trips or safaris, though, this might be just the ticket.

Finally, INSTANT POWER (www.instant-power.com) offers an unusual but popular emergency charger that uses disposable zinc-air batteries that can recharge a typical CLIÉ approximately three times. (See Figure 20-7.) After you buy a full kit that includes the SmartCord adapter for your handheld, you can easily purchase replacement cartridges at a nearby Radio Shack. The company also offers the 2in1 kit, which charges by using the zinc-air battery, car cigarette lighter, or your desktop computer's USB port. If you just can't get enough of charging, check out the 3in1 kit, which adds a wall charger to the 2in1 mix.

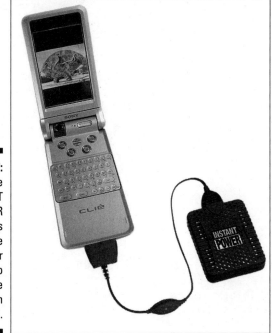

Figure 20-7:
The
INSTANT
POWER
system uses
disposable
zinc-air
batteries to
recharge
your CLIÉ in
the field.

Chapter 21

Caring for Your CLIÉ

*Y*ou spend $400 bucks on a nice piece of jewelry for your spouse. When it's not being worn, it's safely locked away in the jewelry box. You blow a couple hundred dollars on a top-quality, progressive-scan DVD player and set it up on a high shelf where the kids can't get near it. Your CLIÉ is probably jealous of this treatment. Here it is, a fancy, stylish, high-end piece of consumer electronics, and it's tossed on your desk among piles of papers, thrown into briefcases and purses, and even made to suffer the indignity of being carried around in your pants pocket.

Treat your CLIÉ like the faithful companion that it is by keeping its screen and case clean and safe, and it will continue to serve you well. And beware of the toddlers. I don't ever again want to hear a story about a toddler who thought it would be cool to fill a PDA's HotSync port with cake icing. . . .

For the times when something does go awry, I show you the places to get help at the end of this chapter.

Want to see some really scary stories about what can happen to your PDA if you're not careful? Visit the Palm Graveyard at www.palminfocenter.com/graveyard.asp, where you can read such frightening tales as "On Palms and Skateboarding," "Flushed at 30,000 Feet," and the gut-wrenching "5-Wood Meets CLIÉ." (Figure 21-1 highlights another spine-tingling tale.)

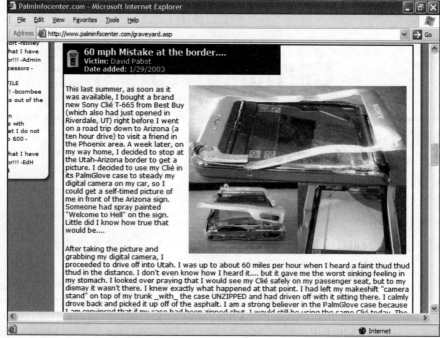

Figure 21-1: The Palm Graveyard features a number of sadly deceased CLIÉs.

Screen Savers

When I say *screen saver,* I'm not talking about the rotating cubes and star fields that you see on your desktop system monitor, but products designed for keeping your CLIÉ's screen safe from damage. A tiny little scratch might not affect your ability to see what's happening on the screen, but it could affect your ability to tap a particular spot on the screen — which can be annoying in some instances and a serious problem if that scratch happens to be in the writing area.

Besides the obvious advice — be careful when using your stylus, and use *only* a stylus designed for PDA use — you can do other things to protect your screen. Creating *screen protectors* (clear film covers for handhelds) is actually quite an industry. You can see a typical screen protector in Figure 21-2.

When buying a screen protector, be sure to get one that's designed for your particular handheld model rather than a generic screen protector. Screen protectors work best and are most unobtrusive when they're *exactly* the same size as your screen, with no gaps at the edges or problem fits caused by trimming them.

Screen protectors are designed to be transparent and inconspicuous in regular use, but some people see a slight reduction in screen clarity with the extra layer of plastic. If this particular problem plagues you, and you have a handheld with a silk-screen text entry area (Chapter 2 covers the silk-screen area), you can always trim the protector so that it covers just the Graffiti area and not the liquid crystal display (LCD) screen. You'll have a little less protection, but the Graffiti area tends to see the most stylus action and is most crucial to protect.

You can find screen protectors at many stores that sell CLIÉs, but because of the slight differences in screen sizes among models, finding one with a perfect fit can sometimes be hard. In some cases, the screens on various models are identical in size — such as the CLIÉ NR-, NX-, and NZ-series handhelds. When in doubt, check with the vendor. One of the best deals around can be found at www.freescreenprotectors.com. Incipio Technologies offers 12-packs of screen protectors (they do wear out after a while) for just $5 even though the retail value is $19.95. But as you might guess from the name, you can enter the coupon code **FREESP** and get the box of screen protectors for just the cost of shipping. The deal sounds too good to be true, but the folks at Incipio have been around for quite a while and have many satisfied customers.

If you want to save a few bucks, and you don't mind a somewhat less elegant solution, you can substitute Scotch Magic Removable Tape 811, which is a clear tape that's designed to be removed and repositioned. I wouldn't want to cover the entire screen with it (the multiple strips would have annoying seams between them), but the ¾-inch-wide version of the tape is just right for covering the writing area. Be sure to get the 811 tape that you see in Figure 21-3 — standard Scotch tape leaves a nasty glue residue when you remove it from your PDA screen.

What if your CLIÉ's screen is already scratched? If the gouge is deep or annoying enough, you unfortunately need to look at sending your PDA back to Sony for repair. But if the scratch is simply light and annoying, you might be able to polish it out yourself. After trying a wide variety of products, the polish that I've found works best is a silica-based polish that's designed for cleaning ceramic-topped stoves. Used with a very soft cotton cloth and light pressure, you can polish out many minor scratches. Of course, any process like this risks doing more damage, so I don't suggest trying polish out a scratch unless it's bad enough that the alternative is sending the PDA in for repair.

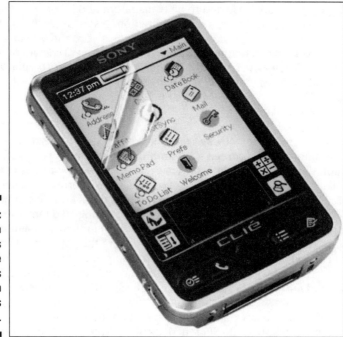

Figure 21-2:
Screen
protectors
can save
your CLIÉ's
display from
scratches
and muck.

Figure 21-3:
Cheap
screen
protection
brought
to you by
Scotch
Removable
Magic Tape.

On the Case

Choosing a case is a matter of how you plan to carry your CLIÉ. Do you plan to toss it in a briefcase? Carry it in your pocket? Snap it onto your belt? Is protection your number-one concern, or style?

You have plenty of choices — many CLIÉs have over a dozen cases available from a variety of third-party manufacturers. Go for classy leather, sleek aluminum, or even a bask-in-my-individualism leopard print.

Do you even need a case at all? If your CLIÉ has solid metal or plastic screen protection (found on the UX and NX series, the PEG-TG50, and the PEG-TH55), you can get by without one because the screen is protected when the cover is closed. You still might want to consider a case, though, to keep the outer shell from getting scratched up or just to add a little additional personalization.

The following are a few things to consider when buying a case:

- **Custom case:** What holds the CLIÉ in the case? Beware of generic case designs that use Velcro to hold your PDA in place. Do you really want to attach an ugly, fuzzy Velcro sticker to the back of your CLIÉ? Look for a custom-fit case that uses straps or a molded design to grip the PDA.

- **Protection:** Are you just looking to protect the CLIÉ from scratches, or do you want basic drop protection as well? For maximum protection, look for a hard case with a soft inner lining.

- **Useful slots:** Some cases have slots for storing Memory Sticks, pens, business cards, etc. If you like to carry extra storage or an additional backup, look for one of these.

- **Travel-readiness:** How do you plan to carry it? If it's going in your pocket, you want the thinnest case possible. (Aluminum cases are a good choice.) If you want to carry it on your belt, a belt loop or clip is a must. If you want to do both, look for a case with a removable belt-clip post.

- **Accessibility:** Does the case give easy access to the HotSync port, headphone jack, jog dial, and all the buttons? You don't want to have to remove your CLIÉ from the case just to look up a phone number.

Dozens of cases are available for the various CLIÉ models. Here are a few of my favorites:

- **Covertec** (www.covertec.com) makes my favorite leather cases. Classy and available in a variety of styles and colors, these cases feature cutouts in all the right places, and they're Velcro-free. (Check out Figure 21-4 for a taste of their offerings.)

- **Krusell** (www.krusell.se) sells quality leather cases with a unique Multidapt attachment system that lets you connect a belt clip, strap, vehicle holder, or other carrying attachment to the case.

✔ **Proporta** (www.proporta.com) offers a wide variety of cases, including slick, thin aluminum cases that boast openings for all the requisite ports and controls. They also sell leather and soft neoprene cases made from the same soft, synthetic rubber used for diving suits. The company even offers a slick, business-card-sized aluminum case for carrying extra Memory Sticks.

Figure 21-4:
Deluxe leather cases like this one from Covertec add both protection and style.

For techies only: Fix it yourself

If you're comfortable digging around inside delicate electronics, you can actually buy the parts to fix obvious problems and repair the unit yourself. I recommend doing this only if your CLIÉ is out of warranty, because if it's not, it *will* be as soon as you crack open the case. One little bit of static electricity can fry the CLIÉ's delicate innards, so home surgery should be performed only if you're willing to accept the chance that you could lose the patient.

If that doesn't scare you, head over to www.pdaparts.com. There you can find replacement batteries, screen glass, jog dials, and other key parts — and most parts are priced at well under $50. The site even offers online guides and videos covering topics such as screen removal and battery replacement.

CLIÉ care do's and don'ts

Some of these do's and don'ts might seem obvious, but I've caught myself making a few of these mistakes when I was in a hurry or distracted.

✔ **Do:** When using a combination stylus/pen, be *sure* that you have it set to Stylus mode before writing on the screen. At best, the pen tip will only get ink on your screen; at worst, it'll ink the screen and scratch it.

✔ **Do:** When carrying your CLIÉ in a belt case, double-check the snap on the cover before leaning over. I was happy to find out that a CLIÉ NX70V can sometimes survive a three-foot fall onto a concrete garage floor, but I'd prefer never to have to perform that kind of torture-testing again.

✔ **Do:** Taking your CLIÉ camping or canoeing? Place it in a Ziploc baggie. This protects it from water and dirt, and you can press buttons and use the stylus without removing the PDA!

✔ **Do:** When your screen gets gunky, clean it with special wipes such as the Companion-Link Screen Cleaners, available from www.freescreenprotectors.com. In a pinch, you can use a soft cotton T-shirt to wipe your PDA's screen clean. Don't use paper towels — they're too abrasive and can scratch the screen.

✔ **Do:** When carrying the CLIÉ in a briefcase or purse, remove small metal objects like paper clips — they could potentially slide into the HotSync connector and cause a short.

✔ **Do:** If you're putting your CLIÉ in your pocket without a case, carry only the CLIÉ models that are equipped with a hard plastic or metal screen. The soft fabric flip covers included on some models don't protect the screen from loose objects in your pocket.

✔ **Don't:** Don't use a voltage transformer when charging your CLIÉ in countries other than the United States. The charging transformer brick included with North American CLIÉ models is a universal power supply that works on 110/220 v and 50/60 Hz electrical systems, so all you need is a simple plug adapter, available at any travel store or online at sites such as www.laptoptravel.com. The cheap travel transformers that are sold for use with hair dryers aren't designed for use with sensitive electronics, and they're not necessary when using the Sony charging brick.

✔ **Don't:** Speaking of loose objects, never put your CLIÉ in your pocket with change, paper clips, or (gasp!) your car keys. You're just begging for a scratched case or screen if you do.

✔ **Don't:** Never put your CLIÉ in your back pocket. If you get distracted and forget it's there before you sit down, you could hear a sound far more disturbing than a whoopee cushion — the crunch of a smushed CLIÉ.

When Bad Things Happen

CLIÉs are like kids. No matter how hard you try to protect them, if you let them out of the house, there's always a chance that they'll fall down and get a nasty scrape or break their glasses. Well, their glass, at any rate.

The cost of the repair depends on whether your warranty is still valid and whether the problem was caused by a technical failure or accident/negligence. A battery that doesn't charge is covered by warranty, but break out your credit card if you drop the CLIÉ and damage the screen.

Here are the ways to find technical support and repair services for your CLIÉ:

- ✔ **Phone support:** Call (877) 760-7669.

- ✔ **Web:** Visit www.sony.com/clie and click the Support tab.

- ✔ **E-Mail:** Send missives to handheld.service@am.sony.com.

- ✔ **User support:** You can often get the fastest answers by running your problems past experienced CLIÉ users in the discussion forums at www.cliesource.com.

Part VII

The Part of Tens

In this part . . .

Top ten lists are a staple of humor and attempted humor. An organization once passed an amendment to its constitution so that I'd stop doing top ten lists at the beginning of meetings. So I introduced the weekly top nine list.

Unencumbered by *ww* here, you get the full top ten — four times! You find out about ten of the best third-party programs for the CLIÉ and ten of the top accessories. The book wraps up with the top ten tips for troubleshooting CLIÉ problems — and for just getting a laugh from some fun secrets hidden in your CLIÉ — as well as a way-more-than-top-ten list of handy Web sites devoted to things CLIÉ.

Chapter 22

Ten Great Third-Party Programs

*F*rom the moment you take it out of the box, the CLIÉ is an amazing device, but with over 20,000 third-party programs available, the possibilities for personalizing your CLIÉ are endless. Which of those 20,000 programs do you start with? Start right here with this top-ten list of the very best programs that are available for the CLIÉ.

Note that my Must Have list also includes programs like Bejeweled, Snapper Mail, and Documents To Go, all of which I cover elsewhere in this book. This list is here to introduce you to gems that I don't cover elsewhere.

Agendus

Agendus integrates all your personal information manager applications into one souped-up program. It's an idea similar to the CLIÉ Organizer that's included with the PEG-TH55, but the Agendus focuses more on accessibility than on flash and dazzle. That's not to say it doesn't have flash — customizable backgrounds, icons for appointments and contacts, and selectable font sizes all make configuring Agendus fun. All sorts of provisions exist for linking your data between modules, and the Pocket PC–style Today screen puts your upcoming appointments and To Dos in one spot. Agendus is available from www.iambic.com.

Contacts 5

Contacts 5 is a sleek Address Book replacement application that offers several different quick lookup techniques that make finding addresses and phone numbers easier than ever. You can customize its look with downloadable graphic skins and even connect to the Mapopolis mapping program to bring up a map of your contact's address. You can even dial your Bluetooth phone directly from Contacts 5. It's not as feature-laden as Agendus or DateBk5, but Contacts 5 has one of the easiest-to-use — and most attractive — interfaces out there. It's available from `www.pdaperformance.com`.

DateBk5

Similar to Agendus in concept, DateBk5 combines the data from the built-in personal information manager applications into one integrated program. A wide variety of views let you customize how you view your data to match your personal work style. Enhanced alarms help ensure you make your appointments, and templates help you automate the entry of commonly repeated events. It offers over a hundred other features, and the best part is that all profits from the program go to support a wildlife habitat for gorillas in Georgia. You can discover more about DateBk5 and find a link to Gorilla Haven at `www.datebk5.com`.

FileZ

FileZ is an extremely powerful file manager for finding, copying, moving, deleting, and beaming files in both Handheld and Memory Stick memory. t's fast, easy to use, and (best of all) free! FileZ is available from `nosleep software.sourceforge.net`.

Lightspeed and PXA Clocker

Okay, this one's a tie because they're both excellent programs, so I suggest trying them both and going with the one that best fits your needs. Lightspeed and PXA Clocker are overclocking programs for your CLIÉ. The idea is that you can get extra speed by running your CLIÉ's processor faster than its rated speed, which can be useful for games and video applications. I don't actually suggest doing this, though — it's extremely rare, but overclocking could damage your CLIÉ. However, both programs can also *under*clock your CLIÉ. When you're doing something that doesn't need much speed, such as reading an eBook or listening to MP3 tunes, underclocking can dramatically extend your battery life. PXA Clocker can be found at `www.palmgear.com` and Lightspeed at `www.clievideo.com`.

RepliGo

RepliGo is one of the most flexible file viewers available for the CLIÉ. The program can convert output from virtually any Windows program that features a Print command to a full-color file that can be viewed on your CLIÉ. This means that you can carry along anything from Word documents to Web sites to Quicken reports. Best of all, it offers a free viewer, so you can create RepliGo documents to distribute to others. It's available from `www.cerience.com`.

SplashWallet Suite

SplashWallet Suite is a bundle of four useful programs:

 ✔ **SplashPhoto:** A super-fast photo-viewing program that's more flexible than the built-in CLIÉ Viewer.

 ✔ **SplashShopper:** A handy list-keeping program.

 ✔ **SplashMoney:** A personal finance manager.

 ✔ **SplashID:** Safely stores personal information such as passwords and credit card numbers.

By themselves, these are all excellent programs. Bundled together at a low price, they're a terrific bargain. The suite is available from `www.splash data.com`.

SwitchSync

Do you need to synchronize your CLIÉ with both Palm Desktop and Outlook? SwitchSync does the trick. You also need to purchase Chapura's PocketMirror Outlook sync program — SwitchSync doesn't work with the IntelliSync Lite application that comes bundled with CLIÉs — but that's a small price to pay if you need your personal information manager data to be in two places at once. SwitchSynch is available from www.livepim.com, and you can get PocketMirror at www.chapura.com.

Vivid Webcam

Now this is a great idea. This program turns your CLIÉ's camera into a full-featured Webcam for your desktop system. It works with any program that supports standard Universal Serial Bus (USB) Webcams, including MSN Messenger and AOL Instant Messenger. It also includes a Web server that lets anyone with a Java-enabled Web browser view your camera. Why spend $100 on a good Webcam when you can use your CLIÉ? Vivid Webcam is available from www.clievideo.com.

ZLauncher

This program is a highly enhanced replacement for the built-in Program Launcher and can be customized to suit your needs and personality. ZLauncher features customizable themes, allowing you to display a background image behind your Launcher screen and even swap images and colors as your mood changes. It lets you arrange your programs in tabbed folders, making it a snap to group similar programs together. A group of customizable icons lets you drag and drop files to beam them, delete them, get info on them, and more. With full support of CLIÉ high-resolution screens, this is the most powerful and attractive Launcher available for Sony CLIÉs. It's available from www.zztechs.com.

Chapter 23

Ten Great CLIÉ Add-Ons

In This Chapter

▶ Juicing up your battery

▶ Improving your listening experience

▶ Cradling your CLIÉ

*H*ere are just some of the accessories that can make your CLIÉ life even more productive and fun. Extend your CLIÉ's battery life, print out the pictures from its camera, listen to MP3s anywhere — your already impressive CLIÉ shines even brighter with these add-ons. Be sure to also check out the must-have travel accessories that I cover in Chapter 17!

Battery Adapter

The PEGA-BC10 battery adapter plugs into all CLIÉ models except the UX series and lets you power or recharge your CLIÉ by using four AA batteries. If you have this device, you'll never find yourself running out of juice on a long flight again. It's available at www.sonystyle.com.

Cyber-shot DSC-V1

Your CLIÉ's built-in camera is great for snapshots, but what about those times when you're shooting something for which quality really matters? The Cyber-shot DSC-V1 makes a great high-end photo companion for your CLIÉ. Shoot pictures with its 5-megapixel resolution and 4X optical zoom, and then pop out the Memory Stick and place it in your CLIÉ to view the images on the CLIÉ's liquid crystal display (LCD) screen. The Cyber-shot DSC-V1 is available at www.sonystyle.com.

Digital Photo Printer

Sony's DPP-EX50 Digital Photo Printer prints top-quality 3.5-x-4-inch and 4-x-6-inch dye-sublimation photos directly from a Memory Stick. You can pop the card out of your camera-equipped CLIÉ, place it in the printer, press a button or two, and a minute later you have a lab-quality print. You can also connect the printer to your television set to do basic editing work on your CLIÉ photos and even display a slideshow of your photos on the TV. The printer works whether it's by itself, connected to a TV, or plugged into your desktop system. If offers both Memory Stick and CompactFlash slots, so it works with a variety of digital cameras. Check it out at www.sonystyle.com.

Extended Battery

Designed for the PEG-UX40 and PEG-UX50 units, the PEGA-EB40 Extended Battery is a Lithium Ion battery pack that snaps on to the bottom of your CLIÉ. It offers double the capacity of the built-in UX battery, giving you three times the overall battery life. It's excellent for long sessions of listening to music, watching videos on the road, or heavy Wi-Fi radio use. You can find it at www.sonystyle.com.

Noise-Canceling Headphones

Noise-canceling headphones actively compensate for background sounds like air conditioners and the ambient noise in an aircraft cabin so that you can hear your music without having to crank the volume to 11. Sennheiser's PXC 250 headphones offer excellent audio quality, effective noise cancellation, and a comfortable design. They're perfect accompaniment for your CLIÉ when you're listening to music or audiobooks on the plane. The PXC 250 headphones are available from www.sennheiser.com.

Pen/Stylus Combo

If you use the stylus for frequent data entry, I recommend purchasing a combination pen/stylus. Your fingers will thank you. The tiny, thin styluses that come with CLIÉs are fine for quick data entry, but they force your hand into an atypical position that can quickly become uncomfortable. The combo styluses are like multicolor pens except that they include a pen in place of the second color. (Always be sure to switch the pen to stylus mode before writing on your CLIÉ's screen!) Models are available from a wide variety of manufacturers. My personal favorite is the Fisher Space Pen. You can find dozens of choices at www.styluscentral.com.

SanDisk Memory Stick PRO

This third-party Memory Stick is fully compatible with Sony's cards, but it has a slightly flashier casing — bling bling fans, take note. What makes the SanDisk cards really special is the price — they're typically dramatically less expensive than Sony's. You can get more info at www.sandisk.com.

SoundFeeder SF250

The perfect accessory if you want to listen to MP3 or audiobook files on your car or home stereo. The SF250 plugs into your CLIÉ's headphone jack and transmits on eight different FM frequencies. What makes it better than some other solutions is its digital tuning — you don't have to worry about jarring a tuning dial and knocking the transmitter off-frequency while you're driving. It's available from www.arkon.com.

SyncDicator Cable

Sony's own HotSync cable requires you to lug along your power brick if you plan to charge on the road. If you're bringing a laptop along anyway, check out Brando WorkShop's SyncDicator cable, which not only HotSyncs your CLIÉ, but also recharges it by using power from your computer's Universal Serial Bus (USB) port. A dual-color LED glows read for battery charging and blue for data synchronization. The cable includes a HotSync button, perhaps the most annoying omission from Sony's model. The SyncDicator cable is available at shop.brando.com.hk.

USB Cradle

Sony is now shipping all its CLIÉs with a USB cable instead of a cradle. The cable is great for travel use but a bit awkward for desktop usage because the charger and USB cables come out of the small adapter, which you have to fumble with to connect to your CLIÉ. With the cable, you also have to load the HotSync application to synchronize. Sony's PEGA-UC55 cradle works with all current CLIÉs except for the UX series. It sits on your desk, where you can simply drop in your CLIÉ to charge and sync it. A HotSync button right on the cradle means no fumbling for the stylus every time you want to sync. It's available at www.sonystyle.com.

Chapter 24

Ten Top Tips and Secrets

• •

• •

*H*aving problems? Want to get the most out of your CLIÉ? Or just looking for a little fun? Here you can find the ten top tips for solving problems and getting a little extra out of your favorite handheld.

HotSync Hassles

Having trouble HotSyncing? First, make sure HotSync Manager is running — you should see the icon in the lower-right corner of your desktop system's screen. If it is, try both rebooting your desktop system and doing a soft reset on the CLIÉ. That fixes the problem 90 percent of the time. If that still doesn't help, try unplugging your HotSync cradle or cable and plugging it into a different Universal Serial Bus (USB) port on your computer, which forces Windows to reinstall the sync driver. If all else fails, reinstall the Palm Desktop software and see whether that helps.

Power Problems

Your CLIÉ won't turn on? Make sure the Hold slider isn't in the active position. If it's not active, plug the CLIÉ into its charging cable and see whether it turns on then. If it still doesn't turn on, try a soft reset.

Oooh, the Colors, Man!

Think the CLIÉ's color scheme is just too staid and businesslike? On units running Palm OS 5.2 or higher, you can change the color scheme to anything from a cool blue to a garish mix that would make artist Jackson Pollock cringe. Open the Prefs application from the Program Launcher. Select General from the drop-down menu arrow in the upper-right corner, and then tap the Colors pop-up menu and select your scheme. Even if orange text isn't your thing, try the Basic scheme, which is similar to the standard colors but spruces up the buttons with a gray background. And if you ever owned an early monochrome Palm or CLIÉ, be sure to try the Nostalgia scheme.

Reset 101

You can reset your CLIÉ in the following three ways when it stops responding:

- **Soft reset:** Just press the Reset button with your stylus tip or with the Reset tool (a small pin) hidden in the styluses that came with older CLIÉ models where the stylus tip doesn't fit in the Reset hole. This type of reset works almost all the time and keeps your memory intact.

- **Warm reset:** Press the Reset button while holding the Up (or Left, in the case of center-mounted jog dials) button. This resets the CLIÉ while disabling any programs and operating system libraries that automatically run on startup. The goal of a warm reset is to find and delete the offending program and then do a soft reset.

- **Hard reset:** This is the reset of last resort because it clears your CLIÉ's memory. Hold down the Power button, press the Reset button, and then release the Power button when the logo appears on the screen.

Need to reset your CLIÉ but can't find your stylus? Just unfold a paper clip and carefully push the tip into your CLIÉ's Reset hole.

This One Will Have You Beaming

Having trouble receiving beamed data? Launch Prefs from the Program Launcher, select General from the drop-down menu arrow in the top-right corner, and make sure that Beam Receive is turned on by tapping the pop-up menu next to Beam Receive and choosing On. If that doesn't help, try moving the CLIÉs to a shadier spot — very bright lights can interfere with the infrared transmission. And make sure that the two units are at least six inches apart.

Unleash Hidden Memory

Really short on memory? Check out JackFlash from Brayder (www.brayder. com), which can take advantage of unused Flash memory inside your CLIÉ to store additional programs, data, and more. Some CLIÉ models have a couple of megabytes available, perfect for squeezing in a couple of your most-used programs without having to put them on a Memory Stick. Best of all, this memory will survive dead batteries and hard resets.

Keeping up to Date

Savvy users make it a habit to periodically check www.sony.com/clie/ support to see whether any improved programs or bug fixes are available for their CLIÉs. Now Sony has made the process of finding and downloading patches completely automatic for most CLIÉ models. Just visit Sony's support site at www.sony.com/clie/support and download the latest version of the CLIÉ Update Wizard. This program can automatically find, download, and install all the latest updates and patches for Palm OS 5 CLIÉ models.

Power to the CLIÉ People

If your battery life isn't what it seems like it should be, try turning down the brightness on your screen by tapping the small sun icon just below the Menu soft button. Also, remember that Bluetooth and Wi-Fi radios love to eat up power, so turn them off when you're not using them.

A Real Easter Egg

This secret is a fun one. You might have heard of *Easter eggs,* the surprises that programmers sometimes hide in software. Well, the CLIÉ has a true, literal Easter egg — in full color! Tap the Prefs icon in the Program Launcher, and then tap the drop-down menu arrow in the upper-right corner of the screen and select General.

Now, draw a small circle, counterclockwise, in the lower-right corner of the Prefs screen, just above the Calculator soft button. An Easter egg appears. See the following section for what you can do with your egg.

Taxi!

The fun doesn't stop at creating the Easter egg. This one's a little tricky and takes some trial and error. After you activate the egg, hold the Down rocker (or the button to the right of the jog dial on units with center-mounted jog dials) and draw a line in the Graffiti area from just above the numeric keypad 1 icon all the way to the left side of the screen between the Home and Menu soft buttons. If you do this right, you see a taxi bounce across the screen! It keeps popping up in the Program Launcher and even in some applications to surprise you. To make it stop appearing, just tap the Easter egg. The egg disappears, and the taxi drives off into the sunset.

Chapter 25

Way More Than Ten Useful Internet Resources

*N*ow that you've unleashed the power of your CLIÉ, you might want to check out these great Web sites. You can chat with fellow CLIÉ fans, read the latest CLIÉ–related news, and find the coolest add-on programs and products.

News, Discussion, and Support

✓ **ClieSource:** It's a huge Web site that's all CLIÉ, all the time. ClieSource offers daily news on the hottest new programs and add-ons, as well as helpful and informative discussion groups for every CLIÉ model. If you visit one CLIÉ Web site, this should be the one. (www.cliesource.com)

✓ **PalmInfoCenter:** Despite the Palm in its name, this site covers all PDAs that use the Palm OS, including the CLIÉ. It's a good source for news and discussion. (www.palminfocenter.com)

✓ **PDA 24/7:** As you might guess from the name, this site prides itself on providing PDA-related news day and night. For sheer volume of information related to the CLIÉ and other PDAs, you can't beat it. (www.pda247.com)

✓ **PDArcade:** This site is devoted to the latest and greatest games for PDAs. It has a very active Palm OS section with lots of discussion and reviews of CLIÉ games. (www.pdarcade.com)

✔ **Sony Support:** On this site, you can find the latest patches and updated software applications for your CLIÉ, as well as a technical support database and frequently asked questions list. (www.ita.sel.sony.com/support)

Downloads

✔ **Fictionwise:** You can find an impressive collection of eBooks and short stories here. (www.fictionwise.com)

✔ **FreewarePalm:** Want to download some new programs for your CLIÉ but don't want to spend any money? Browse this site for some great — and some goofy — CLIÉ applications. (www.freewarepalm.com)

✔ **Handango:** Handango is a multiplatform download site, but despite that, its Palm OS library rivals PalmGear's. Browsing the site will make you feel like a kid in a candy store. Or a geek in an electronics superstore. (www.handango.com)

✔ **Palm Digital Media:** This giant virtual bookstore is packed with eBooks. (www.palmdigitalmedia.com)

✔ **PalmGear:** PalmGear.com is devoted 100 percent to Palm OS programs, eBooks, and other products. At last check, the site had over 22,000 freeware and shareware downloads available. The available choices are mind-boggling. (www.palmgear.com)

✔ **PocketMovies:** The short films, movie trailers, and other eye candy at this site are designed for playback on the Pocket PC, but they work just fine on the CLIÉ. (www.pocketmovies.net)

CLIÉ–Related Manufacturers and Publishers

✔ **Astraware:** If you're a gamer, check out this purveyor of disturbingly addictive puzzle games such as Bejeweled and Text Twist. Caution: Don't visit here when you have a deadline approaching. (www.astraware.com)

✔ **Brando WorkShop:** Yes, it's in Hong Kong, but it has probably the widest variety of CLIÉ accessories of any shop on the planet, and overseas shipping is cheap and reliable. (shop.brando.com.hk)

✔ **DataViz:** DataViz is the creator of Documents To Go and Beyond Contacts, the Outlook equivalent for CLIÉs. (www.dataviz.com)

- ✔ **Handmark:** This company has a large library of dependably good Palm OS software, consisting of both games and productivity applications. (www.handmark.com)

- ✔ **Mark/Space:** This company offers The Missing Sync, the program to have if you want to sync your CLIÉ with a Macintosh. (www.markspace.com)

- ✔ **MobilePlanet:** This online store has so much PDA stuff that it's scary. It offers tons of accessories, even for older CLIÉ models. This site is especially handy when you're looking for a case or an accessory for an out-of-production CLIÉ. MobilePlanet offers the newest toys, too. (www.mobileplanet.com)

- ✔ **PDAparts.com:** If you want to fix your CLIÉ yourself, you can probably find the repair parts here. (www.pdaparts.com)

Index

• H •

Handango Web site, 332
handheld options
  Documents To Go program, 189–190
  Handheld overwrites Desktop action,
    conduit settings, 56
  memory, 214
Handmark Web site, 333
Hands High Software (ToDo Plus), 91
hard buttons, 20–23
hard resets, 60, 328
headers, e-mail, 259
headphones
  noise-canceling, 324
  travel kits, 274
hidden memory, 329
hiding private records, 281–282
highlighting options, Memo Pad, 101
Hold slider, 21
holidays, Date Book appointments, 84
Home button, 24
Home icon, status bar, 25
home movie conversions, 133
home-networking equipment, Wi-Fi, 232
hotspots, Wi-Fi zones, 232
HotSync
  add-on software installation, 57–59
  advanced options, 55–56
  backups, 51
  benefits of, 47–48
  conduits, 55–56
  cradles, 50–51
  Custom window, 56
  data, transferring to Desktop, 52
  discussed, 12
  HotSync command (Options menu), 253
  InfraRed option, 55
  Intellisync Lite application, 52–53
  Local Serial option, 55
  Local USB option, 55
  Modem option, 55

  Network option, 55
  problems, 327
  setting up, 48–50
  user account information, 48
  User Name field, 49
HTML (Hypertext Markup Language),
  58, 258–259

• I •

icons
  Address (Program Launcher), 65
  Bookmark View (Picsel Viewer
    program), 199
  Camera (Program Launcher), 118
  Carousel (Picsel Viewer program), 198
  Date Book (Program Launcher), 75
  Delete Page (Memo Pad), 105
  Documents (Program Launcher),
    191–192
  Memo Pad (Program Launcher), 100
  Mobile Manager (Program
    Launcher), 248
  Move Page (Memo Pad), 105
  PhotoStand (Program Launcher), 123
  Receive Settings (Mail Program),
    260–261
  Scissors (Memo Pad), 105
  Security (Program Launcher), 277
  status bar, 25–27, 39
  View Menu (Open dialog box), 122
  Viewer (Program application), 114
  Voice Rec (Program Launcher), 150
  Wrench (camera options), 119
IEEE (Electrical and Electronics
  Engineers), 232
IM (Instant Messaging), 263
images
  Image Converter application, 121–122
  Image Info option, slideshow
    presentations, 125
  viewing, 116

• N •

• O •

• P •

user account information, HotSync
    setup, 48
User Name field, HotSync set up, 49, 51
user support, 316

• *V* •

VBR (Variable Bit Rate), 140
VCF (VCard) formats, 68
VeriChat instant messaging, 263
Vexed puzzle game, 162
video
  memory card capacity, 217
  shooting, 13
View Menu icon (Open dialog box), 122
Viewer program
  commands, 115
  Delete Files option, 114
  discussed, 113
  files, removing, 115
  images, viewing, 116
  Send to CLIÉ Mail option, 114
  Send to Other Program option, 114
  Send to Photostand option, 114
  sound files, 117
viewing
  addresses in Address Book, 70
  appointments, in Date Book, 76
  images, in Viewer program, 116
  slideshow presentations, 125, 196
Vivid Webcam program, 322
vocabulary builders, Beret Study Buddy:
    Vocabulary activity game, 173
Voice Recorder program, 150–151
volume controls
  AeroPlayer, 140
  Audio Player, 137
  AVLS (Automatic Volume Limiting
    System), 137
  playing movies, 131

Voice Recorder program, 151
Volume Control icon, status bar, 27

• *W* •

Warfare Incorporated strategy game,
    165–166
warm resets, 60, 328
Web browsers
  AvantGo, 264
  NetFront, 261–263
  PocketLink, 264
  WebToGo, 264
Web sites
  action games, 154–158
  adventure games, 168–169
  Arkon, 184
  Astraware, 332
  AvantGo, 264
  Baen, 178
  board games, 164
  Boingo, 243
  Brando Workshop, 332
  card games, 163
  Chapura, 54, 209, 286
  ClieSource, 331
  Contentlink, 179
  Covertec, 313
  DataViz, 208, 332
  DateBk5, 320
  Decuma, 40
  eBooks, 178–179
  Fictionwise, 17, 177–178, 332
  Fitaly Virtual, 44
  FreewarePalm, 332
  Google, 246
  Handango, 332
  Handmark, 333
  Hands High Software, 91
  iTunes, 146
  kid games, 170, 172–174

• Z •

Notes

FOR DUMMIES®

The easy way to get more done and have more fun

ERSONAL FINANCE

0-7645-5231-7

0-7645-2431-3

0-7645-5331-3

Also available:

Estate Planning For Dummies
(0-7645-5501-4)

401(k)s For Dummies
(0-7645-5468-9)

Frugal Living For Dummies
(0-7645-5403-4)

Microsoft Money "X" For
Dummies
(0-7645-1689-2)

Mutual Funds For Dummies
(0-7645-5329-1)

Personal Bankruptcy For
Dummies
(0-7645-5498-0)

Quicken "X" For Dummies
(0-7645-1666-3)

Stock Investing For Dummies
(0-7645-5411-5)

Taxes For Dummies 2003
(0-7645-5475-1)

USINESS & CAREERS

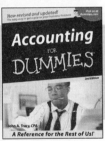

0-7645-5314-3

0-7645-5307-0

0-7645-5471-9

Also available:

Business Plans Kit For
Dummies
(0-7645-5365-8)

Consulting For Dummies
(0-7645-5034-9)

Cool Careers For Dummies
(0-7645-5345-3)

Human Resources Kit For
Dummies
(0-7645-5131-0)

Managing For Dummies
(1-5688-4858-7)

QuickBooks All-in-One Desk
Reference For Dummies
(0-7645-1963-8)

Selling For Dummies
(0-7645-5363-1)

Small Business Kit For
Dummies
(0-7645-5093-4)

Starting an eBay Business For
Dummies
(0-7645-1547-0)

IEALTH, SPORTS & FITNESS

0-7645-5167-1

0-7645-5146-9

0-7645-5154-X

Also available:

Controlling Cholesterol For
Dummies
(0-7645-5440-9)

Dieting For Dummies
(0-7645-5126-4)

High Blood Pressure For
Dummies
(0-7645-5424-7)

Martial Arts For Dummies
(0-7645-5358-5)

Menopause For Dummies
(0-7645-5458-1)

Nutrition For Dummies
(0-7645-5180-9)

Power Yoga For Dummies
(0-7645-5342-9)

Thyroid For Dummies
(0-7645-5385-2)

Weight Training For Dummies
(0-7645-5168-X)

Yoga For Dummies
(0-7645-5117-5)

.vailable wherever books are sold.
o to www.dummies.com or call 1-877-762-2974 to order direct.

FOR DUMMIES®

A world of resources to help you grow

HOME, GARDEN & HOBBIES

Feng Shui
0-7645-5295-3

Gardening
0-7645-5130-2

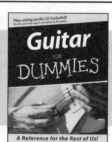

Guitar
0-7645-5106-X

Also available:

Auto Repair For Dummies
(0-7645-5089-6)

Chess For Dummies
(0-7645-5003-9)

Home Maintenance For
Dummies
(0-7645-5215-5)

Organizing For Dummies
(0-7645-5300-3)

Piano For Dummies
(0-7645-5105-1)

Poker For Dummies
(0-7645-5232-5)

Quilting For Dummies
(0-7645-5118-3)

Rock Guitar For Dummies
(0-7645-5356-9)

Roses For Dummies
(0-7645-5202-3)

Sewing For Dummies
(0-7645-5137-X)

FOOD & WINE

Cooking
0-7645-5250-3

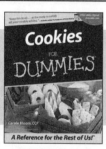

Cookies
0-7645-5390-9

Wine
0-7645-5114-0

Also available:

Bartending For Dummies
(0-7645-5051-9)

Chinese Cooking For
Dummies
(0-7645-5247-3)

Christmas Cooking For
Dummies
(0-7645-5407-7)

Diabetes Cookbook For
Dummies
(0-7645-5230-9)

Grilling For Dummies
(0-7645-5076-4)

Low-Fat Cooking For
Dummies
(0-7645-5035-7)

Slow Cookers For Dummies
(0-7645-5240-6)

TRAVEL

Italy
0-7645-5453-0

Hawaii
0-7645-5438-7

Las Vegas
0-7645-5448-4

Also available:

America's National Parks For
Dummies
(0-7645-6204-5)

Caribbean For Dummies
(0-7645-5445-X)

Cruise Vacations For
Dummies 2003
(0-7645-5459-X)

Europe For Dummies
(0-7645-5456-5)

Ireland For Dummies
(0-7645-6199-5)

France For Dummies
(0-7645-6292-4)

London For Dummies
(0-7645-5416-6)

Mexico's Beach Resorts For
Dummies
(0-7645-6262-2)

Paris For Dummies
(0-7645-5494-8)

RV Vacations For Dummies
(0-7645-5443-3)

Walt Disney World & Orlando
For Dummies
(0-7645-5444-1)

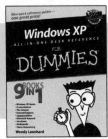
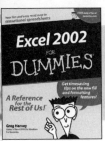

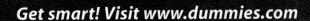
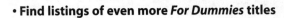

FOR DUMMIES®

Helping you expand your horizons and realize your potential

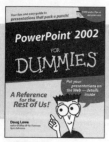
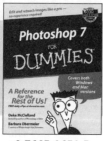